de Smith, Woolf & Jowell

Judicial Review

of

Administrative Action

FIRST CUMULATIVE SUPPLEMENT TO THE FIFTH EDITION

by

The Rt Hon The Lord Woolf
Master of the Rolls
Bencher of the Inner Temple
Fellow of University College London
Pro-Chancellor of the University of London

Jeffrey Jowell, Q.C.
M.A., LL.M., S.J.D.
Professor of Public Law
and Vice Provost,
University College London

EDITOR OF SUPPLEMENT

A.P. Le Sueur, LL.B.
Barrister
Lecturer in Laws, University College London

ASSISTANT EDITOR
Javan Herberg, LL.B., B.C.L.
Barrister

London
Sweet & Maxwell
1998

Published by
Sweet & Maxwell Limited of
100 Avenue Road, London NW3 3PF
(http://www.smlawpub.co.uk)
Typeset by LBJ Typesetting Ltd
of Kingsclere
and printed and bound in Great Britain by
MPG Books Ltd,
Bodmin, Cornwall

No natural forests were destroyed to make this product;
only farmed timber was used and replanted

ISBN Main Work (Fifth Edition) 0 420 46620 7
ISBN First Cumulative Supplement 0 421 607 904

A catalogue record for this book is available from the British Library

PREFACE TO THE FIRST SUPPLEMENT

The Fifth Edition of *Judicial Review of Administrative Law* stated the law as at June 1995. This First Cumulative Supplement brings that work up to date to the end of November 1997. Where it has been possible to do so, important later developments up to January 1998 have also been included. As in the Main Work, our aim has not been to include reference to every reported case; rather it has been to alert readers to those cases which develop principles, or provide particularly useful illustrations of well-established doctrines. In several areas of law (for instance, public sector housing) important new legislation has been enacted since 1995. At the time of writing this Supplement, the Human Rights Bill is being debated in Parliament. Its enactment will bring about some profound changes to the nature of judicial review in the United Kingdom, but detailed analysis of its scope and potential has to await the Sixth Edition of this work.

As in the Fifth Edition, parts of this Supplement rely on the help of those lawyers with special expertise in the operation of judicial review in particular contexts. Our thanks go to the following for assisting with draft chapters: Professor Takis Tridimas (Chapter 21—E.C. Law in English Administrative Law): Dr Jane Holder (Chapter 22—Planning); Jeremy Woolf (Chapter 23—Revenue); Professor Martin Loughlin (Chapter 24—Prison Discipline); Andrew Nicol Q.C. (Chapter 25—Immigration); Stephen Knafler (Chapter 26—Public Sector Housing); Charles Blake (Chapter 27—Social Security); and Richard Gardiner (Chapter 28—Treaties and Foreign Affairs). Professor Gillian Morris contributed to that part of Chapter 3 (Public and Private Law and Their Relation to Judicial Review) dealing with public sector employment and Professor Patrick Birkinshaw to the exposition in Chapter 1 of Extra-judicial safeguards and the disclosure of official information.

We are greatly obliged to a number of distinguished lawyers for informing us of developments in other jurisdictions: Lord Cooke of Thorndon and Dr Yvonne Cripps (New Zealand); Professor Cheryl Saunders (Australia); Professor Hugh Corder (South Africa); Professor Brigid Hadfield (Northern Ireland); Justice Yitzhak Zamir (Israel); Roger Errera (France); Professor Mario Chiti (Italy); Andrew Roman of Miller Thomson, Toronto (Canada); Attorney-General Ashok Desai (India).

Javan Herberg, who worked as a research assistant during the preparation of the Fifth Edition, joins the editorial team for this Supplement. Simmy Viinikka assisted in verifying citations. The continuing support of Sweet and Maxwell and the secretarial assistance of Sylvia Lough have been vital to the project.

Harry Woolf   February 1998
Jeffrey Jowell
Andrew Le Sueur
Javan Herberg

CONTENTS

Contents

Contents

Contents

Contents

TABLE OF CASES

References are to paragraph numbers

Table of Cases

Table of Cases

Table of Cases

Table of Cases

Table of Cases

Table of Cases

Table of Cases

Table of Cases

Table of Cases

Table of Cases

TABLE OF STATUTES

References are to paragraph numbers

Foreign Statutes

TABLE OF STATUTORY INSTRUMENTS

References are to paragraph numbers

References are to paragraph numbers

TABLE OF TREATIES AND CONVENTIONS

References are to paragraph numbers

PART I

JUDICIAL REVIEW AND ADMINISTRATIVE LAW

CHAPTER 1

THE PLACE OF JUDICIAL REVIEW IN ADMINISTRATIVE LAW

ENGLISH ATTITUDES TOWARDS ADMINISTRATIVE LAW

[Add to Note 5:]   **1–006**

and J.W.F. Allison, *A Continental Distinction in the Common Law: a Historical and Comparative Perspective on English Public Law* (1996).

[Add to Note 13:]   **1–009**

For a recent plea on behalf of "the constitutional imperative of judicial self-restraint which must inform judicial decision-making in public law", see Lord Irvine of Lairg, Q.C., "Judges and Decision-Makers: the Theory and Practice of *Wednesbury* Review" [1996] P.L. 59.

[Add to Note 19:]

and J. Jowell, "Restraining the State: Politics, Principle and Judicial Review" *Law of Opinion in Twentieth Century England* (1997) 50 C.L.P. 189.

[Add to Note 26:]   **1–012**

For a recent account of the influence of the United States of America, see I. Loveland (ed.), *A Special Relationship? American Influences on Public Law in the United Kingdom* (1995).

[Add new paragraph:]   **1–019**

In July 1996, Lord Woolf's final report *Access to Justice* was published, recommending far-reaching reforms of the whole civil justice system in England and Wales. Most of the recommendations made by the Law Commission in its 1994 report were endorsed (See *Access to Justice*, Chapter 18). The Government acted quickly to implement proposals on homelessness cases (which in 1995 accounted for over a third of all applications for leave to apply for judicial review). Many challenges to local authorities' decisions in cases involving homelessness are now dealt with initially by new internal appeal mechanisms and then by appeal to the county courts

3

upon judicial review principles: *Access to Justice*, pages 216–217 and see further below, Chapter 26. Other recommendations, which have yet to be implemented, are in summary as follows (see *Access to Justice*, pages 320–321).

"(i)   The procedures in public law cases should be brought into line with one another and with those in private law cases wherever possible. Use of the wrong procedure should not lead to the case being dismissed. Instead it should be dealt with so far as possible under the proper procedure.

(ii)   More judges from Divisions of the High Court other than the Queen's Bench should be nominated to hear Crown Office cases.

(iii)   Certain Crown Office List cases should be heard outside London.

(iv)   Claimants for judicial review should use available methods of Alternative Dispute Resolution (ADR).

(v)   Claimants should notify the defendant of their proposed claim before starting proceedings.

(vi)   A claim for judicial review and any defence should follow the standard claim form and defence. Unless it would inconvenience the hearing of a claim for judicial review, it should be possible for the claimant to include any remedies which could be obtained in a private law action and for the defendant to make a counterclaim.

(vii)   The courts should be able to grant advisory declarations in limited circumstances.

(viii)   At the preliminary consideration stage (formerly "leave"), which should be in writing, the judge should allow the claim to proceed if there is a realistic prospect of success or some other reason why the claim should be disposed of at a substantive hearing. He should consider giving directions for the conduct of the claim and set a timetable.

(ix)   There should be a right to renew the application in non-criminal cases at an oral hearing before a single judge and a further renewal to the Court of Appeal, with leave. Consideration should be given to the same procedure applying in criminal cases.

(x)   The court should be able to grant interim relief before the preliminary considerations but should only do so *ex parte* in a clear and urgent case.

(xi)   The claimant will have standing if he has been or will be adversely affected or if it is in the public interest that the claim should be brought.

(xii)   All cases of judicial review should normally be heard by a single judge. There should be an appeal, with leave, to the Court of Appeal (Civil Division) in non-criminal cases and consideration should be given to enabling appeals in criminal causes to lie, with leave, to the Court of Appeal (Criminal Division).

(xiii)   The court should have a discretion to order costs to be paid out of public funds or to order that the unsuccessful party is not to pay the other party's costs where the proceedings have been brought in the public interest.

(xiv) It should be possible to determine some claims in the Crown Office list in writing where the parties agree.

(xv) The rules on habeas corpus and committal for contempt will be clarified and simplified."

The Civil Procedure Act 1997, ss 1–5, confer powers to make new rules of court (to be called the Civil Procedure Rules) to govern the practice and procedure in the High Court, Court of Appeal (Civil Division) and the county courts. This rule-making power is to "be exercised with a view to securing that the civil justice system is accessible, fair and efficient" (s. 1(3)). The present date for implementing the reforms announced by the Lord Chancellor's Department is April 1999.

External influences

[Correction to Note 49:]   1–020

The Convention on the Prevention and Punishment of the Crime of Genocide came into force in 1951.

[Add to Note 54:]   1–021

See also Murray Hunt, *Using Human Rights in English Courts* (1997). And see further paras 6–048–6–058 and 13–059–13–063, below.

LEGAL REASONING AND JUDICIAL REVIEW

[Add to Note 63:]   1–025

In *Goldsmith v. Bhoyrul* [1998] 2 W.L.R. 435 Buckley J. extended to *Derbyshire* principle to prevent a political party (the Referendum Party) from bringing a libel action.

[Add to Note 67:]   1–027

For a robust defence of orthodox views on parliamentary supremacy, and a justification of judicial review on the basis of implied parliamentary intent, see Christopher Forsyth, "Of Fig Leaves and Fairy Tales: the Ultra Vires Doctrine, the Sovereignty of Parliament and Judicial Review" [1996] C.L.J. 122.

[Add to Note 69:]

See also *R. v. Secretary of State for Social Security, ex p. Joint Council for the Welfare of Immigrants* [1997] 1 W.L.R. 275 (regulations denying asylum seekers welfare benefits held to be unlawful; the effect of this decision was later reversed by the Immigration and Asylum Act 1996, s. 9); *R. v. Lord Chancellor, ex p. Witham* [1997] 2 All E.R. 779 (Laws J. held new rules on court fees to be *ultra vires*; access to the courts is a constitutional right which could only be denied by the government if it persuaded Parliament to pass legislation with express provision permitting the executive to turn poor people away from the court door. Such rights were not "the consequence of the democratic political process but would be logically prior to it"). And see further para. 13–060, below.

1–029   *[Add to Note 70:]*

But see for the possibility that some common law rights lie so deep that even Parliament cannot override them *Fraser v. State Services Commission* [1984] 1 N.Z.L.R. 116 at 121; and *Taylor v. New Zealand Poultry Board* [1984] 1 N.Z.L.R. 394 at 398, *per* Cooke J.

[Add to Note 76:]

Sedley, "Human Rights: a Twenty-first Century Agenda" [1995] P.L. 356; Laws, "The Constitution: morals and rights" [1996] P.L. 622; Lord Irvine of Lairg, "Response to Sir John Laws" [1996] P.L. 636. For an excellent overview of the recent contributions by members of the judiciary to constitutional theory, see Murray Hunt, *Using Human Rights in English Courts* (1997), Chap. 5.

1–032   *[Add to Note 82:]*

See now Eric Barendt, "Separation of Powers and Constitutional Government" [1995] P.L. 599; Sir Stephen Sedley, "Autonomy and the Rule of Law", Chap. 14 in R. Rawlings (ed.), *Law, Society and Economy* (1997). See also the debate in the House of Lords on the relationship between the judiciary, the legislature and the executive, and on judicial participation in public controversy: H.L. Deb., Vol. 572, col. 1449 (July 3, 1996) and col. 1581 (July 4, 1996) and Robert Stevens, "Judges, Politics, Politicians and the Confusing Role of the Judiciary", Chap. 11 in Keith Hawkins (ed.), *The Human Face of Law* (1997).

THE IMPORTANCE OF JUDICIAL REVIEW

1–033   *[Add to Note 85:]*

This statement (and that retained in para. 1–002 of this work) is discussed in G. Richardson and M. Sunkin, "Judicial Review: Questions of Impact" [1996] P.L. 79.

The growing case load

[Add to Note 87:]   1–034

In 1995 there were 3,604 applications for leave to apply for judicial review, an increase of 12 per cent on the previous year: Lord Chancellor's Department, *Judicial Statistics in England and Wales 1995* (Cm. 3290, June 1996). The figure for 1996 is 3901.

[Add to Note 91:]   1–035

See now L. Bridges, G. Meszaros and M. Sunkin, *Judicial Review in Perspective* (2nd ed., 1995).

The response of government

Central government

[Add to Note 98:]

Compare the booklet issued by the Commonwealth Secretariate, *Good Government and Administrative Law: an International Guide* (1996) and that published by the Australian Government, *Legal Issues: a Guide for Policy Development and Administration* (October 1994).

[Add to Note 1:]   1–037

There seems to have been an "absorption of the prospect of legal challenge into . . . departments' political and administrative bloodstream": A. Barker, "The Impact of Judicial Review: Perspectives from Whitehall and the Courts" [1996] P.L. 612, 613. During the mid–1990s, government ministers also became more ready publicly to criticise unfavourable judgments in a confrontational manner, aided by a partisan press: see A.P. Le Sueur, "The Judicial Review Debate: From Partnership to Friction" (1996) 31 *Government and Opposition* 8; Diana Woodhouse, "Politicians and Judges: A Conflict of Interest" (1996) 49 Parl. Aff. 423 and, *In Pursuit of Good Administration: Ministers, Civil Servants and Judges* (1997); and Robert Stevens, "Judges, Politics, Politicians and the Confusing Role of the Judiciary", Chapter 11 in Keith Hawkins (ed.), *The Human Face of Law: Essays in Honour of Donald Harris* (1997).

Local authorities

[Add to Note 2:]   1–038

See also: Martin Loughlin, *Legality and Locality: the Role of Law in Central Government Relations* (1996); Davina Cooper, "Institutional Illegality and Disobedience—Local Government Narratives" (1996) 16 O.J.L.S. 255.

Evaluation

1–040   *[Add to Note 9:]*

See further G. Richardson and M. Sunkin, "Judicial Review: Questions of Impact" [1996] P.L. 79 and Simon James, "The Political and Administrative Consequences of Judicial Review" (1996) 74 Pub. Admin. 613.

Judicial review and political action

1–041   *[Add to Note 10:]*

R. Rawlings, "Litigation as Political Action" in I. Loveland (ed.), *A Special Relationship? American Influences on Public Law in the United Kingdom* (1995).

[Add to Note 15:]

Simon James, "The Political and Administrative Consequences of Judicial Review" (1996) 74 Pub. Admin. 613.

ASPECTS OF THE ADMINISTRATIVE PROCESS IN ENGLAND

1–051   British Rail and British Coal have been privatised.

1–052   Oflot has been created to regulate the National Lottery. Note also Railways Act 1993, s.1 and the Regulator and Director of Passenger Franchising.

Ministers and Parliament

1–084   The Osmotherley Rules which set out the duties of Ministers to Select Committees and the provision of evidence and witnesses have been revised to take into account the Code of Practice on *Access to Government Information* (see paras 1–122 *et seq.* below): *Departmental Evidence and Response to Select Committees* (Cabinet Office, January 1997).

1–086   On the role of national Parliaments and E.C. legislation and policy see: the Select Committee on European Legislation, *The Scrutiny of European Business*, H.C. 51–xxvii (1995–1996) and *The Role of National Parliaments in the European Union*, H.C. 51–xxviii (1995–1996) and P. Birkinshaw and D. Ashiagbor, "National Participation in Community Affairs: Democracy, the UK Parliament and the EU" (1996) 33 C.M.L.Rev. 499. The revised Treaty now has a protocol on the role of national parliaments in the European Union.

The Treasury and Civil Service Committee has been split into the **1–087**
Public Service Committee (now the Public Administration Committee)
and the Treasury Committee. The Select Committee on the Parliamentary
Commissioner has ceased to exist and its functions have been transferred
to the Public Administration Committee.

There are revised practices on answering Parliamentary Questions: (see **1–088**
paragraph 1–130 *et seq.*, below). The "Table Office" of the House of
Commons has also provided a list of "blocking" answers to parliamentary
questions for the 1995–1996 session: H.C. 234 (1996–1997), pages vii–viii.
This does not include those refused because of cost or all of those based on
unavailability of information.

On the Scott Report and reaction to it, (see paragraph 1–122 below). **1–090**

There are 42 national charters and over 10,000 local charters: *The* **1–091**
Citizen's Charter—Five Years On, Cm. 3370 (1996). The Citizen's Charter
Complaints Task Force in the Cabinet Office has produced a series of
publications on, *If Things Go Wrong* . . . advising public bodies on
complaints' procedures. On redress for maladministration (see paragraph
1–108 below). The Cabinet Office under the Labour Government are
engaging in a "Better Government" programme to improve the quality of
government and public service.

Ombudsmen

History

[Add to Note 90:] **1–092**

I.F. Nicholson, *The Mystery of Crichel Down* (1986).

Under Health Service Commissioners (Amendment) Act 1996, s. 6, **1–093**
"clinical judgment" of practitioners, including consideration of the merits
of such decisions, may now be investigated. The Act also extends the
jurisdiction of the Health Service Commissioner to cover family health
services delivered by general medical practitioners, community dentists,
opticians and pharmacists (section 1). The Commissioner may also
investigate bodies which have contracted with the NHS to provide services
for the latter. The Commissioner or his officers are given the power to
disclose otherwise confidential information if they consider it necessary to
do so to protect patients: section 11 amending section 15 of the 1993 Act.
On April 1, 1996 a two tier complaints process was introduced into the
NHS following the Wilson Report *Being Heard* (1994, HMSO). Most
complaints it is hoped will be resolved by the body complained against.

Where that is not possible, a "semi-independent" panel will review the complaint—the second stage. Only after that stage will the Commissioner take up an unresolved complaint for investigation.

A Broadcasting Standards Commission has been formed from a merger of the Broadcasting Complaints Commission and the Broadcasting Standards Council under Part V of the Broadcasting Act 1996. This will deal with complaints concerning fairness and privacy and complaints relating to standards and decency.

Powers and jurisdiction

1–095   The Parliamentary Commissioner for Administration was judicially reviewed in *R. v. Parliamentary Commissioner for Administration, ex p. Balchin* [1997] C.O.D. 146. In this Case, the PCA failed to consider what the impact of correct advice from a government department (which had failed to offer any advice) to a recalcitrant local authority on the latter's legislative powers may have been in a complaint concerning a new discretionary power to compensate for blight. "The Commissioner omitted a potentially decisive element from his consideration of whether the Department of Transport had caused injustice to the Balchins by maladministration in its dealings with the County Council" in the Department's failure to advise on the new power. Sedley J. believed that whether this failure amounted to maladministration by the Department was for the PCA to decide: but the Department "overlooked" its power and it had "failed" to perform a relevant power. The inference seems clear. The PCA had argued that the actions of the County Council were outside his jurisdiction and any advice from the Department would have made no difference to the outcome given the evidence of intransigence by the authority. There is growing evidence that the courts are scrutinising ombudsmen decisions ever more closely in establishing legal errors on their part (see, *e.g. Westminster C.C. v. Haywood and the Pensions Ombudsman* [1977] 3 W.L.R. 641, setting aside, *inter alia*, payments for inconvenience and distress). However, the Court of Appeal has refused to review recommendations of the Parliamentary Commissioner for Standards set up by Standing Orders of the House of Commons: *R. v. Parliamentary Commissioner for Standards, ex p. Fayed* [1998] 1 All E.R. 93.

1–097   *[Add:]*

It has been held that the local government ombudsman is entitled to obtain privileged, confidential files relating to an adoption. The local government ombudsman was given wide investigatory powers, adoption was within his jurisdiction, and it was not contrary to the public interest for the ombudsman to obtain such files: *Re a Subpoena issued by the Commissioner for Local Administration* (1996) 8 Admin. L.R. 577.

The Government reply to the *Channel Tunnel Rail Link*, H.C. 819   **1–098**
(1994–1995) indicated that the Government was prepared to consider the
issue afresh to examine possibilities in order to implement the Select
Committee's recommendations. The Government put proposals for compensation to the Select Committee. (Note that the Select Committee on
the Parliamentary Commissioner has been replaced by the Public Administration Committee).

Under section 10 of the Health Service Commissioners (Amendment)
Act 1996 the Health Ombudsman reports directly to Parliament, not via
the Secretary of State.

[Add:]   **1–100**

For complaints provisions relating to the National Criminal Intelligence
Service, the National Crime Squad and authorisation of actions in relation
to property, see the Police Act 1976, ss 39–40, 83–84 and 102 respectively.
See also the discussion on the Health Service Commissioners (Amendment) Act 1996 at paragraph 1–093 above.

On the position of "clinical judgment" and complaints and the extended   **1–103**
jurisdiction of the HSC in relation to family practitioner services, see
paragraph 1–093 above.

Operation

Mr Michael Buckley has now replaced Mr William Reid as Parliamentary   **1–105**
and Health Commissioners on the latter's retirement. Mr Reid had
brought innovative qualities to the Commissioners' role, particularly on the
side of information complaints. The object of Mr Reid's report was the
Child Support Agency.

Evaluation

In the Government Reply to *Maladministration and Redress*, H.C. 316 (1994–   **1–108**
1995) it was stated that it was not always possible to achieve consistency
through Treasury guidance on compensation and levels of redress. A "Dear
Accounting Officer letter" has replaced the letter of 1992 and contains
advice on maladministration and redress. The Government undertook to
keep the question of a Redress Team in the Citizen's Charter unit under
review. Generally, the tone of the report was noticeably positive. The reply
stated that only in very exceptional circumstances should payments be
made for worry and distress. If exceptional circumstances were present,
and the sums were within the delegated limits, payment might be made.
See the Court of Appeal in *Westminster C.C. v. Haywood* [1997] 3 W.L.R.

641; also *Miller v. Stapleton* [1996] 2 All E.R. 449; *Seifert v. Pensions Ombudsman* [1997] 4 All E.R. 947. Payments for "botheration" may be made where the behaviour causing the botheration amounts to maladministration, *i.e.* a "significant failure" to consider effectively a "clear-cut" case of maladministration.

1–109   On the Channel Tunnel complaint, see paragraph 1–098 above. On December 10, 1996 the Minister for Transport announced to the House of Commons that he would shortly be giving a response to the Select Committee on the outcome of the review conducted in the particularly difficult cases emerging from the building of the Channel Tunnel.

1–110   On information complaints, see paragraph 1–124 below.

1–111   For the first annual report of the Prisons Ombudsman see: *Prisons Ombudsman 1995* (1996). The position and work of this ombudsman have not been without some controversy in relation to his independence of the Home Office. This has caused concern as to whether "ombudsman" is in this case a "misnomer". The Report, Prisons Ombudsman 1996 (1997) has now been published and shows that he is making a small but real contribution to improving standards within prisons.

1–112   On the relationship between the ombudsmen and the courts, see *R. v. Parliamentary Commissioner for Administration, ex p. Balchin* [1997] C.O.D. 146, noted in paragraph 1–095. On the relationship between legal duties and maladministration see: *LGO Issue No. 5* (Commission for Local Administration).

THE DISCLOSURE OF OFFICIAL INFORMATION, THE COURTS AND PUBLIC INTEREST IMMUNITY

Access to information

1–122–   The activity surrounding two official reports will keep constitutional gazers
1–123   in business for generations. In May 1995 the Committee on Standards in Public Life under the chairmanship of Lord Nolan published its first report: *Standards in Public Life*, Cm. 2850. Nolan has since issued a further set of reports on *Local Public Spending Bodies*, Cm. 3270, Vols I and II, and local government: *Local Government*, Cm. 3702, Vols I and II. The Government responded (see Cm. 2931) to the first report in a generally positive manner but with a reluctance to allow civil servants to "whistleblow" outside the established internal procedures within the civil service. Codes of Conduct for Ministers—*Questions of Procedure*—and civil servants have been redrafted. The Code of Conduct for MPs has also been amended: H.C. 604 (1995–1996). Various Commissioners have been

established to overview public appointments and MPs' conduct and standards; and on improper pressure by a Minister on the Committee on Standards and Privileges, see: H.C. 88 (1996–1997).

In February 1996 the Scott Report was published: Sir Richard Scott, *Inquiry into the Export of Defence Equipment and Dual-Use Goods to Iraq and Related Prosecutions*, H.C. 115 (1995–1996). Scott famously reported on two major concerns in addition to the control and licensing of arms exports and the troublesome nature of the actions and office of the Attorney-General—and, one might add, its potential political compromise—and various departmental failings. The major concerns were: the misleading of Parliament by Ministers and the use of public interest immunity certificates (see below at paragraph 1–130 *et seq.* for the latter). His report was critical of the misleading of Parliament and subsequently he has suggested that an independent officer of Parliament should have power to investigate cases where Ministers refused to answer parliamentary questions. The refusal to answer parliamentary questions "of their nature secret" was removed and the refusal to answer where there had been a prior refusal by a Minister was relaxed, both in 1993. The Public Service Committee has reported on *Ministerial Accountability and Responsibility* (H.C. 313, Vols I & II) and there is a *Government Reply*, H.C. 67 (1996–1997). The latter accepted that where parliamentary questions were not answered, the Minister should cite some statutory justification or the reliance upon the harm to the public interest test in the non-statutory Code of Practice on *Open Government*. In early 1997 there was still debate about when Ministers who knowingly misled the House should resign although it seemed to be apparent that where Ministers knowingly misled the House, the House would expect them to offer their resignations to the Prime Minister: Public Service Committee, *Ministerial Accountability and Responsibility*, H.C. 234 (1996–1997). On March 20, 1997 a draft resolution by the Government affirming the duty of Ministers to account to Parliament for the policies, decisions and actions of their departments and Next Steps Agencies was approved by Parliament. See the statement of Nicholas Soames MP in the House of Commons on December 10, 1996 about organophosphates and the misleading of the House because Ministers had not been given the correct advice by officials.

The Code on *Open Government* was amended in January 1997, along with the Code on Interpretation. The Osmotherley Rules, covering the giving of evidence to Select Committees, was also amended to reflect the more liberal approach in the Code on *Open Government* (and see para. 1–124 below).

See *Attorney-General v. Blake* [1996] 3 All E.R. 903 and Scott V.-C.'s   **1–123** decision on the inability of the Crown, on the facts of the case, to restrain a former member of the secret Intelligence Service from publishing his memoirs. The contents were no longer confidential. On appeal the Attorney-General was granted an injunction by the Court of Appeal to prevent Blake receiving the royalties for his memoirs. Leave to appeal to the House of Lords has been granted. See also *Attorney-General v. Blake (Jonathan Cape Ltd, third party)* [1998] 1 All E.R. 833, noted at para. 2–089 below.

The role of confidentiality

1–124   The Code of Practice on *Access to Government Information* was published in a second edition in January 1997 and followed a report by the Select Committee on *Open Government*, H.C. 84 (1995–1996) and a *Government Reply*, H.C. 75 (1996–1997). In spite of some relaxations the Government remained committed to a code and not a statute, to the provision of information and not documents and to the exclusion of Cabinet material from the Code. The Code was becoming a "bench-mark against which access to information in all areas of government activity is being judged" (*Reply*, p. vii). The Select Committee itself did not see the need for a body above the Ombudsman to enforce the code, *e.g.* courts. See further P. Birkinshaw *Freedom of Information: the Law, the Practice and the Ideal* (2nd ed., 1996). The Office of Public Service has produced annual reports on the Code and its operation and the Parliamentary Commissioner has displayed a combative spirit in investigating complaints although on some occasions he appears to have been thwarted by departmental sleight of hand: (see H.C. 84 (1995–1996), pages 47–49). On other occasions he has managed to persuade departments to hand over documents and not simply information. The Government also produced for departments *The Ombudsman in Your Files* without any public reference to the document at the time of its production. On December 10, 1996 the Shadow Chancellor of the Duchy of Lancaster gave an undertaking that a Labour Government would introduce a freedom of information statute. The Queen's Speech in May 1997 stated that there was to be a White Paper on Freedom of Information to discuss the options. *Your Right to Know* (Cm. 3818, December 1997) outlines the Government's plans for a Freedom of Information Statute.

The Health Service Commissioner's First Report of 1996–1997 covered his selected investigations on *Access to Official Information in the National Health Service*, H.C. 62 (1996–1997).

The code of practice of the E.C. Council and Commission has been shown to be rather narrow in its impact: *Carvel v. E.U. Council* Case T-194/94 [1996] All E.R. (E.C.) 53 where practices of the Council were successfully challenged and also *Netherlands v. EU Council*; Case C-58/94, April 30, 1996 (E.C.J.). A subsequent Code was agreed on access to the minutes and statement in the minutes of the Council acting as legislator: (PRES/95/271, October 2, 1995. See generally P. Birkinshaw, "Freedom of Information and Open Government: The European Community/Union Dimension" (1997) 14 *Government Information Quarterly* 27). The European Union Ombudsman has conducted an audit of the practices on disclosure of those E.U. bodies not covered by the Code. Further litigation occurred

in *WWF v. Commission* Case T-105/95 [1997] All E.R. (E.C.) 300. (See also
J. Michael, "Freedom of Information comes to the European Union"
[1996] P.L. 31). The revised E.C. Treaty now provides for access for
information of Council, Commission and Parliament documents: Art. 255
E.C.

The European Convention

[Note 18:]　　　　　　　　　　　　　　　　　　　　　　　　　　　　**1–125**

In *Goodwin*, on March 27, 1996 the European Court of Human Rights
found the U.K. in breach of Art. 10: *Goodwin v. United Kingdom, The Times*,
March 28, 1996. See, however, *Camelot Group plc v. Centaur Communications
Ltd* [1998] 1 W.L.R. 379 (C.A.) and *Saunders v. Punch Ltd* [1998] 1 All E.R.
234.

Local government

Although a Code on Access to local government information was promised　　**1–127**
by the Government in its 1993 White Paper, the local authority associations
were left to produce what turned out to be a "practice note" on *Open
Government* (AMA, ADC and ACC, 1995). It was recommended that local
authorities develop their own policies on access. Where authorities had
adopted policies on access and had not followed them that may well
amount to maladministration. Where a policy had not been adopted that
may also amount to maladministration and non-adoption would certainly
not be a defence to an allegation of maladministration: *LGO Issue 6*, March
1996.

[The last sentence of the paragraph should read:]

This has established that members possess a prima facie right to documents
addressed to or by the authority of which they are members.

Personal information

An E.C. Directive has been adopted on data protection which will seek to　　**1–128**
harmonise laws throughout the Community on access to personal data.
The Directive, which applies to computer and paper documents, is closer
in some respects to a privacy protection law, but there are notable areas
which are excluded from its operation. It has to be implemented within
three years of its adoption and applies to both public and private holders of
personal data (European Parliament and Council Directive 95/46/E.C.

15

([1995] O.J. No. L281, page 31)). A Data Protection Bill was introduced into the House of Lords in the Autumn of 1997. It will be crucial to see how data protection and freedom of information operate together and how the balance is struck between privacy and access. Note also, in this regard, the Human Rights Bill.

1–129   *[Add to Note 40:]*

R. v. Secretary of State for the Home Department, ex p. Fayed [1997] 1 W.L.R. 228, where although there was no duty to provide reasons for refusing British nationality, the Home Secretary was bound in fairness to provide the applicant with sufficient information relating to any concerns the Home Secretary may have in relation to the application and which were not covered by public interest protection. (See also *R. v. Secretary of State for the Home Department, ex p. Venables* [1997] 2 W.L.R. 67 (C.A.) and [1997] 3 W.L.R. 23.

[Add to Note 41:]

See also Statutory Instruments (Production and Sale) Act 1996.

Public interest immunity

1–130   This part of the chapter now has to be read in the light of the extraordinary events surrounding the Matrix Churchill Trial, its collapse and the report by Sir Richard Scott into the events leading to the prosecution and collapse of the prosecution arising from, as well as the question of, the export of dual use equipment to Iraq. In a very damning report (see paragraph 1–122 above), Sir Richard was critical of the use of class claims for public interest immunity (PII) in criminal trials, the extension of principles developed in civil cases to criminal cases and the advice that the Attorney-General had given to Ministers that they were under a duty to sign PII certificates even in relatively routine matters. Although doubt was expressed in government and judicial circles about the accuracy of Sir Richard's interpretation of the law and his opinion, and after some initial reluctance to accept his recommendations, eventually statements were made in both Houses on December 18, 1996 by the Lord Chancellor and the Attorney-General that guidelines would be produced under which claims for public interest would only be made where disclosure would damage substantially the public interest because of the contents of the documents. Class claims would no longer be made (H.C. Deb., Vol. 287, col. 949 and H.L. Deb., Vol. 576, col. 1507; and H.C. Deb., Vol. 297, Col. 616 (July 11, 1997)). The Attorney-General confirmed that real damage or harm meant "substantial damage" quoting Lord Templeman in *ex p. Wiley*. The nature of the harm will be clearly explained in the certificate which will contain greater detail than before. Policy advice would not be protected on a candour or internal operations of government basis but it would be protected when appropriate by a contents claim.

A detailed review of the questions raised by the Scott Report can be found in [1996] P.L. 357–527 and (1997) 50 Parl. Aff., No.1. (See also: P. Birkinshaw, "Government and the End of its Tether: Matrix Churchill and the Scott Report" (1996) 23 *Journal of Law and Society* 406).

[Add to Note 99:]   **1–145**

See *Savage v. Chief Constable of the Hampshire Constabulary* [1997] 2 All E.R. 631 (C.A.).

[Add to Note 1:]

And see *Re Barings plc* [1998] 1 All E.R. 673 (Ch.D.) where it was held that statutory reports made by administrators under the Company Directors Disqualification Act 1986 were not protected by legal professional privilege where no public interest immunity claim was made.

Public interest immunity and criminal trials

Scott believed that where the demands of justice required that the defence   **1–148** in a criminal trial should have access to information held by the prosecution then no question of a "balance" of public interests emerged; it should be disclosed or the prosecution should be withdrawn. Under the Criminal Procedure and Investigations Act 1996 and its accompanying Code of Practice, new rules govern the disclosure of relevant information to the defence. These take effect from April 1, 1997. The basic test is that information should be disclosed where it might undermine the prosecution case or assist the defence disclosed by the accused. Criticism has been made to the effect that this will not bring about a fairer position for the defence. The Code deals with questions of definition, recording of information and retention of material, preparation of material for the prosecution including that which it is not in the public interest to disclose, which in turn includes that which can only be given to the prosecution under certain safeguards. Where it is in the public interest that material be given to the defence, the case will not proceed unless there is disclosure although the defence is not necessarily entitled to unrelated documents.

The duty to withhold?

The statement made by the Attorney-General on December 18, 1996 (see   **1–153—** paragraph 1–130 above) would appear to undermine his previous opinion   **1–154** that Ministers were under a duty to sign PII certificates even for routine materials. The duty to sign only operates after the Minister believes, on the basis of advice, that disclosure of the contents of documents would harm the public interest. Much was made of the fact that the Attorney-General's advice was given *before* the decision in *ex p. Wiley* (see for instance the exchange between the Lord Chancellor and Lord Simon of Glaisdale in the House of Lords on December 18, 1996).

Immunity and the public interest sphere beyond the Crown

1–155   *[Add to Note 30:]*

Re L (A Minor) (Police Investigation: Privilege) [1997] A.C. 16 (H.L.); *Re G (A Minor) (Social Worker: Disclosure)* [1996] 1 W.L.R. 1407 (C.A.).

PART II

THE SCOPE OF REVIEW

CHAPTER 2

WHO MAY BRING PROCEEDINGS: STANDING TO SUE

INTRODUCTION

The general approach to standing: comparative perspectives

[Correction to spelling in Note 8:]   2–007

Jürgen Schwarze.

The court's jurisdiction

[Note 32:]   2–016

R. v. Secretary of State for Foreign and Commonwealth Affairs, ex p. World Development Movement Ltd is now reported at [1995] 1 W.L.R. 386 and noted by P. Cane, "Standing up for the Public" [1995] P.L. 276.

[Note 34:]

Delete the final sentence.

LOCUS STANDI ON APPLICATIONS FOR JUDICIAL REVIEW

The absence of a "decision" capable of being reviewed

[Add to Note 55:]   2–026

See also R. v. Secretary of State for Trade and Industry, ex p. Greenpeace Ltd [1998] C.O.D. 59, where Laws J. dismissed as "quite misconceived" an argument that an announcement contained in a press release issued by the DTI, publicising the Government's decision to consider applications for licences to drill for oil, did not constitute a reviewable decision. Laws J. stated that quite apart from the fact (*pace* Sir William Wade Q.C.) that the law was long past the stage when judicial review bit only on a distinct executive decision itself having direct consequences upon affected persons' rights, the DTI announcement was a specific act by government—not a piece of advice as might be contained in a circular—with at once affected third party rights: the oil companies could bid only for the sites then promulgated.

The National Federation of Self-Employed case

2–031 *[Add:]*

In *R. v. Somerset C.C. and ARC Southern Ltd, ex p. Dixon* [1997] C.O.D. 323 Sedley J. reaffirmed the position that it is entirely misconceived, at the leave stage, to elevate the question of standing "above the elementary level of excluding busybodies and troublemakers and to demand something akin to a special private interest in the subject matter".

The relevance of the relief claimed

2–034 *[Add to Note 68:]*

In the High Court of New Zealand it has been held that Television New Zealand and other members of the news media have standing to challenge the permanent suppression of the name of a convicted offender: *R v. L* [1994] 3 N.Z.L.R. 568.

The broad and flexible approach

2–037 *[Add new paragraph:]*

The judgment of Sedley J. in *R. v. Somerset C.C. and ARC Southern Ltd, ex p. Dixon* [1997] C.O.D. 323 serves to re-emphasise the need for a broad approach to standing, particularly at the leave stage. The applicant in that case sought leave to apply for judicial review of the conditional grant of planning permission to extend a limestone quarry. He was, *inter alia*, a local resident, a parish councillor and a member of more than one body concerned with the environment. The local planning authority contended that the applicant, having no interest as a landowner or as possessor of a personal right or interest threatened by the proposed quarrying, had no "sufficient interest" to be granted leave to apply for judicial review within the meaning of section 31(3) of the Supreme Court Act 1981. Sedley J. rejected these submissions and the notion that there always exists a simple dichotomy between, on the one hand, the generality of the public which has a general interest in seeing public bodies comply with the law and, on the other, the person who has a particular interest in the matter above the generality (a distinction drawn in *R. v. Canterbury C.C., ex p. Spingimage Ltd* (1994) 68 P. &. C.R. 171). There was, Sedley J. held, no authority for a proposition that a court is necessarily compelled to refuse leave where the interest of the applicant is shared with the generality of the public (and if *dicta* of Schiemann J. in *R. v. Secretary of State for the Environment, ex p. Rose Theatre Co. Ltd* [1990] Q.B. 504 at 506 suggested otherwise they were not to be followed). While accepting that in the majority of cases such a greater interest may be necessary to establish that an applicant is more than a mere busybody, Sedley J. stated that "there will be, in public life, a certain number of cases of apparent abuse of power in which any individual, simply as a citizen, has a sufficient interest to bring the matter before the court". One such case is *R. v. Secretary of State for Foreign and Commonwealth Affairs, ex p. Rees-Mogg* [1994] Q.B. 552 where there was no dispute as to the applicant's *locus standi* (he was *inter alia* a former editor of *The Times* newspaper) and the Divisional Court accepted "without question that Lord Rees-Mogg brings the proceedings because of his sincere concern for constitutional issues".

This broad approach has not been adopted in some other jurisdictions. In Australia, the Federal Court has held that the Right to Life Association did not have standing under the Administrative Decisions (Judicial Review) Act 1977 (Cth) to challenge a decision not to stop trials of an abortion drug. The interest of the Association was no greater than that of an ordinary member of the public; and standing cannot be created merely by forming an association: *Right to Life Association (NSW) v. Secretary of the Department of Human Services and Health* (1995) 128 A.L.R. 238. The decision affects the rules of standing under the general law of Australia as well, because the courts have kept it broadly in line with the definition of "person aggrieved" under the 1977 Act.

The standing of a representative body or a pressure group

[Add to Note 78:]   2–038

and *R. v. Traffic Commissioner for the North Western Traffic Area, ex p. BRAKE* [1996] C.O.D. 248 in which Turner J. disapproved *Darlington Taxi Owners* and refused to set aside leave to move for judicial review which had been granted to an unincorporated association the aim of which was to promote greater safety in the use of lorries on public roads. See also para. 15–104, below.

[Add to Note 83:]   2–040

R. v. Secretary of State for Social Security, ex p. Joint Council for the Welfare of Immigrants [1997] 1 W.L.R. 275.

[Note 86:]

R. v. Secretary of State for the Environment, ex p. Friends of the Earth is now reported at (1995) 7 Admin. L.R. 26.

2–041   *[Add to Note 87:]*

In *R. v. Somerset C.C. and ARC Southern Ltd, ex p. Dixon* [1997] C.O.D. 323 Sedley J. comments that the decision in *ex p. World Development Movement Ltd* reasserts, without expressly referring to, "a very strong and old line of authority of which the courts have lost sight"—including; *R. v. Speyer* [1916] 1 K.B. 595 (affirmed at [1917] 2 K.B. 858).

[Add to end of first paragraph in 2–041:]

In *R. v. Secretary of State for Trade and Industry, ex p. Greenpeace Ltd* [1998] C.O.D. 59, Laws J. held that a pressure group bringing a public interest challenge to the validity of a statutory instrument had to "act as a friend to the court". Litigation of this kind was now an accepted and greatly valued dimension of the judicial review jurisdiction, but it had to be controlled with particular strictness—particularly as regards the requirement that applications for leave be made promptly and in any event within three months of the impugned decision.

Law Commission proposals for reform

2–042   *[Add:]*

The proposals of the Law Commission were supported by Lord Woolf in *Access to Justice—final report* (1995), page 255.

[Add to Note 89:]

Note that the Australian Law Reform Commission has recommended a new standing test in public law proceedings under which a person should be entitled to commence proceedings unless: (1) the relevant legislation provides otherwise; or (2) the litigation would unreasonably interfere with the ability of a person, with a private interest in the matter, to deal with it as he or she wishes: *Beyond the Door-keeper: Standing to Sue for Public Remedies* (1996).

Third party intervention

2–043   *[Add new Note 90a:]*

See further JUSTICE/Public Law Project, *A Matter of Public Interest: the Law and Practice on Interventions in Public Interest Cases* (1996), Chap. 2 and Sir Konrad Schiemann, "Interventions in Public Interest Cases" [1996] P.L. 240.

The contrast between the approach at the leave stage and at the stage when the court is reaching its final conclusion

[Add to Note 91:]   2–044

R. v. Somerset C.C. and ARC Southern Ltd, ex p. Dixon [1997] C.O.D. 323.

STANDING: STATUTORY APPLICATION TO QUASH AND APPEALS

The person aggrieved

[Add to Note 13:]   2–055

See *Warren Felsted Parish Council v. Uttlesford D.C.* [1996] C.O.D. 262 (Town and Country Planning Act 1990, s. 287 did not involve private litigation and did not amount to a "cause or matter" under R.S.C. Order 15, r. 6(2)(b). A company's application to be joined as a party to a challenge to a local plan was refused).

The use of person aggrieved in other contexts and as including rate payers

[Note 38:]   2–061

Re S is now reported as *Re S (Hospital Patient: Court's Jurisdiction)* [1995] Fam. 26.

STANDING IN PRIVATE LAW PROCEEDINGS

Private proceedings by public bodies

[Note 88:]   2–083

Public Health Act 1936, s. 100 is repealed.

The Attorney-General

[Add to Note 3:]   2–087

See further:
   R. v. Solicitor General, ex p. Taylor and Taylor (1996) 8 Admin. L.R. 206 (exercise of discretion by Attorney-General or Solicitor-General as to

whether or not to bring proceedings under Contempt of Court Act 1981, s. 7 is not susceptible to judicial review); *R. v. Attorney-General, ex p. Eady,* February 26, 1992 (unreported). (Court of Appeal rejected a renewed application for leave to apply for judicial review of the Attorney-General's refusal to bring prosecutions for Sunday trading contrary to Shops Act 1950, s. 47 now repealed by Sunday Trading Act 1994); *R. v. Attorney-General, ex p. Ferrante* [1995] C.O.D. 18. (Popplewell J. refused an application for judicial review of decision of Attorney-General not to give his authority for an application to be made to the High Court under Coroners Act 1988 for an order that a new inquest be held).

2-089   *[Add new Note 4a at end of paragraph:]*

See also *Att.-Gen. v. Blake (Jonathan Cape Ltd, third party)* [1998] 1 All E.R. 833 (on application of Attorney-General, the C.A. granted an injunction restraining a criminal from receiving further benefit from crime—royalties from a book published contrary to the Official Secrets Act 1989).

2-090   *[Delete this paragraph.]*

CHAPTER 3

PUBLIC AND PRIVATE LAW AND THEIR RELATION TO JUDICIAL REVIEW

THE HISTORICAL DEVELOPMENT

[Add to Note 8:] 3–008

For further analysis of the public/private law divide, see J.W.F. Allison, *A Continental Distinction in the Common Law: a Historical and Comparative Perspective on English Public Law* (1996).

The public sector today

[Note 34:] 3–015

In relation to electricity, see *Norweb plc v. Dixon* [1995] 1 W.L.R. 636 in which it was held that where there was an agreement under section 16 for the supply of electricity between a tariff customer and a public electricity supplier the legal compulsion as to both the creation of the relationship and the fixing of its terms was not compatible with the existence of a contract and supplies to tariff customers were governed by statute and not by contract. See also the Northern Irish decision in *Re Sherlock and Morris*, November 29, 1996 (unreported), discussed in paragraph 3–046 below, which concerned the question whether a decision to withdraw the supply of electricity from a customer was subject to judicial review. In *R. v. Director General of Electricity Supply, ex p. Scottish Power plc*, February 3, 1997 (unreported) the Court of Appeal quashed a decision of the Director-General not to propose modifications to the applicants' licence to give effect to a report of the Monopolies and Mergers Commission. See further Colin Scott, "Regulatory Discretion in Licence Modification: the *Scottish Power* case" [1997] P.L. 400.

In respect of telecommunications, see *Mercury Communications Ltd v. Director-General of Telecommunications and another* [1996] 1 W.L.R. 48 (considered in paragraph 3–070, below); and *R. v. Director of Telecommunications, ex p. British Telecommunications plc*, December 20, 1996 (unreported, CO/3596/96) in which the Divisional Court held that the Director-General had acted lawfully in modifying a licence to run a telecommunications system. See also *R. v. H.M. Treasury, ex p. British Telecommunications plc* [1996] Q.B. 615 (E.C.J.).

3–020   *[Note 52:]*

Tesco Stores v. Secretary of State for the Environment is now reported at [1995] 1 W.L.R. 759.

3–021   *[Add to Note 53:]*

R. v. Secretary of State for the Environment, ex p. South Lakeland D.C. [1996] 7 C.L. 430; *R. v. Secretary of State for the Environment, ex p. Oswestry B.C.* [1995] C.O.D. 357; *R. v. Greater Manchester Police Authority, ex p. Century Motors (Farnworth) Ltd, The Times,* May 31, 1996.

[Add to Note 54 after ". . . which may now provide a remedy".:]

Cf. *R. v. Legal Aid Board, ex p. Donne & Co. (a firm)* [1996] 3 All E.R. 1 (decision of legal aid committee to award contract to a firm of solicitors for the conduct of the multi-party Gulf War Syndrome litigation was amenable to judicial review) in which Ognall J. held (at p. 11) that the question whether the matter was one justiciable in public law fell to be decided as "one of overall impression, and one of degree. There can be no universal test", *ex p. Hibbit and Saunders (a firm)* was applied in *R. v. Leeds C.C., ex p. Cobleigh* [1997] C.O.D. 69 (a local authority's refusal to sell land was not amenable to judicial review because it lacked the necessary statutory underpinning).

THE IDENTIFICATION OF PUBLIC FUNCTIONS AND PUBLIC LAW

3–024   *[Add to Note 60:]*

Implied terms as fair procedures will not, however, always exist. In *Andreou v. Institute of Chartered Accountants for England and Wales* [1998] 1 All E.R. 14 the C.A. rejected A's submission that in membership contracts with the Institute there were implied terms that "(a) the power of the Institute to make byelaws . . . would be exercised fairly and reasonably and (b) that the Institute would act fairly in the conduct of its disciplinary procedures". Such implied terms were inconsistent with the express provisions of the Institute's Charter.

3–025   *[Add new Note 64a after "Charities,":]*

Where an application for judicial review of a decision taken by a charitable organisation is a "charitable proceedings" under Charities Act 1993, s. 33, they may proceed only if the authorisation of the Charity Commissioners is first obtained, or leave is granted by a judge of the Chancery Division: see *R. v. The National Trust for Places of Historic Interest or Natural Beauty, ex p. Scott and Others* [1998] 1 W.L.R. 228, considered at para. 3–037.

[Add to Note 66:]

See also Julia Black, "Constitutionalising Self-Regulation" (1996) 59 M.L.R. 24; A.I. Ogus, "Re-thinking Self-Regulation" (1995) 15 O.J.L.S. 97; Colin Munro, "Self-regulation in the media" [1997] P.L. 6.

[Add to Note 67:]   **3–026**

Cf. C. Forsyth, "Of Fig Leaves and Fairy Tales: the ultra vires doctrine, the sovereignty of Parliament and Judicial Review" [1996] C.L.J. 122.

[Add to Note 70:]

  Nor are decisions of officers of the House of Commons itself amenable to judicial review. In *R. v. Parliamentary Commissioner for Standards, ex p. Fayed* [1998] 1 All E.R. 93 the Court of Appeal held that the Commissioner for Standards, an officer established by the Standing Orders of the House of Commons, was part of Parliament's own processes and as such outside the court's jurisdiction.

[Add to Note 72:]   **3–027**

R. v. Press Complaints Commission, ex p. Stewart-Brady (1997) 9 Admin. L.R. 247 considered in para. 3–050, below; *R. v. London Beth Din (Court of Chief Rabbi), ex p. Bloom* [1998] C.O.D. 131; *R. v. Panel of the Federation of Communication Services Ltd, ex p. Kubis* [1998] C.O.D. 56; *Andreou v. Institute of Chartered Accountants in England and Wales* [1998] 1 All E.R. 14.

[Note 88:]   **3–028**

See now *Access to Justice* (1996), Final Report to the Lord Chancellor on the Civil Justice System in England and Wales.

[Add to Note 99:]   **3–032**

See also *National Union of Teachers v. Governing Body of St Mary's Church of England (Aided) Junior School* [1997] I.C.R. 334 and *Griffin v. South West Water Services Ltd* [1995] I.R.L.R. 15 (and para. 21–028, below).

JUDICIAL REVIEW AND PUBLIC FUNCTIONS

Statutory bodies and office holders

[Add to Note 6:]   **3–037**

See now *R. v. Crown Court at Leeds, ex p. Hussain* [1995] 1 W.L.R. 1329 in which the Divisional Court held that the arraignment of a defendant and the conduct of a plea and directions hearing were clearly matters directly relating to trial on indictment; the High Court accordingly had no jurisdiction to consider an application for judicial review. *R. v. Maidstone Crown Court, ex p. Clark* [1995] 1 W.L.R. 831 and *R. v. Crown Court at Maidstone, ex p. Hollstein* [1995] 1 W.L.R. 1329 were not followed. See also *R. v. Chester Crown Court, ex p. Cheshire County Council* (1996) 8 Admin. L.R. 224 and *R. v. Dorset Magistrates' Court, ex p. Cox* [1997] C.O.D. 86

[After ". . . the High Court does not exercise its supervisory jurisdiction where an alternative remedy exists." add new Note 6A:]

cf. R. v. Hereford Magistrates' Court, ex p. Rowlands [1998] Q.B. 110 in which the Divisional Court held that the existence of a right of appeal by way of retrial in the Crown Court did not preclude a person convicted in the Magistrates' Court from applying for judicial review on the grounds of procedural impropriety, unfairness or bias.

[Add new Note 6b to end of paragraph:]

Thus in *R. v. The National Trust for Places of Historic Interest or Natural Beauty, ex p. Scott and Others* [1998] 1 W.L.R. 228 Tucker J. refused leave to move for judicial review in respect of the National Trust's decision to ban deer hunting on Trust land. The Trust, a statutory body established by the National Trust Act 1971, was exercising public functions in making its decision. However, the Trust was also a charity, its Council members were charity trustees, and accordingly it was protected by the provisions of the Charities Act 1993, s. 33 which regulated legal proceedings against charities. The applicants had neither obtained an order of the Charity Commissioners authorising the proceedings nor the leave of a judge of the Chancery Division. The present application was in the nature of "charity proceedings" and as consent had not been obtained in accordance with the 1993 Act, the court had no jurisdiction over the matter.

Bodies established and decisions taken under the prerogative

3–038   *[After "—though in this context much government action may be non-justiciable." add new Note 6c:]*

For a recent illustration, see the Privy Council opinion in *Reckley v. Minister of Public Safety and Immigration and others (No. 2)* [1996] A.C. 527 in which it was held that the exercise of the prerogative of mercy conferred on the Governor-General by Art. 92(1) of the Constitution of The Bahamas in death sentence cases (which was of the same legal nature as the royal prerogative of mercy which once pertained in England) was not justiciable. *R. v. Secretary of State for the Home Department, ex p. Bentley* [1994] Q.B. 349 was distinguished as "an exceptional situation" which had no bearing on the instant case *de Freitas v. Benny* [1976] A.C. 239 (in which Lord Diplock said "Mercy is not the subject of legal rights. It begins where legal rights end.") remained good law.

[Add to Note 9:]   3–039

It has been suggested, *obiter*, that the BBC exercising powers conferred on it by its Charter and Agreement with the Secretary of State for National Heritage is amenable to judicial review: see *R. v. British Broadcasting Corporation, ex p. Referendum Party* [1997] C.O.D. 460. See also *R. v. British Broadcasting Corporation, ex p. Pro-Life Alliance Party* [1997] C.O.D. 457 (counsel for BBC accepted, for the purposes of an application for leave to move for judicial review, that it was arguable that the BBC was amenable to judicial review).

Contract and judicial review

[Add to Note 13:]   3–040

See also *R. v. Panel of the Federation of Communication Services Ltd, ex p. Kubis* [1998] C.O.D. 5 (application for judicial review refused to applicant who, while not a member of the non-statutory self-regulatory organisation, was nevertheless in a contractual relationship with it in respect of an anti-theft scheme; see further n. 36, below); *R. v. The Showman's Guild of Great Britain, ex p. Flint* (July 31, 1997, unreported, CO/2014/96); and *Andreou v. Institute of Chartered Accountants in England and Wales* [1998] 1 All E.R. 14.

PRIVATE FUNCTIONS OF PUBLIC BODIES

[Add to Note 21:]   3–042

See also *R. v. Secretary of State for the Environment, ex p. Oswestry B.C.* [1995] C.O.D. 357; *R. v. Greater Manchester Police Authority, ex p. Century Motors (Farnworth) Ltd, The Times,* May 31, 1996; *R. v. Legal Aid Board, ex p. Donne & Co. (a firm)* [1996] 3 All E.R. 1; *R. v. Secretary of State for the Environment, ex p. Harrow L.B.C.* (1997) 29 H.L.R. 1; *R. v. Portsmouth City Council, ex p. Coles* (1997) 9 Admin. L.R. 535.

Nationalised and privatised industries

[Add to Note 26:]   3–046

and see *R. v. Director of Passenger Rail Franchising, ex p. Save Our Railways and others, The Times,* December 18, 1995. In Northern Ireland, Kerr J.

considered the question whether a decision of Northern Ireland Electricity plc (NIE) to withdraw electricity supply from a customer was subject to judicial review: see *Re Sherlock and Morris*, November 29, 1996 (unreported). The company is a privatised industry. *Per* Kerr J.:

> "I consider the discharge of NIE's functions [under the legislation] falls clearly within the field of public law. Before NIE was privatised it could not have been argued that the supply of electricity was not a public law function. It is now recognised that it is the public nature of the function which is discharged which provides the primary, if not the exclusive, guide to the question whether it will be amenable to judicial review."

Self-regulatory bodies

3–050   *[Add to Note 36:]*

In *R. v. Panel of the Federation of Communication Services Ltd, ex p. Kubis* [1998] C.O.D. 5, Tucker J. held that the non-statutory body regulating the mobile telephone retail sector was not amenable to judicial review. Although the applicant was not a member of that body, he had become contractually bound to the terms of a scheme run by the Federation (designed to prevent trade in stolen telephones) by entering into contracts with other dealers and service providers who were members of the Federation. Moreover, the applicant had consented to the Federation's jurisdiction by requesting an appeal hearing after a decision to declare him a trader "not in good standing". Although the Federation's anti-theft scheme had been set up with the support of the Home Office and Department of Trade and Industry, the Federation had no governmental underpinning and was not exercising governmental powers. Accordingly, any remedy against the Federation lay in contract law. (Tucker J. nevertheless went on to deal with the merits of the applicant's complaint of procedural impropriety and *Wednesbury* unreasonableness, and refused the application on those grounds also.) See also, *Andreou v. Institute of Chartered Accountants in England and Wales* [1998] 1 All E.R. 14 (the fact that the Institute is a public body established by Royal Charter does not prevent it entering into contractual relations giving its members private rights.

[After "the Press Complaints Commission, which replaces the Press Council," add new Note 36a:]

In *R. v. Press Complaints Commission, ex p. Stewart-Brady* (1997) 9 Admin. L.R. 247 the Court of Appeal held that it was arguable that the P.C.C. was a body subject to judicial review, but the matter would not be determined in the instant application for leave to move for judicial review. Any jurisdiction which the court did have over the P.C.C. should be reserved for clear breaches of its Code and not merely technical ones. See further, Colin Munro, "Challenging the Press Complaints Commission" (1996) 1 Comms L. 177 and Giles Crown, "Judicial Review and Press Complaints" (1997) 147 N.L.J. 8.

Regulation in higher education: University Visitors

[Add to Note 43:]   3–052

In *R. v. University of Nottingham, ex p. Ktorides* [1998] C.O.D. 26, the Court of Appeal rejected submissions that the court should accept jurisdiction over a challenge to a decision that the applicant failed part of her postgraduate teacher-training course (and about which no complaint had been made to the Visitor) because there had been a statutory intrusion into the University's role in the provision of teacher-training by virtue of the Education (Teachers) Regulations 1993 which enabled a minister to withdraw accreditation of an institution. This was not sufficient to remove the Visitor's exclusive jurisdiction.

[Add to the end of paragraph 3–052:]

Not all universities have Visitors, though where comparable appellate committees exist, an applicant will be required to exhaust those alternative remedies before making an application for judicial review (on which generally, see 20–018). Nor are all disciplinary and other decisions taken by universities which do have a Visitor necessarily within the ambit of the Visitor's jurisdiction: see, *e.g. R. v. University College London, ex p. Christofi* (September 12, 1997, C.A., unreported). (The court considered and rejected on its merits a judicial review challenge brought by a former student against findings of an ad hoc committee of senior academics from outside University College London that he had falsified scientific data published in international journals while engaged in post-doctoral research).

Sporting bodies

[Add new paragraph:]   3–053

Even if under current English law a sporting body is not regarded as amenable to judicial review, the courts may nevertheless invoke a broad supervisory jurisdiction in private law in the form of the doctrine that contracts in unreasonable restraint of trade are unenforceable. Such a contract may be challenged by a person with no contractual nexus to the body in question: see *Pharmaceutical Society of Great Britain v. Dickson* [1970]

A.C. 403 and *Buckley v. Tutty* (1971) 125 C.L.R. 353. In *Stevenage Borough Football Club Ltd v. The Football League Ltd* (1997) 9 Admin. L.R. 109 the Court of Appeal accepted it had jurisdiction to grant a declaration that criteria applied by the Football League to refuse the plaintiff membership were in restraint of trade, but declined to grant a declaration because of the plaintiff's delay and the affect of the decision on third parties. See also *Newport Association Football Club Ltd v. Football Association of Wales Ltd* [1995] 2 All E.R. 87. Moreover, European Community law prohibiting discrimination on the ground of nationality may apply to sport in so far as the sport constituted economic activity: see *Union Royale Belge des Sociétés de Football Association ASBL v. Bosman* [1996] All E.R. (E.C.) 97; *Wilander v. Tobin* [1997] 1 Lloyd's Rep. 195 (arguable that provision on drug testing in rules of International Tennis Federation fell within Article 59 of E.C. Treaty); and *Edwards v. British Athletic Federation and Another, The Times*, June 30, 1997 (Articles. 59–66 had no application to drug control rules of International Amateur Athletic Federation, which were of an exclusively sporting nature). See also *Jones and Another v. Welsh Rugby Football Union, The Times*, January 6, 1998.

Religious bodies

3–054   *[Add to Note 52:]*

R. v. London Beth Din (Court of the Chief Rabbi), ex p. Bloom [1998] C.O.D. 131.

PUBLIC EMPLOYMENT

3–056   *[Note 54 should now read:]*

Under the Employment Rights Act 1996, s. 94.

3–057   *[Line seven:]*

delete "prison officers".

[Add:]

The Northern Ireland Court of Appeal held *Re Phillips*, February 12, 1996 (unreported), considering a dispute concerning an applicant who was a mobile non-industrial civil servant, that "the preferable approach [is] to consider the nature of the issue itself and whether it has characteristics which impart an element of public law, rather than to focus upon the classification of the civil servant's employment or office."

[Note 57 should now read:]

Employment Rights Act 1996, s. 200. The Criminal Justice and Public
Order Act 1994, s. 126(1)–(2) provides that prison officers, who were
previously held to be "in prison service" for the purposes of unfair
dismissal legislation (*Home Office v. Robinson* [1981] I.R.L.R. 524) are not to
be so treated. Workers at GCHQ are excluded by certificate issued
pursuant to Employment Rights Act 1996, s. 193. In addition, civil servants
are in no better position than other employees if they have been employed
for less than two years (Employment Rights Act 1996, ss. 108(1), 191)
although the House of Lords has referred to the European Court of Justice
the question whether this qualifying period infringes Article 119 of the
E.C. Treaty: *R. v. Secretary of State for Education and Employment, ex p.
Seymour-Smith and Another* [1997] 1 W.L.R. 473. In addition, the relationship between a Police Authority and an individual member of the police
force is not that of an employer and employee: *Fisher v. Oldham Corp.*
[1930] 2 K.B. 364; *Rodwell v. Minister of Health* [1947] K.B. 404; *Metropolitan
Police District Receiver v. Croydon Corp.* [1957] 2 Q.B. 154.

[Note 60:]   3–059

R. v. Secretary of State for Education, ex p. Prior is now reported at [1994]
I.C.R. 877.

[Add:]

(private law action appropriate for the challenge of a teacher at a grant
maintained school to the validity of an *ultra vires* dismissal *vis-à-vis* his
employer but challenge to Secretary of State's decision not to intervene
justiciable in public law).

[Note 64:]   3–061

R. v. C.P.S., ex p. Hogg is now reported at (1994) 6 Admin. L.R. 778.

[Note 70:]   3–065

Add after ". . . *ex p. Vardy* [1993] I.C.R. 720,": and *R. v. City of Sunderland,
ex p. Baumber* [1996] C.O.D. 211.

[Add to Note 71:]

R. v. Lambeth L.B.C., ex p. Thompson [1996] C.O.D. 217.

WHEN PROCEEDINGS SHOULD BE BY WAY OF JUDICIAL REVIEW
(THE PROCEDURAL DIVIDE)

The general rule

3–068   *[Add to Note 74:]*

For a recent illustration of the application of *O'Reilly v. Mackman*, see *The Great House at Sonning Ltd v. Berkshire C.C.*, *The Times*, March 25, 1996 (C.A., Saville L.J. dissenting). It was held, striking out a writ for an action in public nuisance, that a person affected by a road closure order made under Road Traffic Regulation Act 1984, s. 14 had no private right to assert; the only remedy lay in public law proceedings.

[Note 76:]

M v. Home Office is now reported at [1994] 1 A.C. 377.

3–071   *[Add:]*

The decision in *Cocks* was considered by the House of Lords in *O'Rouke v. Camden L.B.C.* [1997] 3 W.L.R. 86. Their Lordships followed *Cocks* in holding that until a local housing authority had made its inquiries and decided whether or not it was satisfied as to the various matters upon which the existence of the statutory duty depended, any decision by the authority could be challenged only by judicial review (if at all). Their Lordships went on, however, to disapprove of the dicta of Lord Bridge in *Cocks* to the effect that once a public law decision had been reached, private law rights and obligations capable of being enforced by injunction and the breach of which would give rise to liability in damages. The Court of Appeal decision in *Thornton v. Kirklees M.B.C.* [1979] Q.B. 626, holding that an action in tort for breach of statutory duty lay for a failure to provide accommodation, was accordingly overruled.

Collateral public law qualities

3–073   *[Add:]*

In *Mercury Communications Ltd v. Director-General of Telecommunications and another* [1996] 1 W.L.R. 48 the House of Lords refused to strike out an originating summons where it was argued that the matters in question ought to have been raised in an application for judicial review. Lord Slynn of Hadley stated (at 57D) that it was

"of particular importance . . . to retain some flexibility, as to the precise limits of what is called 'public law' and what is called 'private law' are by no means worked out. . . . It has to be borne in mind that the overriding question is whether the proceedings constitute an abuse of the process of the court."

In the instant case, the dispute as to the correct interpretation by the Director General of a condition in a licence granted to British Telecommunications plc was "in substance as well as form" a dispute over terms of a contract. See further, P.P. Craig, "Proceeding Outside Order 53: A Modified Test?" (1996) 112 L.Q.R. 531.

The approach of the House of Lords in *Roy v. Kensington and Chelsea and Westminster Family Practitioner Committee* [1992] 1 A.C. 624—that it is not an abuse of process to proceed by way of a private law action, even though there is a public law issue which may need to be determined, as long as there is a clearly identified private law right—has been applied by the Court of Appeal in two recent decisions: see *Andreou v. Institute of Chartered Accountants in England and Wales* [1998] 1 All E.R. 14 and *Trustees of the Dennis Rye Pension Fund and another v. Sheffield City Council* [1997] 4 All E.R. 747.

Relying on public law as a defence to private law proceedings

[Add new paragraph:]   3–074

In *British Steel plc v. Customs and Excise Commissioners* [1996] 1 All E.R. 1002 Laws J. at first instance struck out a writ claiming restitution and repayment of excise duty on hydrocarbon oils. The plaintiffs claimed that the demands for payment of duty were unlawful because the plaintiffs were entitled to relief from paying duty under the relevant legislation. The plaintiffs had neither sought to challenge the defendants' demands by way of judicial review, nor declined to pay and await action by the commissioners with a view to pleading a defence to the effect that they were entitled to relief under the legislation. Laws J. held that whereas the illegality of the tax demands was the premise of *Woolwich Building Society v. I.R.C. (No. 2)* [1992] A.C. 70, in the instant case it was the very question falling for decision. "Where the statute confers what is plainly a private right, if on the Act's true construction the right enures only after and in consequence of a purely public law decision in favour of the claimant, any complaint directed to the public decision-making stage must be brought by Order 53" (*per* Laws J.). The Court of Appeal allowed an appeal against Laws J.'s decision: see [1997] 2 All E.R. 366. It held that applying the reasoning in *Woolwich* to the facts of the instant case justified the conclusion that a demand for tax following an unlawful refusal to grant relief from tax was an "unlawful demand" for the purposes of Lord Goff's reformulation of the law. The writ action could continue as British Steel might be able to prove that it was an "approved person" and, if it could, it would have a restitutionary claim.

The position in criminal proceedings

3–075   [*Substitute:*]

In *R. v. Wicks* [1997] 2 W.L.R. 876 the House of Lords considered the question whether a defendant in a criminal trial may challenge the validity of the public law decision, order or subordinate legislation upon which the prosecution is based. On the facts of the case, the defendant was prosecuted for failure to comply with an enforcement notice served upon him pursuant to section 172 of the Town and Country Planning Act 1990. He elected for trial on indictment and his counsel sought to argue that the local planning authority had had regard to immaterial considerations in its decision to serve the enforcement notice, which was accordingly invalid. On appeal, their Lordships held that it was not possible to lay down a general rule; the question whether issues could be raised at a criminal trial to impugn a decision or legislation depended entirely on the construction of the statute under which the prosecution was bought. In the instant case, it was held that "enforcement notice" meant a notice issued by the planning authority that was formally valid and had not been quashed. One important factor which compelled this conclusion was that the 1990 Act contained an elaborate code with detailed provisions regarding appeals. Parliament had intended the Divisional Court, not criminal proceedings arising from a failure to comply with an enforcement notice, to be the appropriate forum to question such notices. It was therefore not permissible for the defendant to seek to impugn the enforcement notice in the Crown Court. Their Lordships expressed strong doubt over the analysis adopted by the Divisional Court in *Bugg v. D.P.P.; D.P.P. v. Percy* [1993] Q.B. 473 where a distinction had been drawn between "substantive" invalidity (regarded by the Divisional Court as a permissible defence in a criminal trial) and "procedural" invalidity (which was not viewed by the court as a basis for a defence) as a method of limiting the scope of an *ultra vires* defence. See further A.W. Bradley, "Collateral challenge to enforcement decisions—a duty to apply for judicial review?" [1997] P.L. 365.

Note also that in *Percy v. Hall* [1997] Q.B. 924 the Court of Appeal held that in relation to the test of uncertainty, the decision in *Bugg* based on the failure to describe the boundary for the protected area in the byelaws could not be accepted. Whether applying the test in *Kruse v. Johnson* (above); or that in *Fawcett Properties Ltd v. Buckingham C.C.* [1961] A.C. 636 of which the latter was to be preferred, the words "lands belonging to the Secretary of State" described the protected area with sufficient certainty to provide adequate information to those who had to obey the byelaws.

Where private law dominates the proceedings

3–077   [*Add to Note 93:*]

and *Mercury Communications Ltd v. Director-General of Telecommunications and another* [1996] 1 W.L.R. 48; *British Steel plc v. Customs and Excise Commissioners* [1997] 2 All E.R. 366; *Trustees of the Dennis Rye Pension Fund v.*

Sheffield City Council [1997] 4 All E.R. 747; *Andreou v. Institute of Chartered Accountants in England and Wales* [1998] 1 All E.R. 14.

The disadvantages of the present situation

[Add to Note 4:]   **3–083**

See also Woolf, *Access to Justice* discussed in Chapter 15, below.

CHAPTER 4

THE SPECIAL POSITION OF THE CROWN

INTRODUCTION

Judicial review: in outline

[Add to Note 1:]   **4–002**

On the changing nature of the legal status of the Crown, see further Joseph M. Jacob, *The Republican Crown: Lawyers and the Making of the State in Twentieth Century Britain* (1996).

[Note 3:]

R. v. Blackledge and others is now reported at (1996) 8 Admin. L.R. 361.

DEFINITIONS OF THE CROWN

The indivisibility of the Crown

[Add to Note 16:]

See also *R. v. Blackledge and others* (1996) 8 Admin. L.R. 361 at 372, *per* Lord Taylor C.J., holding that a failure to disclose the documents in the Matrix Churchill prosecution amounted to a material irregularity:

> "In reaching this conclusion we consider that the documents in the possession of one or other government department involved in the inter-departmental consideration of licences are to be regarded for the purposes of this case as in the possession of the Crown as an indivisible entity. Mr Lawson. Q.C., on behalf of the Crown, did not argue to the contrary".

CHAPTER 5

JURISDICTION, VIRES, LAW AND FACT

THE ULTRA VIRES DOCTRINE

[Add to Note 32:] **5–013**

And see H. Rajak, "Judicial Control: Corporations and the Decline of Ultra Vires" [1995] Cambrian L.R. 9.

STATUTORY RESTRICTION OF JUDICIAL REVIEW

Time-limited clauses

[Add to Note 70:] **5–024**

"Six weeks" is to be equated with six times seven days: see *Okolo v. Secretary of State for the Environment* [1997] 4 All E.R. 242.

Cases after 1978

[Add to Note 35:] **5–036**

R. v. Dacorum D.C., ex p. Cannon [1996] 2 P.L.R. 45.

[Add to Note 38:] **5–037**

and *R. v. Honourable Society of the Middle Temple, ex p. Bullock* [1996] C.O.D. 376 (in an educational matter the judges qualified to sit as Visitors did not have an unfettered power to overrule decisions made by an expert review body under statutorily approved regulations and the Visitor was therefore right to conclude that he should only interfere if satisfied that the review board has acted irrationally or unlawfully). On the powers of Visitors, see *R. v. Visitor of the University of London, ex p. Vijayatunga* [1990] 2 Q.B. 444. See also *R. v. University of Nottingham, ex p. Ktorides* [1998] C.O.D. 26 and *R. v. University College London, ex p. Christofi*, September 12, 1997, C.A. (unreported), considered at para. 3–052, Note 43, above.

JURISDICTION AND VIRES TODAY

5–040   *[Add to Note 52:]*

See *Century National Merchant Bank Ltd v. Omar Davies*, Privy Council, March 16, 1998 (10-day appeal from minister's action to Court of Appeal carried "a necessary implication" of finality. *Barraclough v. Brown* [1897] A.C. 615 applied).

5–041   *[Add to Note 56:]*

See *British Columbia (Milk Board) v. Grisnich (c.o.b. Mountainview Acres)* [1995] 2 S.C.R. 895.

5–043   *[Add to Note 68:]*

C. Forsyth, "Of Fig Leaves and Fairy Tales, The Ultra Vires Doctrine, The Sovereignty of Parliament and Judicial Review" [1996] C.L.J. 122; Sir William Wade, "Habeas Corpus and Judicial Review" (1997) 113 L.Q.R. 55. And see the helpful discussion by Lord Cooke of the concept of jurisdiction in *R. v. Bedwellty JJ, ex p. Williams* [1997] A.C. 225 (although remedy for error of law at court's discretion, where a committal procedure was so influenced by inadmissible evidence as to amount to an irregularity, a remedy would normally follow (although express use of "jurisdiction" was avoided). And see Michael Taggart, "The Contribution of Lord Cooke to Scope of Review Doctrine in Administrative Law: A Comparative Common Law Perspective", in *The Struggle for Simplicity in the Law: Essays for Lord Cooke of Thorndon* (1997), p. 189. And see D. Dyzenhaus, "The Politics of Deference: Judicial Review and Democracy" in M. Taggart (ed.), *The Province of Administrative Law* (1997), p. 279.

[Add to Note 69:]

In New Zealand it has been said that, assuming Parliament can (at least within unexplored limits) empower an administrative tribunal to determine some questions of law conclusively, such power must at least be given clearly and it would be surprising if an administrative officer were not to be given such power. Hence a privative clause would not protect a statutory misinterpretation by such an officer. *Bulk Gas Users Group v. Attorney-General* [1983] N.Z.L.R. 129. In *Regan v. Lousich* [1995] 2 N.Z.L.R. 620 Tipping J., after a full examination of modern authorities, held that a privative clause does not protect a decision of an inferior court if it is erroneous in law, unfair or unreasonable.

[Add to Note 70:]

See *New Zealand Rail Ltd v. Employment Court* [1995] 3 N.Z.L.R. 179 (privative clause confines judicial review to jurisdictional errors in Lord

Reid's "narrow and original sense", but provision for appeal on questions of law).

[Add to Note 80:]

In *R. v. Hereford Magistrate's Court ex p. Rowlands* [1998] Q.B. 110 it was held that the existence of a right of appeal by way of a retrial in the Crown Court did not preclude a person convicted in the Magistrate's Court from applying for judicial review. And see *British Steel plc v. Customs and Excise Commissioners* [1997] 2 All E.R. 366 (C.A.).

(6) *Precedent fact*

[Add to Note 79:]

R. v. Secretary of State for the Home Department, ex p. Onibiyo [1996] Q.B. 768 (*Bugdaycay* and *Khawaja* considered; court no power to review as an objective precedent fact whether fresh "claim for asylum" had been made). But see *Tan Te Lam v. Superintendent of Tai A Chau Detention Centre* [1997] A.C. 97 (P.C.) (question whether applicant could be repatriated to Vietnam from Hong Kong is a matter of jurisdiction for the court) and see also, *Re Rahman (Saidur)* [1997] 3 W.L.R. 990.

[Add to Note 84:]

See also the importance attached to certainty in respect of the assumption of management of a bank in *Century National Merchant Bank Ltd*, Note 52 above.

VOIDNESS AND NULLITY

The situation today

[Add to Note 28:]   **5–048**

R. v. Leeds, ex p. Hussain [1995] 1 W.L.R. 1329 (whether arraignment a nullity).

[Add to Note 31:]

British Steel plc v. Customs and Excise Commission [1997] 2 All E.R. 366 (where there was an unlawful demand for tax, the taxpayer was entitled to a common law restitutionary right to repayment unless removed by legislation. Therefore the plaintiff was not restricted to judicial review proceedings but entitled to bring common law action for restitution): see para. 3–074, above.

COLLATERAL CHALLENGE

5–053   *[Add to Note 45:]*

See also *R. v. Parking Adjudicator for London, ex p. Bexley L.B.C.* [1998] C.O.D. 116 (parking adjudicator exercising appellate functions under Road Traffic Act 1984, s. 32 was entitled and bound to consider validity of byelaw; he had correctly held that a provision was *Wednesbury* unreasonable).

5–054   *[Add to Note 48:]*

R. v. Blackledge and others is now reported at (1996) 8 Admin. L.R. 316. Strong doubts were expressed about *Bugg v. D.P.P.* [1993] Q.B. 473 by the House of Lords in *R. v. Wicks* [1997] 2 W.L.R. 876 considered in para. 3–075. See further A.W. Bradley, "Collateral challenge to enforcement decisions—a duty to apply for judicial review?" [1997] P.L. 365.

5–055   *[Add to Note 52:]*

See *Re Jamison* (N.I.Q.B.D.) unreported October 14, 1996. Kerr J. referring to *Foster* said "I would be slow to conclude, on the authority of that decision alone, that a Social Security Commissioner does not have jurisdiction to decide whether the refusal of an adjournment amounted to a breach of natural justice".

DISREGARD OF STATUTORY REQUIREMENTS

5–066   *[Add to Note 79:]*

Re Akomolede [1995] Crim. L.R. 161. (Application for habeas corpus. A was arrested and charged by customs officers with indictable offences under the Customs and Excise Management Act 1979. The day after he was remanded in custody by magistrates. A argued that the charging had been fundamentally defective and that the magistrates had no jurisdiction to deal with him. Held: although customs officers had the power to arrest A, they lacked the power to charge him. The defect in procuring A's appearance was cured by his appearance before the magistrates, who did have jurisdiction). *Duffield v. Pensions Ombudsman* [1996] C.O.D. 406 considers *London & Clydeside Estates Ltd v. Aberdeen D.C.* [1980] 1 W.L.R. 182 (failure to comply with section 149 of Pension Schemes Act 1993 vitiated P's decision).

SCOPE OF REVIEW OF FINDINGS OF LAW AND FINDINGS OF FACT

Error of fact a ground of judicial review?

[Note 75:]   5–092

R. v. Independent Television Commission, ex p. TSW Broadcasting Ltd is now
reported at [1996] E.M.L.R. 291.

[Add new Note 79a:]   5–094

See, *e.g. South Glamorgan C.C. v. Long* [1996] C.O.D. 213; *R. v. Secretary of
State for Education, ex p. Skitt* [1995] C.O.D. 270 and [1996] C.O.D. 31; *R.
v. Secretary of State for the Home Department, ex p. Canbolat* [1997] 1 W.L.R.
1569; *R. v. Radio Authority, ex p. Guardian Media Group plc* [1995] 1 W.L.R.
334 (factual evaluation was for the Radio Authority). And see *Shetland Line
(1984) Ltd v. Secretary of State for Scotland* 1996 S.L.T. 653 (noted [1996] P.L.
694).

PART III

THE GROUNDS OF REVIEW

[Add to Note 5:]   **III–044**

Under South Africa's new constitution (Act 108 of 1996, s. 33(1)): "Everyone has the right to administrative action that is lawful, reasonable and procedurally fair". See further H. Corder and T. Malawa (eds) *Administrative Justice in Southern Africa* (1997).

CHAPTER 6

ILLEGALITY

REVIEW OF DISCRETIONARY POWER

Discretion and duty

[Add to Note 30:]   **6–011**

For a recent analysis of the uses of "may" and "shall", "duty" and "power", see, *R. v. Berkshire County Council, ex p. Parker* [1997] C.O.D. 64.

Discretion and justiciability

[Add to Note 98:]   **6–032**

On similar facts see the recent case in the South African Constitutional Court, *T. Soobramoney v. Minister of Health Kwazula Natal*, 1997 (12) BCCR 1696 (CC).

Contractual powers

[Add to Note 12:]   **6–036**

See cases listed under Chapter 3 above, especially paras 3–015, 3–021 and 3–040.

REVIEW OF THE PREROGATIVE POWERS

The previous limits on reviewing prerogative powers

Add to Note 38:   **6–041**

See now *R. v. Solicitor General, ex p. Taylor and Taylor* (1996) 8 Admin. L.R. 206. *R. v. Attorney-General ex p. Edey* (Transcript February 26, 1992) and *R. v. Attorney-General ex p. Ferrante* [1995] C.O.D. 18, considered above at para. 2–087, Note 3.

The present approach

6–043   *[Add to Note 48:]*

For recent cases where national security has been relevant see *R. v. Secretary of State for the Home Department, ex p, McQuillan* [1995] 4 All E.R. 400; *R. v. Secretary of State for the Home Department, ex p. Adams* [1995] All E.R. (E.C.) 177; *R. v. Secretary of State for the Home Department, ex p. Chahal* [1995] 1 W.L.R. 931 (C.A.) and *Chahal v. United Kingdom* (1997) 23 E.H.R.R. 413.

6–044   *[Add to Note 50:]*

See also *R. v. Inland Revenue Commissioners ex p. Mead* [1993] 1 All E.R. 772; and *R. v. Haringey Justices, ex p. DPP* [1996] Q.B. 351 (in both the Crown Court and in magistrates' courts the prosecution had an "unfettered discretion" which witnesses to call). But see n. 38 above.

6–046   *[Add to Note 57:]*

Bentley was distinguished in *R. v. Reckley v. Minister for Public Safety and Immigration* [1996] 1 A.C. 527 where the Privy Council held that the prerogative of mercy was not reviewable under the particular procedures of the Bahamas' Constitution.

6–047   *[Add to Note 60:]*

This paragraph was cited with approval by Baragwanath J. in the High Court of New Zealand in *Patel v. Chief Executive of the Department of Labour* [1997] 1 N.Z.L.R. 102, 108. In *New Zealand Maori Council v. Attorney-General* [1996] 3 N.Z.L.R. 140, a majority of the Court of Appeal held that a Cabinet approval of a course of action was not reviewable (but see the dissent of Thomas J.).

[Add to Note 61:]

The *Fire Brigades Union* case is now reported at [1995] 2 A.C. 583 (and noted by Barendt [1995] P.L. 357 and E.W. Thomas (1996) 112 L.Q.R. 177). In *R. v. Secretary of State for the Home Department, ex p. Launder (No. 2)* [1997] 1 W.L.R. 839 (the House of Lords held that the Home Secretary's discretion under Extradition Act 1989 was normally justiciable); *R. v. Secretary of State for Foreign and Commonwealth Affairs, ex p. Manelfi* [1996] 12 C.L. 65 (judicial review of decision that M was ineligible for employment at GCHQ because of the foreign nationalities of his parents—M claimed application of the rules without waiver were *Wednesbury* unreasonable and contrary to the common law and the International Covenant on Civil and Political Rights 1996, Art. 26. Held, dismissing the application: the decision in the making of the rules and their application were made in the interests of national security and were non-justiciable); see also *R. v. Lord Chancellor ex p. Maxwell* [1997] 1 W.L.R. 104 (allocation of judges between High Court and Court of Appeal justiciable but not normally reviewable).

FUNDAMENTAL HUMAN RIGHTS

[Add the following paragraph at the end of the paragraph:]   6–048

At the time of writing the Human Rights Bill is proceeding with its passage through Parliament. If enacted, it would permit courts directly to enforce provisions of the European Convention on Human Rights in respect of the exercise of public functions. In respect of legislation, however, courts would only be permitted to issue a "declaration of incompatibility" with the Convention and it would thus lie with Parliament whether to remedy the incompatibility (which it could do through a "fast track" procedure, by means of a statutory instrument).

[Add to Note 64:]

For an excellent account of the extent of the use of human rights in English courts see Murray Hunt, *Using Human Rights Law in English Courts* (1997). And see M. Beloff and H. Mountfield, "Unconventional Behaviour? Judicial Uses of the European Convention on Human Rights in England and Wales" 1996 E.H.R.L.R. 467.

The European Convention as the source of a treaty obligation in international law

[Add to Note 67:]   6–050

See also *Governor of Pitcairn v. Sutton* [1995] 1 N.Z.L.R. 426, 430 ("generally worded statutory discretions are not to be exercised without taking into account international obligations" *per* Cooke P.); *Rajan v. Minister of Immigration* [1996] 3 N.Z.L.R. 543. As a result of the *Tavita* Judgment immigration policies were introduced in New Zealand to give better effect to Art. 23 of the International Covenant on Civil and Political Rights: see *Patel* (cited at n. 60 above). In Australia, where legislation implements an international commitment, it is appropriate for the courts to have regard to the interpretation of the international instrument by the international community in settling the domestic interpretation; *Rocklea Spinning Mills Ltd v. Anti-Dumping Authority* (1995) 129 ALR 401 (Federal Court of Australia). And see the discussion of *Minister for Immigration and Ethnic Affairs v. Teoh* (1995) 183 CLR 273 below Chapters 8 and 13.

Fundamental rights in English law

6–055   *[Add to Note 1:]*

The approach in *Leech* was expressly followed by Laws J. in *R. v. Lord Chancellor, ex p. Witham* [1997] 2 All E.R. 779 (court fees deprived the citizen of his constitutional right of access to the courts. Such rights were not "the consequence of the democratic political process but would be logically prior to it"). *Leech* was also followed by Lathan J. in *R. v. Secretary of State for the Home Department, ex p. Simms* [1997] C.O.D. 217 (prohibition on the use by a journalist of material gathered on a visit to a prisoner violated prisoners' right to free speech and the restriction not necessary or justified; but the Court of Appeal overruled this judgment, holding no right of a prisoner to communicate with a journalist) see (1998) 95 L.S.G. 23 and para. 24–016, below. *Leech* was taken a step further in *R. v. Secretary of State for Social Security ex p. Joint Council for the Welfare of Immigrants* [1997] 1 W.L.R. 275 where it was held that regulations excluding from income support entitlement those who sought asylum otherwise than on immediate arrival in the U.K. or whose claims were rejected and awaiting appeal, both conflicted with and rendered rights in other legislation nugatory and were so Draconian to an extent that "no civilised nation can tolerate." *per* Simon Brown L.J. Dictum of Lord Ellenborough C.J. was in *R. v. Eastbourne (Inhabitants)* (1803) 4 East 103 at 107 cited: "the law of humanity, which is anterior to all positive laws obliges us to afford [poor foreigners] relief, to save them from starving". (See further under para. 6–068 n. 41 below). And see also Lord Steyn's acceptance of the concept of "substantive fairness", based on the rule of law in *Pierson v. Secretary of State for the Home Department* [1997] 3 W.L.R. 492.

EXERCISE OF A DISCRETIONARY POWER FOR EXTRANEOUS PURPOSE

Where purposes are specified in the statute

6–065   *[Add to Note 27:]*

A distinction should be made between the use of *Hansard* to resolve an ambiguity in a statutory provision, and its use to determine the general purpose of a statutory scheme. In the latter case, *Pepper v. Hart* is not relevant and the court accordingly is not bound by its restrictions and thus, for example, may look at statements other than those of the Minister promoting the bill: see *Three Rivers D.C. v. Bank of England (No. 2)* [1996] 2 All E.R. 363.

[Add to Note 36:]   **6–066**

Some recent cases holding various financial or housing schemes of local authorities to be *ultra vires* include: *Credit Suisse v. Allerdale BC* [1997] Q.B. 306; *Credit Suisse v. Waltham Forest LBC* [1997] Q.B. 362; *Sutton London LBC v. Morgan Grenfell and Co. Ltd* (1997) 9 Admin L.R. 145. But see *R. v. Greater Manchester Police Authority, ex p. Century Motors (Farnworth) Ltd, The Times*, May 31, 1996 (necessary implication that power to levy charges for vehicle recovery operation); *R. v. Powys CC ex p. Hambidge, The Times*, November 5, 1997 (Local authority may charge for services under section 2 of the Chronically Sick and Disabled Persons Act 1970).

[Add to Note 41:]   **6–068**

Following the case of *Joint Council for the Welfare of Immigrants* (see para. 6–055 n. 1 above): *R. v. Kensington and Chelsea R.L.B.C., ex p. Kihara* (1997) 9 Admin. L.R. 25 (total resourcelessness of asylum seeker a special reason for purposes of vulnerability and priority needs in section 59 of the Housing Act 1985). Note that the Immigration and Asylum Act 1996, s. 9 overturns *Joint Council* and *Kihara* cases. *R. v. Hammersmith and Fulham L.B.C., ex p. M* (1997) 9 Admin. L.R. 504 a destitute asylum seeker who had no money and therefore lacked the means of supporting himself could be said to be "in need of care and attention" within the meaning of National Assistance Act 1948, s. 21(1)(a). (See also: *R. v. Secretary of State for the Home Department, ex p. Shelter and The Refugee Council* [1997] C.O.D. 49. Declaration sought as to the effect of Asylum and Immigration Act 1996, s. 9); *R. v. Southwark L.B.C., ex p. Bediako* (1998) 30 H.L.R. 22 Housing Act 1985 and Asylum and Immigration Act 1996, s. 9; *R. v. Kensington and Chelsea R.L.B.C., ex p. Koneva* (1997) 29 H.L.R. 709; *R. v. Newham LBC ex p. Gorenkin* [1997] C.O.D. 391 (an asylum seeker could be in need of care and attention for the puposes of the National Assistance Act 1948 and therefore in need of residential accommodation even though he had accommodation). And see generally *re* the duty of local authorities to offer suitable accommodation under the Housing Act 1985, s. 65(2); *Awua v. Brent LBC* [1996] 1 A.C. 55 (noted D. Cowan, "Doing the Court's Work" (1997) 60 M.L.R. 267) and *R. v. Wandsworth LBC ex p. Mansoor* [1997] Q.B. 953.

[Note 45:]   **6–069**

Fewings is now reported at [1995] 1 W.L.R.1037. And see Davina Cooper, "For the Sake of the Deer: Land, Local Government and the Hunt (1997) 45 *Sociological Review* 668.

[Add the following to the end of the paragraph:]   **6–070**

The powers of the Home Secretary in respect of the continued detention of life prisoners have been the subject of particular recent attention, both by Parliament and the courts. In respect of discretionary life-sentenced prisoners, detainees and those detained during Her Majesty's pleasure, the "danger to the public" was the only ground on which to justify the Home Secretary continuing the prisoner's detention after the punitive term set for his release. The relevant statute under which the Home Secretary was acting was the Criminal Justice Act 1991 (especially sections 34 and 35). A series of cases thus set out that matters extraneous to the danger to the public are unlawful considerations which the Home Secretary may not take into account. (See for example, the two most recent cases in the House of Lords, both overturning the Home Secretary's exercise of his powers: *R. v. Secretary of State for the Home Department, ex p. Venables and Thompson* [1997] 3 W.L.R. 23; *R. v. Secretary of State for the Home Department ex p. Pierson* [1997] 3 W.L.R. 492. In 1997, however, the Home Secretary's powers were revised by section 29 of the Crime (Sentences) Act. It has recently been held that these powers permit the Home Secretary to take into account, in his decision, whether or not to release a mandatory life prisoner, factors broader than public risk; in this case whether or not the prisoner was likely to commit an imprisonable offence fail to comply with the terms of his release. *R. v. Secretary of State for the Home Department ex p. Stafford, The Times*, Nov. 28, 1997. The Lord Chief Justice in that case held that the discretion conferred on the Home Secretary was "extraordinarily wide" and, although lawfully exercised, it "lay uneasily with the rule of law."

Unspecified purposes

6–073   *[Add to Note 57:]*

And see generally: *R. v. Greenwich L.B.C., ex p. W (a minor), sub nom. R. v. Greenwich L.B.C., ex p. Williams*. Macpherson J.'s judgment at first instance is reported (1996) 8 Admin. L.R. 423; the Court of Appeal refused leave to appeal [1996] C.O.D. 459. W argued that the Road Traffic Regulation Act 1984, s. 14, which enables local authorities to restrict traffic when there was "a danger to the public" should be exercised when there was damage to the public from pollutants in the air, which were in excess of international guidelines, on days when there was a temperature inversion. Held: section 14 only applied to the risk of damage caused directly by vehicles or pedestrians by way of accidents. See also: *R. v. National Rivers Authority, ex p. Haughey* (1996) 8 Admin. L.R. 567; *U.K. Waste Management Ltd v. West Lancashire D.C., The Times*, April 5, 1996, (unlawful to use the power under the Road Traffic Regulation Act 1984 to make an order "for the purpose of carrying out an experimental scheme of traffic control" if the only purpose was to ban heavy vehicles from a road and there was no element of "experiment").

Planning powers and the notion of changing purpose

[Add to note 69:]   6–075

West Midland Probation Committee v. Secretary of State for the Environment, Transport and the Regions, The Times, December 1, 1997 (fear of residents can be a material planning consideration).

EXERCISE OF A DISCRETIONARY POWER ON IRRELEVANT GROUNDS
OR WITHOUT REGARD TO RELEVANT CONSIDERATIONS

Financial considerations

[Add to Note 34:]   6–091

The question of the relevance of resources was decided in a number of cases. Cases where resources were held to be relevant considerations were: *R. v. Gloucestershire C.C., ex p. Barry* [1997] A.C. 584 (duty to assess need for care arrangements made under Chronically Sick and Disabled Persons Act 1970, s. 2. Financial resources may lawfully be taken into account in determining whether the obligation exists at all. This case was followed in *R. v. East Sussex CC ex p. Tandy* [1997] 3 W.L.R. 884. See also *R. v. Southwark L.B.C., ex p. Udu* (1996) 8 Admin. L.R. 25 (policy of refusing grants to courses at private colleges, including the College of Law. Held: the Local Authority was a political body with limited funds, and it was entitled to have policies and to decide how to allocate those funds). *R. v. Chief Constable of Sussex, ex p. International Trader's Ferry* [1997] 3 W.L.R. 132 a Chief Constable's decision to provide policing on only two days a week to protect the transport of livestock where animal rights' protestors were demonstrating was reasonable under domestic and E.C. law because of restraints on resources.); *R. v. Registered Homes Tribunal, ex p. Hertfordshire C.C., The Times,* February 28, 1996 (financial considerations relevant to the registration of homes).

Cases where resources were held not relevant were: *R. v. Sefton MBC ex p. Help the Aged* [1997] 4 All E.R. 532 (C.A.) (lack of financial resources does not entitle a local authority to defer compliance with their duty under section 2 of the Chronically Sick and Disabled Persons Act 1970); *R. v. Cheshire C.C., ex p. C, The Times,* August 8, 1996 (the decision about special educational needs should be made on purely educational grounds without reference to financial considerations); *Case C–44/95, R. v. Secretary of State for the Environment, ex p. RSPB* [1997] Q.B. 206. (On Art. 177 reference from House of Lords). ECJ held that economic considerations are not relevant to determining wild bird protection areas under Directive 79/409; *R. v. Secretary of State for the Environment, ex p. Kingston-Upon-Hull City Council* [1996] C.O.D. 289 (the cost of the treatment of waste water

was not a relevant consideration); But see *R. v. National Rivers Authority,
ex p. Moreton* [1996] Env. L.R. D17 (investment budget relevant to decision
of NRA to allow discharge); *R. v. Hillingdon L.B.C., ex p. Governing Body of
Queensmead School* [1997] E.L.R. 331 (Collins J. held that budgetary
constraints and lack of funds could play no part in the assessment of a
child's special educational needs); *R. v. Social Fund Inspector, ex p. Taylor*
[1998] C.O.D. 152.

It is important in the above cases to note that under any given statutory
scheme a distinction is often made between (a) determining whether a
person's need exists and (b) whether that need can be satisfied within
available resources. Normally (depending upon the statutory scheme) need
should be initially determined without regard to resources. See further,
notes to Chap. 27–020 below.

6–092   *[Add to Note 35:]*

R. v. Coventry City Council ex p. Phoenix Aviation is now reported at [1995] 3
All E.R. 37 (D.C.). It was held that the authorities operating air and sea
ports were not entitled, in the absence of an emergency, to ban the passage
of livestock by animal exporters so as to avoid the disruptive consequences
of unlawful protesters. To do so would, *per* Simon Brown L.J., conflict
with the rule of law. But compare *R. v. Chief Constable of Sussex ex p.
International Traders Ferry Ltd* [1997] 3 W.L.R. 132 (reducing policing to
two days per week in the light of insufficient resources, lawful).

6–097   *[Add to Note 54:]*

In New Zealand there is a line of cases in which the fiduciary concept has
been applied: see *Lovelock v. Waitakere City Council* [1996] 3 N.Z.L.R. 310.

Government policy as a relevant consideration

6–099   *[Add to Note 62:]*

R. v. Islington L.B.C., ex p. Rixon, The Times, April 17, 1996 (statutory policy
guidance issued under section 7 of the Local Authority Social Services Act
1970 binding on local authorities). See also *R. v. Sutton L.B.C. ex p. Tucker*
[1997] C.O.D. 144.

DELEGATION OF POWERS

Delegation and agency

6–111   *[Add to Note 4:]*

See Mark Freedland, "The Rule Against Delegation and the Carltona
doctrine in an Agency Context" [1996] P.L. 19.

The Carltona principle

[Add to Note 43:]   **6–114**

R. v. Secretary of State for the Home Department, ex p. Mensah [1996] Imm.
A.R. 223.

[Add to Note 66:]   **6–117**

R. v. Secretary of State for the Home Department, ex p. Sherwin (1996) 32
B.M.L.R. 1. (*Carltona* applied to the Benefits Agency which was held to be
part of the Department of Social Security and the agency staff belonged to
the Civil Service). See also *R. v. Greater Manchester Police Authority ex p.
Century Motors (Farnworth) Ltd The Times*, May 31, 1996. But see, *R. v.
Oxfordshire C.C., ex p. Pittick* [1995] C.O.D. 397 (Education Act 1981,
s. 7(2)—council had not improperly delegated its duty to provide special
needs education to the school); *R. v. Harrow L.B.C., ex p. M* [1997] 3
F.C.R. 761 (obligations on a local education authority under Education Act
1993, s. 168 to arrange that special educational provision be made for a
child was not delegable); *MFI Furniture Centre Ltd v. Hibbert* [1996] C.O.D.
100 (validity of council's Minutes of Delegation).

CHAPTER 7

PROCEDURAL FAIRNESS: INTRODUCTION AND HISTORY

Introduction

[Add to Note 2:] **7–004**

D.J. Galligan, *Due Process and Fair Procedures* (1996).

Historical Development

The concept of natural justice

[Add new Note 32a after ". . . the Founding Fathers of the American Constitution **7–007**
or the notion of "due process" ":]

The term "due process" has itself recently been invoked in a number of English decisions; see, for example *R. v. Secretary of State for the Home Department, ex p. Moon* (1996) 8 Admin. L.R. 477 at 485c and *R. v. Camden L.B.C., ex p. Paddock* [1995] C.O.D. 130.

Early development of the right to a fair hearing

[Add to Note 64:] **7–012**

Compare, as a possible modern parallel, *R. v. Secretary of State for the Home Department, ex p. Fayed* [1997] 1 All E.R. 228 (C.A.).

Revisionism revised

The duty to act fairly

[Note 51]: The correct citation for *R. v. Secretary of State for the Home* **7–038**
Department, ex p. Swati is [1986] 1 W.L.R. 477.

CHAPTER 8

PROCEDURAL FAIRNESS: ENTITLEMENT

Natural Justice and the Duty to Act Fairly Today

[Add to Note 4:]   **8–004**

Denis Galligan, *Due Process and Fair Procedures* (O.U.P., 1996); Nick Wikeley, "Natural Justice and non-disclosure of medical evidence" (1996) J.S.S.L. 98–99; (proper approach to non-disclosure in Social Security Appeal Tribunal hearings).

[Add to Note 10:]   **8–007**

In *R. v. Secretary of State for the Home Department, ex p. Fayed* [1997] 1 All E.R. 228, the Court of Appeal held: (Woolf M.R., Phillips L.J.—Kennedy L.J. dissenting), that the applicants for British citizenship were wrongly deprived of an opportunity to make representations in advance of the refusal of their applications. The statute itself precludes a requirement for reasons. The *ratio* appears to be (*per* Lord Woolf at 237–238; Phillips L.J. at 251) that, although the applicants had no vested rights to citizenship (as in *Attorney-General v. Ryan* [1980] A.C. 718 (P.C.)—constitutional entitlement to citizenship of the Bahamas), the refusal of the application would in the circumstances of this case lead to adverse inferences being drawn about the applicants' characters. *Quare* whether the applicants would have been successful simply because their interest in citizenship was in issue. The matter is on appeal to the House of Lords. For a recent case where "serious allegations of misconduct" against the applicant grounded a right to make representations (despite the lack of a finding of any adverse public inferences on the applicant's character), see *R. v. Immigration Board, ex p. Kirk Freeport Plaza Ltd and Island Companies Ltd* Cayman Island Court of Appeal, November 28, 1997. For another case where an applicant was afforded the right to a fair hearing see *R. v. Secretary of State for the Home Department, ex p. Moon* (1996) 8 Admin. L.R. 477.

[Add to Note 19:]   **8–011**

Thus a passage in a decision or a public report criticising a person who has not had a fair opportunity of answering the allegation may be reviewable:

63

O'Regan v. Lousich [1995] 2 N.Z.L.R. 620, developing *Mahon v. New Zealand Ltd* [1984] A.C. 808.

[Add to Note 21:]

In South Africa a "Legislation" decision recently attracted the duty of *audi alteram partem. S.A. Roads Board v. Johannesburg City Council*, 1991 (4) S.A. 1(A). See also *Hailowsky Estates Ltd v. Harlow D.C.* [1997] J.P.L. 541 (fairness required in local plan inquiry). The fairness of a number of procedures in English law and practice have recently been under scrutiny in the European Court of Human Rights. See, *e.g. Benham v. United Kingdom* (1996) 22 E.H.R.R. 293 (no provision for legal aid for committals to prison for non-payment of community charge. Held, upholding the complaint: there had been a breach of Art. 6 of the E.C.H.R.); *Pullar v. United Kingdom* (1996) 22 E.C.H.R. 391 (dismissed complaint about juror being an employee of a prosecution witness). *Bryan v. United Kingdom* (1996) 21 E.H.R.R. 342 (appeal to inspector in planning matter did not satisfy Art. 6—but subsequent review by the High Court did); *Saunders v. United Kingdom* (1997) 23 E.C.H.R. 313; *Findlay v. United Kingdom* (1997) 24 E.H.R.R. 221. (Court Martial was not a fair hearing;) (leave to apply for judicial review had been refused); *Gregory v. United Kingdom, The Times*, February 27, 1997; (judge's direction sufficient to counter bias); *Murray v. United Kingdom* (1996) 22 E.C.H.R. 29 (access to solicitor).

[Add to Note 27:]

R. v. Monopolies and Mergers Commission, ex p. Stagecoach Holdings Ltd, The Times, July 23, 1996. Application to quash MMC decisions recommending that applicant should limit its percentage holdings in rival bus companies. Applicant contended that MMC had failed to clarify certain evidential material upon which the recommendations were based. Held, dismissing the application: the propriety of the MMC's decision was to be decided on the basis of natural justice and fairness and not (as the MMC contended) by the principles of *Wednesbury* unreasonableness. "The court is the arbiter of what is fair", although the court would give great weight to the MMC's own view of fairness.

A. STATUTORY REQUIREMENTS AND THE FAIR HEARING

8–013   *[Add the following cases to Note 29:]*

R. v. Secretary of State for Education and Employment, ex p. McCarthy, The Times, July 24, 1996. Education (Special Educational Needs) (Approval of Independent Schools) Regulations 1994, reg. 5 imposed on Secretary of State an obligation to consult the proprietor of an independent school before withdrawing approval of the school, except in circumstances where withdrawing approval without consultation was required in the interests of the children's health, safety or welfare.

R. v. Lambeth L.B.C., ex p. N [1996] E.L.R. 299. Challenge to decision to close a maintained boarding school for children with special educational needs. N argued that the authority had failed to comply with the statutory obligation to consult parents as to the closure under section 184, Education Act 1993. Held, allowing the application: section 184(1) provided that an authority had a duty to consult such persons as were appropriate, and parents were clearly intended to be consulted under Circular 3.94 issued by the Secretary of State for Education. The authority also had an obligation to ensure that parents were invited to make oral or written representations on the proposed closure and its impact on their children. The failure to do so vitiated the consultation process and the notice of closure was quashed accordingly. *R. v. Brent L.B.C., ex p. Gunning* (1985) 84 L.G.R. 168; and *R. v. Secretary of State for Social Services, ex p. A.M.A* [1986] 1 W.L.R. 1 considered.

Duffield v. Pensions Ombudsman [1996] C.O.D. 406. Held: under section 149 Pension Schemes Act 1993, the ombudsman was required to consult not only current trustees but also previous trustees who were under investigation. *Seifert v. Pensions Ombudsman*, [1997] 1 All E.R. 214. (Pensions Ombudsman had to comply with the statutory procedure, designed to ensure fairness, contained in section 149 and with the principles of natural justice; appeal on merits allowed in part [1997] 4 All E.R. 947.) *R. v. Merton L.B.C., ex p. Wiggins* [1996] E.L.R. 332. (Council had erred by failing to follow the correct appeal procedures). *R. v. Secretary of State for the Home Office, ex p. Hickey (No. 1)* [1995] Q.B. 43; (right of a hearing under Mental Health Act 1983 was conferred only on persons subject solely to the provisions of the Act). *R. v. Bristol Magistrates' Court, ex p. Hodge* [1997] Q.B. 974 applicant not given the opportunity to make representations to the court within the provisions of Magistrates' Courts Rules 1981, r. 44(1)).

Statute and legitimate expectations

[Add to Note 48:]   8–019

R. v. Secretary of State for Wales, ex p. Emery [1996] 4 All E.R. 1 (legitimate expectation that the Secretary of State would fairly subject a case to a public inquiry).

B. Where a Hearing is Required to Safeguard Rights and Interests

[Add to Note 62:]   8–028

See the discussion of the *Fayed* case above at para. 8–005 n. 12.

The scope of interests attracting a right to a hearing

8–029   *[Add to Note 65:]*

See the cases under 8–013, above n. 29 and see also the Canadian case *Telecommunications Workers Union v. Canada (Radio-Television and Telecommunications Commission)* [1995] 2 S.C.R. 781 (notice not required to be given, under the statutory provision which specified direct parties, to the union, when questions of broad policy are decided by the Commission). *cf. R. v. North Yorkshire Family Health Services Authority, ex p. Wilson* (1996) 8 Admin. L.R. 613 (doctors who provided pharmaceutical services in rural areas had no right to be consulted over a decision to grant permission to a pharmacist already on the pharmaceutical list for the area to open a shop in the village. It was only under reg. 12, where an application was made by someone not already on the area's pharmaceutical list, that local doctors had an express right to make representations. Whether principles of natural justice breached when a party is denied the opportunity to present an argument which is based on an irrelevant consideration). See also *ex p. R. v. Central Criminal Court, Crook* [1995] 1 W.L.R. 139, C.A. (no statutory authority which limited the persons from whom the court was entitled to receive representations on whether in a particular case an order should be made under Children and Young Persons Act 1933, s. 39).

[Add to Note 66:]

R. v. Ealing Justices, ex p. Fanneran (1996) 8 Admin. L.R. 351; (applicant was not informed of a hearing before justices at which they made a destruction order in relation to her pit bull terrier following her nephew's conviction of having the dog in a public place without a muzzle. Held that even though the applicant's presence at a hearing may not have made any difference to the outcome, it was important that justices acted in accordance with the rules of natural justice. The destruction order was quashed).

C. THE LEGITIMATE EXPECTATION

Introduction

8–038   *[Add to Note 86:]*

P.P. Craig, "Substantive Legitimate Expectations in Domestic and Community Law" [1996] C.L.J. 289.

Development

8–044   *[Add after Note 6:]*

After reference to *New Zealand Maori Council v. Attorney-General* [1994] A.C. 466: and see [1996] 3 N.Z.L.R. 140, 183–85 *per* Thomas J. dissenting (reasonable expectation that the Crown would comply with the Treaty of Waitanga obligations to protect the Maori language). The point is not separately considered in the majority judgment, where legislative intent to the contrary is discerned. See also *Whangarei Deep Sea Anglers Club v. Marshall* [1995] 1 N.Z.L.R. 286.

The scope of the legitimate expectation

[Add to Note 21:]   **8–053**

Ramburan v. Minister of Housing 1995 (1) S.A. 353 (D).

The nature of the representaiton

[Add to Note 22:]

R. v. IRC, ex p. Unilever plc [1996] C.O.D. 369; [1996] S.T.C. 681 (C.A.). (claim for tax relief made in similar form to that accepted in previous years and therefore unfair for the IRC to resile from previous practice without notice).

[Add to note 27:]   **8–055**

R. v. Funding Agency for Schools, ex p. Bromley L.B.C. [1996] C.O.D. 375 (B argued that the FAS's grants to grant-maintained schools in the Bromley area was too high. One argument was that B was led to believe that FAS would use B's pupil figures and had budgeted in that belief. Held: B was unable to show that FAS had made a clear and unqualified representation that it would use their figures. Thus, the issue of legitimate expectation failed). See also *R. v. Secretary of State for the Home Department, ex p. Dey; sub nom. Dey v. Secretary of State for the Home Department* [1996] Imm. A.R. 521, (return of passport did not give legitimate expectation to remain). *cf. R. v. Gaming Board of Great Britain, ex p. Kingsley (No. 2)* [1996] C.O.D. 241.

[Add to Note 34:]   **8–057**

See the controversial Australian case of *Minister for Immigration and Ethnic Affairs v. Teoh* (1995) 183 C.L.R. 273, where the High Court held that the UN Covenant on the Rights of the Child, which was not incorporated into Australian law, may nevertheless give rise to a legitimate expectation that the executive decision-maker would comply with it, at least to the extent of giving an affected person a hearing on the matter. For a critical article see Taggart (1996) 112 L.Q.R. 50 and para. 28–023 below.

8–065 *[Add to Note 51:]*

And see the cases discussed in this Supplement under paras 13–030 and
13–035.

CHAPTER 9

PROCEDURAL FAIRNESS: CONTENT

[Add to Note 2:]   **9–002**

For a recent example, see *R. v. Leicester Crown Court, ex p. Phipps* [1997]
C.O.D. 299 (where there is no customary general practice, an individual
judge will have to devise a procedure that is fair and just and meets the
particular circumstances of the case). But for the dangers of excessive
informality, see *Dyason v. Secretary of State for the Environment, The Times,*
February 9, 1998 (C.A.).

[Add to Note 4:]   **9–003**

See further, his Lordship's remarks in *Re D (Minors) (Adoption Reports:
Confidentiality)* [1996] A.C. 593, 609.

[Add to Note 5:]

See further Chap. 8 above, paras 8–015 to 8–020.

PRIOR NOTICE OF THE DECISION

[Add to Note 8:]   **9–005**

It should be noted, however, that as the knowledge of the basic requirements of fairness has increased among both potential Applicants and
Respondents, the proportion of cases involving a complete failure to give
notice or to hear has fallen, as compared to those cases involving a
challenge to the extent or nature of the hearing.

[Add to Note 14:]   **9–006**

R. v. Ealing Magistrates' Court, ex p. Fanneran (1996) 8 Admin. L.R. 351 (dog-
owner entitled to be heard before destruction order is made).

[Add to Note 22:]   **9–007**

R. v. Guildford Justices, ex p. Rich [1997] 1 Cr. App. R. (S) 49 (sufficient notice of distress order must be given to allow affected individual opportunity to make representations); *R. v. Devon County Council, ex p. Baker* [1995] 1 All E.R. 73 (insufficient notice given to residents of proposed closure of old people's home to enable proper representations or objections); *R. v. Secretary of State for the Home Department, ex p. Moon* (1996) 8 Admin. L.R. 477.

[Add to Note 24:]

R. v. LAUTRO, ex p. Tee (1995) 7 Admin. L.R. 289; see further, the duty of adequate disclosure, below, at para. 9–18 *et seq.*

[Add to Note 25:]

R. v. Chance, ex p. Coopers & Lybrand (1995) 7 Admin. L.R. 821, 835H (surprise as the enemy of justice).

9–011   *[Add to Note 45:]*

In the absence of such express provision, however, the courts will not normally imply a requirement that prejudice be shown; see below, Chap. 10, at paras 10–31 to 10–36.

CONSULTATION AND WRITTEN REPRESENTATIONS

9–014   *[Add to Note 58:]*

Per contra, it may be unfair to require written evidence when the individual is not at liberty to provide it: *R. v. South Western Magistrates, ex p. Doyle* [1996] C.O.D. 309.

9–017   *[Add to Note 69:]*

R. v. Lambeth L.B.C., ex p. N [1996] E.L.R. 299; *R. v. Secretary of State for Trade and Industry, ex p. UNISON* [1996] I.C.R. 1003; *Desmond v. Bromley L.B.C.* (1996) 28 H.L.R. 518 (distinguishing *ex p. AMA*); *R. v. Secretary of State for Transport, ex p. Richmond-upon-Thames L.B.C.* [1996] 1 W.L.R. 1460 (level of detail in consultation sufficient to enable representations).

[After "received by way of reasons.⁷¹" add:]

Further, there is generally no duty to consult further where the decision-maker makes alterations to a proposal as a result of responses received during a consultation process, unless, *semble*, the proposal alters radically: *R. v. Islington L.B.C., ex p. East* [1996] E.L.R. 74; *R. v. Secretary of*

State for Wales, ex p. Williams [1996] C.O.D. 127 (no duty to prolong consultation period).

DUTY OF ADEQUATE DISCLOSURE

[Add to Note 73. After ". . . decision to maintain him as a "category A" prisoner"   **9–018**
add:]

See further, *R. v. Secretary of State for the Home Department, ex p. McAvoy* [1998] C.O.D. 148 (categorisation of non-life sentence prisoner; gist of report sufficient). *R. v. Secretary of State for the Home Department ex p. Hickey (No.2)* is now reported at [1995] 1 W.L.R. 734.

[Add to Note 74:]

The House of Lords has now upheld the decision of the Court of Appeal; see [1996] 1 W.L.R. 298. See also *Re D (Minors) (Adoption Reports: Confidentiality)* [1996] A.C. 593: ("It is a first principle of fairness that each party to a judicial process shall have the opportunity to answer by evidence and argument any adverse material which the tribunal may take into account when forming its opinion", *per* Lord Mustill at p. 603H) See also *Camden L.B.C. v. Paddock* [1995] C.O.D. 130.

[After "information prejudicial to his case.⁷⁴", add:]

The requirement of disclosure will be interpreted flexibly, and may extend to disclosure of the fact that the decision-maker has doubts as to the credibility of the applicant (*R. v. Kensington and Chelsea R.L.B.C., ex p. Campbell* (1996) 28 H.L.R. 160); or, more widely, to disclosure of the subject matter of the decision-maker's concern so that the applicant is able to make submissions to meet that concern, even where there is no duty to give reasons post-decision: *R. v. Secretary of State for the Home Department, ex p. Fayed* [1997] 1 All E.R. 228, C.A. (application for citizenship); *R. v. Governors of Sheffield Hallam University, ex p. R* [1995] E.L.R. 267; *R. v. Southwark L.B.C., ex p. Ryder* (1996) 28 H.L.R. 56; *R. v. Home Secretary, ex p. Venables* [1997] 2 W.L.R. 67 (Secretary of State failed to disclose to applicants all material of which he had taken account in order).

[Add to Note 78, after "ex p. Georghiades (1992) 5 Admin. L.R. 457 (parole   **9–019**
board).":]

; *R. v. Faversham and Sittingbourne Justices, ex p. Stickings* [1996] C.O.D. 39 (conversation between Justices' Clerk and prosecution).

[Add to Note 81, after "not obliged to reopen the inquiry.":]

cf. Robert Hitchens Ltd v. Secretary of State for the Environment [1995] E.G.C.S. 101 (undisclosed correspondence could not objectively be said to have caused injury or unfairness to the applicant, particularly since applicant's status as objector was not one of right, but of discretion; compare *R. v. Secretary of State for the Environment, ex p. Slot* [1998] C.O.D. 118 (C.A.) (failure to provide appellant with copy of objector's letters was unfair, and gave rise to risk that her case was prejudiced).

[Add to Note 82:]

cf. Siefert v. Pensions Ombudsman [1997] 1 All E.R. 228 (Ombudsman's failure to send letter of complaint by a member of Scheme to the Trustees of Scheme was a breach of rules of natural justice which vitiated his award against Trustees).

9–020   *[Add to Note 84, after "on ground of confidentiality)":]*

; *R. v. Joint Higher Committee on Surgical Training, ex p. Milner* (1995) 7 Admin L.R. 454 (Committee not obliged to disclose references to applicant for accreditation as surgeon; interests of confidentiality outweighed applicant's interest in disclosure).

JUDICIAL AND OFFICIAL NOTICE

9–021   *[Add to Note 91:]*

And see cases at Note 95 below.

[Add to Note 95:]

; *Bowman v. D.P.P.* [1991] R.T.R. 263; *Norbrook Laboratories (GB) Ltd v. Health and Safety Executive, The Times*, February 23, 1998 (justices proposing to rely upon local knowledge should let both prosecution and defence know to give them opportunity to comment); and see *Mullen v. Hackney L.B.C.* [1997] 2 All E.R. 906 (C.A. held judge entitled to take judicial notice of matters which were notorious, or clearly established, or susceptible of demonstration by reference to a readily obtainable and authoritative source. He could rely on his local knowledge provided he did so properly and within reasonable limits).

RIGHT TO AN ORAL HEARING

9–023   *[After "opportunity of putting his own case.", add:]*

As noted above (paragraph 9–012), he will normally be entitled to that opportunity, particularly where there is some dispute as to material facts or other matter on which oral argument will be of assistance to the decision-maker: see *R. v. Criminal Injuries Compensation Board, ex p. Dickson* [1997] 1 W.L.R. 58 (applicant not entitled to oral hearing because no dispute as to primary facts); *R. v. Criminal Injuries Compensation Board, ex p. Cook* [1996] 1 W.L.R. 1037 (C.A.); *cf. R. v. Criminal Injuries Compensation Board, ex p. Singh (Amrik)* [1996] C.O.D. 149. See also *R. v. Secretary of State for Wales, ex p. Emery* [1996] 4 All E.R. 1 (conflict of documentary evidence as to footpath should have been tested at public inquiry; Secretary of State acted unfairly in deciding without convening inquiry); *R. v. Secretary of State for the Home Department, ex p. Khanafer* [1996] Imm. A.R. 212; *R. v. Cardinal Newman's School, Birmingham, ex p. S, The Times*, December 27, 1997.

[Add to Note 10:]

R. v. Worcester Justices, ex p. Daniels (1997) 161 J.P. 121 (Magistrate appearing not to pay attention); *Jones v. Welsh Rugby Football Union, The Times*, March 6, 1997 (noted, [1997] P.L. 340) (arguable that failure by RFU to let applicant challenge by question or evidence the factual basis of the evidence against him, or to vary procedure for viewing video evidence, was unfair). *R. v. Clerkenwell Metropolitan Stipendiary Magistrate, ex p. Hogner, The Times*, January 28, 1998 (oral hearing before bindover and/or order for surety).

[Add to Note 22, after "R. v. Chance, ex p. Smith":]   **9–025**

now reported, *sub nom. R. v. Chance, ex p. Coopers & Lybrand* (1995) 7 Admin L.R. 821. See also, *R. v. Executive Council of the Joint Disciplinary Scheme, ex p. Hipps* (unreported, June 12, 1996).

RIGHT TO CALL WITNESSES

[After "a breach of natural justice.[28]" add:]   **9–026**

And Magistrates' refusal of an adjournment to enable "vital" defence witnesses to attend was held to have deprived the applicant of a reasonable opportunity to present his defence: *R. v. Hereford Magistrates Court, ex p. Rowlands* [1998] Q.B. 110.

RIGHT TO LEGAL REPRESENTATION

[Add to Note 35, after "Zellick (1975) 38 M.L.R. 683":]   **9–029**

; *Murray v. United Kingdom* (1996) 22 E.H.R.R. 29 (lack of access to lawyer during first 48 hours in detention violated right to fair hearing under Article 6(1) and (3)).

9–030   *[Add to Note 36, after "ex p. Dikko [1985] Q.B. 630":]*

; *R. v. Secretary of State for the Home Department, ex p. Vera Lawson* [1994] Imm. A.R. 58.

9–032   *[Add to Note 44:]*

cf. Murray v. United Kingdom (1996) 22 E.H.R.R. 29; *R. v. Governor of Whitemoor Prison, ex p. Main* [1997] C.O.D. 400 (search of correspondence did not prevent free flow of information between applicant and solicitor); *cf. R. v. London Borough of Newham, ex p. Ajayi* (1996) 28 H.L.R. 25.

RIGHT TO CROSS-EXAMINATION

9–035   *[After "declines to allow those witnesses to be tested in cross-examination", add:]*

, and indeed it may be unfair for the tribunal not to grant an adjournment to allow witnesses to attend for the purpose of being cross-examined: *R. v. Criminal Injuries Compensation Board, ex p. Cobb* [1995] C.O.D. 126.

[Add to Note 52:]

However, in judicial review proceedings, very limited use has thus far been made of the ability to order cross-examination of deponents on their affidavits; see, below, para. 15–031, and see, recently, *R. v. Arts Council of England, ex p. Women's Playhouse Trust, The Times,* August 20, 1997 (Laws J.).

RIGHT TO REASONS

No general duty to give reasons?

9–039   *[Add, at the end of the paragraph, new Note 62A:]*

Both the general proposition and the explanation that procedural propriety does not require reasons must be treated with ever-increasing caution, in the light of the cases referred to at 9–041 and thereafter.

9–040   *[Add to Note 64, after "ex p. Dave, below, n. 66":]*

; *R. v. Ministry of Defence, ex p. Murray* [1998] C.O.D. 134 (court-martial).

[Add to Note 64, after "the absence of reasons is not in itself a ground of appeal).":]

See also, in relation to decisions of Magistrates, *R. v. Southend Stipendiary Magistrate, ex p. Rochford D.C.* [1995] Env. L.R. 1 (no general duty on

Magistrates to give judgments or reasons for decisions); *R. v. Haringey Magistrates, ex p. Cragg* [1997] C.O.D. 160 (no general duty to give reasons, even where no appeal from Magistrates' decision); *Harrison v. Department of Social Security* [1997] C.O.D. 220. But see *R. v. Burton-upon-Trent Justices, ex p. Hussein* (April 29, 1996, unreported). (Magistrates obliged to give reasons where determining appeal by way of rehearing from licensing authority which was itself obliged to give reasons).

[Add to Note 67:]

See also *R. v. Stafford Crown Court, ex p. Reid, The Independent,* March 13, 1995 (no duty to give reasons for Crown Court refusal to extend time for appealing against conviction before Magistrates); *R. v. Southwark Crown Court, ex p. Samuel* [1995] C.O.D. 249; *R. v. Winchester Crown Court, ex p. Morris* [1996] C.O.D. 104; *R. v. Southwark Crown Court ex p. Brooke* [1997] C.O.D. 7 (following *Dave*); *R. v. Bozat* (1997) 9 Admin. L.R. 125 (Crown Court Judge should give reasons for recommending deportation).

[Add to Note 68:]   **9–041**

R. v. Kensington and Chelsea R.L.B.C., ex p. Grillo is now reported at (1996) 28 H.L.R. 94 and (1996) 8 Admin. L.R. 165. Neill L.J. did, however, foresee that "there may come a time when English law does impose a general obligation on administrative authorities to give reasons . . ." (at p. 105); see further, Sir Louis Blom-Cooper Q.C. in *R. v. Islington L.B.C., ex p. Hinds* (1995) 27 H.L.R. 65; (1996) 28 H.L.R. 302 (C.A.). But the general proposition was reaffirmed *R. v. Ministry of Defence, ex p. Murray, The Times,* December 17, 1997 [1998] C.O.D. 134 (Div. Ct, Lord Bingham L.C.J. and Hooper J.).

[Add to Note 69:]

The rapid development of the law in the years since the *Dental Surgery* case has amply confirmed the correctness of that rejection; see the cases cited below at paras 9–047 to 9–048.

[Add at the end of the paragraph:]

Indeed, so fast is the case law on the duty to give reasons developing, that it should now be added that fairness or natural justice will "often" require a decision-maker to give reasons for its decision, even in the absence of any statutory indication: see *ex p. Murray,* above, n.68, which contains an important and valuable general summary of the present extent of the duty to give reasons, and records and reflects the "perceptible trend towards an insistence on greater openness in the making of administrative decisions" (*per* Hooper J.). See also *R. v. Secretary of State for Education, ex p. G* [1995]

E.L.R. 58, 67 (*per* Latham J.); and see De La Mere, [1996] J.R. 88; Toube [1997] J.R. 68.

The advantages of a duty to give reasons

9–042   *[Add to Note 70:]*

For recent judicial consideration of the purpose and advantages of the duty to give reasons, see the important survey in *ex p. Murray*, above, n.68. See also, *ex p. Hinds*, above, n.68.

The disadvantages of a duty to give reasons

9–045   *[Add to Note 78:]*

See also the disadvantages listed by Hooper J. in *ex p. Murray*, above, n.68; and see *R. v. Mayor, Commonality and Citizens of the City of London, ex p. Matson* (1996) 8 Admin. L.R. 49, 70, where Swinton Thomas L.J. cast doubt upon the argument that it would be wrong to require a collegiate body to articulate a reason or set of reasons for its decision.

The distinction between the duty to give reasons and the duty of adequate disclosure

9–046   *[Add to Note 83:]*

An important recent example of the distinction is *R. v. Secretary of State for the Home Department, ex p. Fayed* [1997] 1 W.L.R. 228, C.A. (no duty to give reasons because of statutory exclusion, but duty to disclose to applicant the subject matter of the decision-maker's concern to allow meaningful representations); see update to para. 9–018, above.

Circumstances in which reasons will be required

9–047   *[Add to Note 89:]*

; *Leigh Estates (U.K.) Ltd v. Secretary of State for the Environment* [1996] J.P.L. 217 (duty to explain why grant of planning permission would prejudice preparation of development plan). But see *R. v. Aylesbury Vale D.C., ex p. Chaplin* [1998] J.P.L. 49 (Town and Country Planning Act 1990 did not impose on local planning authority a general duty to give reasons for *granting* application for planning permission). See also, outside the context

of planning, *Berridge v. Benjies Business Centre* [1997] 1 W.L.R. 53 (P.C.)
(adequacy of statutory reasons); *R. v. Secretary of State for Health,
ex p. R.P. Scherer Ltd* (1996) B.M.L.R. 12 (requirement of reasons under
E.C. Council Directive 89/105 was equivalent to common law duty to give
reasons; Minister's decision letter sufficient); *R. v. Doncaster M.B.C., ex p.
Nortrop* (1996) 28 H.L.R. 862 (failure of Housing Benefit Review Board to
give sufficient reasons to discharge statutory duty); *R. v. Brent L.B.C., ex p.
Baruwa* (1996) 28 H.L.R. 361.

[Add to Note 92:]

Recent cases have built on the suggestion (which may also be seen in *ex p.
Cunningham*, below) that reasons may be required to explain a decision
which departs from a policy or usual practice, or is otherwise unexplained,
even if there is no general duty to give reasons: *R. v. Islington L.B.C., ex p.
Rixon* [1997] E.L.R. 66 (authority should have given reasons for departing
from statutory guidance).

[Add to end of sub-paragraph (2):]

The courts have recently demonstrated a greater willingness to intervene in
such circumstances (provided always that they do not discern a statutory
intention to *exclude* reasons) simply on the basis that procedural fairness
requires that reasons be given: *ex p. Murray*, above, n.68. Interestingly, that
case also suggested that the converse situation—*i.e.* where the statutory
framework does not provide for any appeal—may *also* be a factor in favour
of requiring the provision of reasons (relying on *ex p. Cunningham* and
Doody, below).

[Replace, in sub-paragraph (3), third line, "in certain circumstances." with:]

in a wide range of circumstances.

[Add to Note 96:]

Dicta of Hobhouse L.J. in *R. v. Criminal Injuries Compensation Board, ex p.
Cook* [1996] 1 W.L.R. 1037, 1051c (which were not essential to the
decision), which appear to suggest that the giving of inadequate reasons
does not constitute a procedural impropriety, must be treated with reserve.

[Add to Note 97:]

R. v. Secretary of State for the Home Department, ex p. Chetta [1996] C.O.D.
463, where the court criticised the practice of only given reasons after a
challenge had been brought for this reason.

[Add to Note 99, after "ex p. Duggan [1994] 3 All E.R. 277;":]

R. v. Secretary of State for the Home Department, ex p. Follen [1996] C.O.D. 169
(decision to refuse release on licence quashed where no adequate reasons

for not following recommendations of Parole Board); *R. v. Secretary of State for the Home Department, ex p. Lillycrop, The Times,* December 13, 1996 (Parole Board should summarise in decision letter reasons why parole not recommended);

[Add to end of Note 99:]

The "oracular" effect of an unreasoned decision will, naturally, be greater in a case where there is no right of appeal, and this has led to the suggestion that the fact that there is *no* right of appeal may be a factor in favour of requiring reasons: see *ex p. Murray,* above, n.68, and the update to para. 9–047, sub-para. (2), above. The position would therefore appear to be that *both* the existence of a right of appeal (or judicial review), and the absence of any appeal, may be factors predisposing the courts to require reasons.

[Add to Note 3:]

The decision is now reported at (1996) 28 H.L.R. 94. See now the factors identified in *ex p. Murray,* above, n.68.

9–048   *[Add to Note 4:]*

See also the prisoners' cases at the update to n.99, above.

[Add to Note 5:]

The decision is now reported at (1995) 27 H.L.R. 307. See also, in the housing context, *R. v. Camden L.B.C., ex p. Adair* (1997) 29 H.L.R. 236 (nature of duty to give reasons under section 64 of the Housing Act 1985 for decision that applicant not in priority need); *R. v. Kensington and Chelsea R.L.B.C., ex p. Campbell* (1996) 28 H.L.R. 160; *R. v. Lambeth L.B.C. Housing Benefit Review Board, ex p. Harrington, The Times,* December 20, 1996 (duty to supply material facts and reasoning); *R. v. Housing Benefit Review Board of South Tyneside M.B.C., ex p. Tooley* [1996] C.O.D. 143.

[After "regarding an individual's housing application.⁵", add:]

A host of further examples can now be given of circumstances where reasons are required; see, for example, *R. v. Mayor, Commonality and Citizens of the City of London, ex p. Matson* (1996) 8 Admin L.R. 49 (Court of Aldermen, in relation to decision not to confirm election of Alderman following victory in ward vote); *R. v. Secretary of State for the Home Department, ex p. Erdogan (Resul)* [1995] Imm. A.R. 430 (Home Secretary's decision not to extend exceptional leave to remain); *R. v. Islington L.B.C., ex p. Rixon* [1997] E.L.R. 66 (Council's decision as to community care and educational for disabled person, where Council was departing from guidelines); *R. v. Criminal Injuries Compensation Board, ex p. Cook* [1996] 1 W.L.R. 1037, C.A. (reasons for refusal of compensation; considering a number of earlier CICB cases); *Secretary of State for Social Security v. Richards* [1996] C.O.D. 507 (Pensions Appeal Tribunal). See, however, *R. v. Secretary of State for the Home Department, ex p. Owalabi* [1995] Imm. A.R. 400 (immigration; no reasons required for refusal to exercise extra-statutory discretion); *R. v. Solicitor-General, ex p. Taylor and Taylor* (1996) 8 Admin L.R. (no reasons required for decision not to institute contempt proceedings against newspaper editors (*obiter*); *R. v. General Medical Council, ex p. Salvi, The Times,* February 24, 1998 (no reasons required for GMC's refusal to re-register doctor on register of GPs).

[Add to Note 6:]

Nevertheless, it has recently been suggested that the fact that a tribunal is carrying out a "judicial" function, particularly in cases concerning personal liberty, is at least a consideration in favour of requiring reasons: *ex p. Murray,* above, n.68.

The standard of reasons required

[Add to Note 8:]   9–049

Bolton M.B.C. v. Secretary of State for the Environment (No. 2) [1995] 3 PLR 37 and (1995) 71 P. & C.R. 309 (H.L.).

[Add to Note 11:]

See also, *Bolton M.B.C.,* n.8 above; *MJT Securities Ltd v. Secretary of State for the Environment* [1998] J.P.L. 138; (1998) 75 P. & C.R. 188 (C.A.); *S v. Special Educational Needs Tribunal* [1995] 1 W.L.R. 1627, 1636; *R. v. Immigration Appeal Tribunal, ex p. Jebunisha Patel* [1996] Imm. A.R. 161, 167; *Arulandandam v. Secretary of State for the Home Department* [1996] Imm. A.R. 587, 592; *R. v. Secretary of State for Education, ex p. G* [1995] E.L.R. 58, 67; *R. v. Lancashire C.C., ex p. Maycock* (1995) 159 L.G. Rev. 201 ("standard letter" with individual variations sufficient in circumstances); *R. v. Islington L.B.C., ex p. Hinds* (1996) 28 H.L.R. 302; *R. v. Criminal Injuries Compensation Board, ex p. Cook* [1996] 1 W.L.R. 1037, 1043; *R. v. Secretary of State for Transport, ex p. Richmond-upon-Thames L.B.C.* [1996] 1 W.L.R. 1460 (C.A.).

[Add to Note 12:]

Reasons which might be obscure to an outsider may be sufficient for a party who has attended a hearing: *R. v. Chorley B.C., ex p. Bound* (unreported, October 20, 1995, Rich Q.C.); see further, n.21, below.

9–052   *[Add to Note 23:]*

Outside the planning field, however (where the requirement to demon-
strate substantial prejudice is required by statute), the courts will not
readily conclude that an applicant is not prejudiced by an inadequately
reasoned decision. The test may be whether any other conclusion than that
reached was realistically possible: *ex p. Murray*, n.68, above, or whether it is
"obvious" that there is no injustice (*R. v. Winchester Crown Court, ex p.
Morris* [1996] C.O.D. 104).

9–053   *[Add to Note 25:]*

In *R. v. Secretary of State for Transport, ex p. Richmond-upon-Thames L.B.C.*,
the Court of Appeal ([1996] 1 W.L.R. 1460) did not rely upon the
suggestion of Jowitt J. at first instance ([1996] 1 W.L.R. 1005) that there
was no duty to give reasons in respect of a voluntary consultation.

[Add to Note 26:]

Reported at [1994] P.I.Q.R. P314. The case has now been overruled, as to
the obligation on the Board to establish a nexus and as to whether the
reasoning of the Board disclosed any illegality, by *R. v. Criminal Injuries
Compensation Board, ex p. Cook* [1996] 1 W.L.R. 1037 (C.A.).

The effect of a failure to give any or any proper reasons

9–055   *[Add to Note 35:]*

This view is now ordinarily to be preferred; see the cases referred to below.

[Add, after "and need merely be required to produce them.":]

Recent authority has firmly come down in favour of quashing a decision
flawed by inadequate or no reasons; see, in particular, the decision of the
Court of Appeal in *R. v. Westminster C.C., ex p. Ermakov* [1996] 2 All E.R.
302 (C.A.), which concerned statutory reasons; and *R. v. Mayor, Commonality and Citizens of the City of London, ex p. Matson* (1996) 8 Admin. L.R.
49 (C.A.), where the decision was quashed because the failure to give
reasons offended the principles of fairness.

[Add at end of paragraph:]

Recent examples of cases in which the courts have been prepared to accept
affidavit evidence as curing the absence or inadequacy of the reasons
originally given include *R. v. Secretary of State for the Home Department, ex p.*

Moon (1996) 8 Admin. L.R. 477 (where the point was, however, apparently not taken); *R. v. Secretary of State for the Home Department, ex p. Jahromi* (1996) 8 Admin. L.R. 197 (C.A.); *R. v. Criminal Injuries Compensation Board, ex p. S* (1995) 7 Admin L.R. 693 (no objection taken; additional reasons "truly supplementary") *R. v. Northamptonshire C.C., ex p. W* [1998] C.O.D. 110 (no "shift of ground" between decision letter and affidavit; no reason to doubt that affidavit was genuine and adequate recalling of actual basis of decision). All the above cases involved supplementation, not contradiction, of existing reasons. Even here, however, the courts will so far as possible be astute to ensure that later reasons are a genuine expansion of the reasons for the decision at the time, rather than an *ex post facto* justification. A more robust line against subsequent reasons may be seen in the decision of the Court of Appeal in *R. v. Westminster C.C., ex p. Ermakov* [1996] 2 All E.R. 302 at 315–316, a case where there was a statutory duty to give reasons. Hutchison L.J., with whom the other members of the Court agreed, held that whilst courts can, and in appropriate cases should "admit evidence to elucidate or, exceptionally, correct or add to the reasons, . . . [they] should . . . be very cautious about doing so . . . To permit wholesale amendment or reversal of the stated reasons is inimical to [the purposes for which reasons are required]". He also noted that to allow wholesale amendment would give rise to practical difficulties; there would be (justified) applications for cross examination on affidavit and for discovery, which would add to the length and expense of hearings. Although Hutchison L.J. expressly confined his judgment to statutory reasons (and, indeed, to the particular statute under consideration), it is suggested that the reasons which he advanced are equally applicable where reasons are required by virtue of fairness, and the judgment constitutes a powerful warning against allowing substantial supplementation, let alone correction, of reasons in both statutory and common law contexts. *Ermakov* has been followed in a number of cases; see, for example, *R. v. Secretary of State for the Home Department, ex p. Lillycrop, The Times*, December 13, 1996; *R. v. Doncaster M.B.C., ex p. Nortrop* (1996) 28 H.L.R. 862 (Court declined to look at supplemental affidavit of reasons, and quashed decision, because no exceptional circumstances). However, in *R. v. Secretary of State for the Home Department, ex p. Peries* [1998] C.O.D. 150, Jowitt J. suggested that Court of Appeal's decision in *Ermakov* had no application to the situation where the decision maker failed to give any reasons *at all* initially; in such case, the court should permit the respondent to articulate his reasons for the first time by way of affidavit, in the absence of any suggestion that the subsequent reasons were not the true reasons. However, it is suggested that many of the factors relied upon in *Ermakov* are present with equal force in the situation where no reasons are given, and that the decision in *Peries* is, at most, confined to the situation where it is clear that the reasons were articulated (even if not given) at the earlier stage.

The implications which can be Drawn from a failure to provide reasons

9–056   *[Add to Note 39:]*

See also *Bolton M.D.C. v. Secretary of State for the Environment (No. 2)* [1995] 3 PLR 37; (1995) 71 P. & C.R. 309, where Lord Lloyd quoted the *Lonrho* test with approval (at p.43). The nature of the test, however, was not directly in issue in that case. See also, *R. v. Secretary of State for the Home Department, ex p. Pegg* [1995] C.O.D. 84.

[Add to Note 42:]

Gambles has now been overruled, although not on this point; see n.26, above.

9–057   This was described as an "Alice in Wonderland" situation in *Re Chetta, The Times*, July 11, 1996; [1996] C.O.D. 463 (Div. Ct, habeas corpus application).

CHAPTER 10

PROCEDURAL FAIRNESS: EXCEPTIONS

Express statutory exclusion of a fair hearing

[Add:] 10–003

Similarly, an express statutory provision excluding a duty to give reasons has been held not to exclude a duty to disclose the substance of the case so that an applicant for citizenship could make representations: *R. v. Secretary of State for the Home Department, ex p. Fayed* [1997] 1 All E.R. 228.

[Note 10:] 10–004

The Employment Act 1980 has been replaced by the Trade Union and Labour Relations (Consolidation) Act 1992 (see ss 64–67, 174–176).

Where the legislation expressly requires notice and hearing for certain purposes but imposes no procedural requirements for other purposes.

[Add at the end of the paragraph:] 10–005

A number of recent decisions have sought to distinguish those cases where the omission of a procedural safeguard from a statutory framework represents a settled legislative intention that the procedural safeguard should be excluded, from the case of a "mere omission" which may be filled by the courts: see, *e.g. R. v. Secretary of State for the Home Department, ex p. Abdi* [1996] 1 W.L.R. 298; *R. v. Secretary of State for Education and Employment, ex p. M* [1996] E.L.R. 162; *R. v. Secretary of State for Wales, ex p. Emery* [1996] 4 All E.R. 1; and see further, paras 8–013 to 8–020, above.

Where disclosure of information would be prejudicial to the public interest

[Add to Note 15, after ". . . ex p. Chahal [1995] 1 W.L.R. 526":] 10–007

; (1997) 23 E.H.R.R. 413 (*sub nom. Chahal v. United Kingdom*) (European Court of Human Rights found violations of Art. 13 (read with Art. 3) and Art. 5.4 of the Convention); see further, below.

[Note 15:]

Replace "But see *R. v. Secretary of State for the Home Department* [1995] 2 All E.R. 1042, 1050–1051 (C.A.)" with: but see *T v. Secretary of State for the Home Department* [1995] 1 W.L.R. 545 (C.A.); aff'd [1996] A.C. 742 (H.L.).

10–009   *[Replace ". . . the Courts have, as yet, been unwilling to intervene by examining . . ." with:]*

. . . domestic courts have, as yet, been unwilling under the common law to intervene by examining . . .

[Add to Note 22, after ". . . ex p. McQuillan, The Times, September 23, 1994 (Sedley J.) (exclusion order).":]

But see now the decision of the European Court of Human Rights in *Chahal v. United Kingdom* (1997) 23 E.H.R.R. 413, which calls into question the common law position (see below).

[Note 22:]

R. v. Secretary of State for the Home Department, ex p. Gallagher, The Times, February 16, 1994 is now reported at [1995] E.C.R. I–4253; and see also [1996] 1 C.M.L.R. 543 (E.C.J.) (although the point did not directly arise on the Article 177 reference); *R. v. Secretary of State for the Home Department, ex p. Adams, The Independent,* April 28, 1995 is now reported at [1995] 3 C.M.L.R. 476. *R. v. Secretary of State for the Home Department, ex p. McQuillan, The Times,* September 23, 1994 is now reported at [1995] 4 All E.R. 400.

10–010   *[Add to Note 26:]*

The decision of the Divisional Court in *R. v. Ministry of Defence, ex p. Smith,* now reported at [1995] 4 All E.R. 427, was affirmed by the Court of Appeal at [1996] Q.B. 517, where the argument from national security had less prominence.

[Note 27, after "McQuillan, above; transcript at 40" add:]

[1995] 4 All E.R. 400, 423.

10–011   *[Note 29, after "McQuillan, above, n. 22 at 39, transcript" add:]*

[1995] 4 All E.R. 400, 423

[Add to Note 31:]

; *cf. R. v. Secretary of State for the Home Department, ex p. Raghbir Singh* [1996] Imm. A.R. 507, 512; *Jahromi v. Secretary of State for the Home Department* [1996] Imm. A.R. 20.

[Add:]

It should be borne in mind, however, that such an abstentionist stance by domestic courts may leave the United Kingdom in breach of its obligations under the European Convention. In *Chahal v. United Kingdom* (1997) 23 E.H.R.R. 413, the European Court of Human Rights held unanimously that the failure of the courts to carry out or supervise effectively a balancing test (weighing national security considerations) was a breach of Article 5.4, since Mr Chahal's deprivation of liberty had not been subject to any effective judicial control. The Court considered that it must be possible to employ techniques which both accommodated legitimate security concerns about the nature and sources of intelligence information and yet accorded the individual a substantial measure of procedural justice. The domestic case-law set out above must now be considered in the light of this more searching approach.

Where an obligation to give notice and opportunity to be heard would obstruct the taking of prompt action

Statutory relaxation of procedural propriety

[Add to Note 35, after "July 1980, under s.33 of the Act)."":]   **10–012**

Under the Prevention of Terrorism (Temporary Provisions) Act 1989, the Home Secretary may make an exclusion order prior to affording the affected person a hearing before an advisor appointed to hear any objection; for its compatibility with Art. 9(1) of E.C. Directive 64/221 (co-ordination of special measures concerning movement and residence of foreign nationals), see *R. v. Secretary of State for the Home Department, ex p. Gallagher* [1996] 1 C.M.L.R. 543 (E.C.J.): expulsion decision should not be taken before hearing save in cases of urgency.

[Note 44, delete "Listed Buildings Act 1990, s. 1"; insert:]

Planning (Listed Buildings and Conservation Areas) Act 1990.

[Add to Note 47:]   **10–013**

The Public Health Act 1936 has been repealed by the Water Act 1989.

Judicial relaxation of procedural propriety for urgency

[Add to Note 54:]   **10–015**

The rules of natural justice do not apply to the making a Notice of Intervention in a solicitor's practice on the ground of suspected dishonesty under the Solicitors Act 1974, so that there is no requirement to give particulars of the reasons for intervention in the Notice: *Giles v. Law Society* (1996) 8 Admin L.R. 105, C.A. However, the Act does afford a right of judicial consideration *ex post facto.*

Where for other reasons it is impracticable to give prior notice or opportunity to be heard

10–018   *[Add to Note 68:]*

; *R. v. Secretary of State for Wales, ex p. Williams* [1996] C.O.D. 127 (Secretary of State, having consulted in relation to a proposal to close special schools, was not required to consult further in relation to representations of local authority made during consultation process; it was undesirable so to prolong the consultation process).

10–019   *[Add at the end of the paragraph:]*

The same principle may be seen in the jurisprudence of the European Court of Justice: *E.C. Commission v. Lisrestal* [1997] 2 C.M.L.R. 1 (right to be heard is fundamental principle of Community law which cannot be ignored for reasons of administrative inconvenience; decision that grant from European Social Fund should be repaid because of fraud, without consulting grantee, was annulled).

[Add to Note 72:]

See now also *R. v. Brent L.B.C., ex p. O'Malley; R. v. Secretary of State for the Environment, ex p. Walters* [1998] C.O.D. 121, where the Court of Appeal upheld the decision of Schiemann J. that notwithstanding that the extensive consultation process (relating to the redevelopment of council housing estates) carried out by the Respondents was flawed, no relief should be granted since there was overwhelming evidence that the granting of review would damage the interests of a large number of other individuals, and it would be "absurd" to ignore such disbenefits; the courts' discretion to refuse relief was said to be a broad one to be exercised in the light of the particular circumstances. The Court rejected a submission that where there was no "undue deay" under section 31(6) of the Supreme Court Act 1981, the court could not take into account substantial hardship or prejudice to third parties which would be caused by delay or abandonment of this scheme.

Where a procedurally flawed decision has been followed by an ex post facto hearing or by an appeal which complies with the requirements of fairness

10–022   *[Add to Note 86:]*

R. v. LAUTRO, ex p. Tee (1995) 7 Admin L.R. 289; *R. v. Legal Aid Board, ex p. Donn & Co. (a firm)* [1996] 3 All E.R. 1 (Area Committee's unfairness in failing to consider full representations of solicitors seeking legal aid contract not cured by chairman subsequently confirming individually with six of seven members of committee that full representations made no difference to their decision).

[Add to Note 90:]   **10–023**

See similarly, *R. v. Secretary of State for the Home Department, ex p. Sasay (Santigie)* [1995] Imm. A.R. 521.

Where the decision complained of is only a preliminary to a decision subject to procedural fairness

Proximity between investigation and act or decision

[Add to Note 95, after "It does not do anything which adversely affects the man   **10–027**
concerned or prejudices him in any way" (at 427))":]

; *Giles v. Law Society* (1996) 8 Admin. L.R. 105, 114 (decision to issue notice of intervention against solicitor).

[Note 98:]

The correct citation for *Knight v. Indian Head School Division No. 19* is (1990) 69 D.L.R. (4th) 489.

[Add to Note 99:]

; *Brooks v. DPP of Jamaica* [1994] 1 A.C. 568 (decision of DPP to prefer indictment, or of Judge to consent to preferral, was a purely procedural step and neither principles of fairness nor Jamaican Constitution entitled person indicted to be given prior notice of DPP's decision, or to attend before Judge).

Preliminary investigations subject to procedural fairness

[Note 4:]   **10–028**

Section 60 of the Companies Act 1985 has been partly repealed by the Financial Services Act 1986.

[Add to Note 7:]

And see now the decision of the European Court of Human Rights in *Saunders v. United Kingdom* 23 E.H.R.R. 313.

Binding nature of preliminary decision

10–029   *[Note 18:]*

See now Health Service Commissioners Act 1993.

[Note 20:]

See now Criminal Justice Act 1991 and Crime (Sentences) Act 1997, s. 28.

[Add at the end of the paragraph:]

However, where the Parole Board merely reviewed (as an extra-statutory practice) and confirmed the decision of the Secretary of State to recall to prison a discretionary life sentence prisoner who had been released on licence, prior to a full statutory review, the Court of Appeal held that the requirements of full hearing do not apply, because that review was only intended to be "tentative and provisional": *R. v. Parole Board, ex p. Watson* [1996] 1 W.L.R. 906 (*per* Sir Thomas Bingham M.R.); *cf. R. v. Secretary of State for the Home Department, ex p. Seton* (April 25, 1996, unreported).

Where the defect of natural justice has made no difference to the result; where to require fairness or natural justice would be futile; where no prejudice has been caused to the applicant

10–032   *[Add to Note 23:]*

Fulop (Imre) v. Secretary of State for the Home Department [1995] Imm. A.R. 323, C.A. ("no possibility" of a different decision since missing documents unhelpful to applicant); *R. v. London Borough of Camden, ex p. Paddock* [1995] C.O.D. 130 (case "falls within the narrow margin of cases in which the court can say with confidence that the [unfairness] has caused no actual injustice"); *R. v. Islington L.B.C., ex p. Degnan* [1998] C.O.D. 46 (C.A.) ("exceptional case"; judge "near to certainty" that the flawed decision made no difference to the result).

10–034   *[Add to Note 33:]*

R. v. Solicitors Complaints Bureau, ex p. Curtin (1994) 6 Admin. L.R. 657, 664–665, 669; *R. v. Camden London Borough Council, ex p. Cran* (1996) 94 L.G.R. 8.

[After "to decide the matters in question.³³", add:]

As it has recently been put, in a case involving a destruction order under the Dangerous Dogs Act 1991, "the notion that when the rules of natural justice have not been observed, one can still uphold the result because it would not have made any difference, is to be treated with great caution. Down that slippery slope lies the way to dictatorship. On the other hand, if it is a case where it is demonstrable beyond doubt that it would have made no difference, the court may, if it thinks fit, uphold a conviction even if natural justice had not been done"

: *R. v. Ealing Magistrates' Court, ex p. Fanneran* (1996) 8 Admin. L.R. 351, 358, *per* Staughton L.J. A possibly more extreme formulation was set out by Rougier J. in the same case (at p.359):

". . . no one can ever say for certain what must have happened in the circumstances which have not, in fact, arisen. The robing rooms up and down this land are full of strange tales of seemingly impregnable cases foundering on some unforseen forensic reef. It is not, in my opinion, for this court to employ its imagination to postulate facts which might or might not have occurred or arguments which might or might not have succeeded had the rules of natural justice been followed".

[Add to Note 34:]

R. v. Highgate Magistrates Court, ex p. Riley [1996] C.O.D. 12 (following *Dallaglio*, in case of bias, no need to show actual unfairness or prejudice, but simply a real possibility that there was not a wholly impartial adjudication).

[Add to Note 37:]   **10–035**

R. v. London Borough of Camden, ex p. Paddock, above, n.23.

Where the absence of a hearing is not due to any fault on the part of the decision-maker

[Add to Note 45:]   **10–037**

See also the case in this Supplement immediately below.

[Add at the end of the paragraph:]   **10–038**

The courts have continued to struggle with the *Al Mehdawi* proposition (which was, strictly, *obiter*) that review is limited to cases of fraud or breach of duty by the prosecution. On the one hand, there are a number of cases where the courts have been prepared to intervene even though there was clearly nothing akin to fraud on the part of the prosecution: see, for example, *R. v. Kingston-upon-Thames Justices, ex p. Khanna* [1986] R.T.R. 364 (intoximeter calibration beyond limits of tolerance); *R. v. Liverpool Crown Court, ex p. Roberts* [1986] Crim. L.R. 622 (police sergeant inadvertently failed to include in witness statement note in notebook that victim admitted assault was accident); *ex p. Scally*, above, Note 46; *R. v. Harrow Crown Court, ex p. Dave* [1994] 1 W.L.R. 98 (prosecution inadvertently failed to notify defence of convictions of prosecution witnesses). In other cases, however, review has been refused because the conduct of the prosecution could not be characterised as analogous to fraud: *R. v. Burton-upon-Trent Magistrates Court, ex p. Woolley, The Times*, November 17, 1994; *R. v. Dolgellau Justices, ex p. Cartledge* [1996] C.O.D. 106. It is suggested that the analogy with fraud is not helpful; that at the very least "serious error" by the prosecution is sufficient (see *R. v. Thames Stipendiary Magistrate, ex p. Bates* [1995] C.O.D. 6) and furthermore, that the "seriousness" of the error may be measured by its effect upon the fairness of the conviction, rather than the degree of fault of the prosecution: a "misunderstanding, confusion, or failure of communication", in the words of Bingham L.J., may be productive of serious injustice sufficient to found relief (see *Bagga Khan*, above, Note 48. As, for example, in *ex p. Scally*, above, Note 46).

10–038A *[Add new paragraph 10–038A:]*

A further unresolved question is the extent to which this jurisdiction extends beyond errors by the prosecution in criminal proceedings. The Court of Appeal has recently held that it is limited to cases which are "essentially criminal processes", and declined to extend it to a challenge to a decision of the Criminal Injuries Compensation Board which was alleged to be vitiated by a misrepresentation in police officers' evidence of the contents of a medical report: *R. v. Criminal Injuries Compensation Board, ex p. A* [1997] 3 W.L.R. 776, 796a–e (*per* Simon Brown L.J.); 799e (per Peter Gibson L.J.); now on appeal to the House of Lords: [1998] 1 W.L.R. 277. On the other hand, the House of Lords in *Al-Mehdawi* did not expressly so confine the jurisdiction, and it clearly extends to at least some formal disciplinary processes, such as hearings before Prison Boards of Visitors: *ex p. Fox-Taylor*, above, n.43. It may also be detected underlying a recent decision relating to committal proceedings, in which an extradited defendant sought to resist committal on the basis that his extradition was flawed by reason of (deliberate) failure by the authorities to follow extradition procedures and foreign law. The House of Lords (which did not directly refer to the "prosecution" cases) held that in such circumstances, the Magistrates should have adjourned the committal to allow consideration, by the Divisional Court in the exercise of its supervisory jurisdiction, of the lawfulness of the extradition: *R. v. Horseferry Road Magistrates' Court, ex p. Bennett* [1994] 1 A.C. 42; and see *Dixon* [1997] J.R. 86 for the suggestion that *Bennett*, and perhaps the "prosecution" cases, represent the emergence of a head of review separate from the traditional grounds of illegality, irrationality and procedural impropriety, since they are not founded upon any error of the decision-maker. But see *Al-Mehdawi*, above, n.46.

[Add to Note 49:]   **10–039**

; *R. v. Newport Justices, ex p. Carey*, (1996) 160 J.P. 613, Div. Ct (applicant's absence from hearing his own fault); *R. v. Secretary of State for the Home Department, ex p. Kikaka* [1996] Imm. A.R. 340 (applicant had chosen to represent herself).

[Add to Note 52:]   **10–040**

See also, all following *Al Mehdawi*: *Secretary of State for the Home Department v. Mohammed Yasin* [1995] Imm. A.R. 118, 121–122 (failure of applicant's advisors to draw Tribunal's attention to brother's case); *Samuel Dele Adeniyi v. Secretary of State for the Home Department* [1995] Imm. A.R. 101 (failure of solicitors to send notice of appeal to correct address); *R. v. Governors of Sheffield Hallam University, ex p. R* [1995] E.L.R. 267 (failure of applicant's solicitor to seek sufficient adjournment to consider new material); *R. v. Secretary of State for the Home Department, ex p. Osei Yaw Yeboah* [1995] Imm. A.R. 393 (applicant not represented at appeal through fault of solicitor); *R. v. Monopolies and Mergers Commission, ex p. Stagecoach Holdings Plc, The Times*, July 23, 1996.

CHAPTER 11

PROCEDURAL FAIRNESS: FETTERING OF DISCRETION

FETTERING OF DISCRETION BY SELF-CREATED RULES OF POLICY

[Add to Note 2:]   **11–004**

See also *R. v. Secretary of State for the Home Department, ex p. Venables* [1997] 3 W.L.R. 23, 47, where Lord Browne-Wilkinson restated the distinction between a proper policy and an over-rigid or inflexible one, and referred to the passage in the text.

[Add to Note 5 after "R. v. Herrod, ex p. Leeds C.C. [1976] Q.B. 540, 559–560,   **11–005** *563–564":]*

[Note 20:]   **11–006**

The note should read: ". . . The vital words, here as italicised by S.A. de Smith in the first edition of this work, are omitted . . .".

cf. R. v. Gaming Board of Great Britain, ex p. Kingsley [1996] C.O.D. 241.

[Add after "allocation of land for gypsy sites.":]   **11–007**

The Secretary of State for the Home Office was held (by a majority of the House of Lords) to have fettered his discretion in setting a "tariff" period of 15 years for a person sentenced to be detained at Her Majesty's Pleasure, because the "tariff" period did not permit review on grounds other than those relating to the circumstances of the commission of the crime and the applicant's state of mind, contrary to the Secretary of State's statutory power which was not fettered in this way: see *R. v. Secretary of State for the Home Department, ex p. Venables* [1997] 3 W.L.R. 23, *per* Lord Browne-Wilkinson (45e–50g), Lord Steyn (69c–73d, although his Lordship did not use the language of fettering of discretion) and Lord Hope (80c–f, 82d–84f). Compare, in the Court of Appeal, [1997] 2 W.L.R. 67 at 90b–e, *per* Lord Woolf M.R. See also *R. v. Secretary of State for the Home Department, ex p. Zulfikar* [1996] C.O.D. 256 (blanket policy of strip-searching prisoners after every visit not unlawful); *R. v. Secretary of State for the Home Department, ex p. Hastrup* [1996] Imm. A.R. 616 (Minister's discretion as to whether to deport a person married to a British citizen with a British child not fettered by Home Office policy document).

[Add to Note 30 after "(. . . no flexibility whatsoever)":]

R. v. Lambeth L.B.C., ex p. Njomo (1996) 28 H.L.R. 737 (local authority entitled to take into account rent arrears in deciding rehousing priorities (and generally in housing management functions), but policy rigidly applied in particular case and hence an unlawful fetter); *R. v. Brent L.B.C., ex p. Baruwa* (1996) 28 H.L.R. 361.

[Add to Note 32:]

However in *R. v. Newham L.B.C., ex p. Dada* [1996] Q.B. 507 the Court of Appeal held that a housing appeals procedure that required the appellant to sign a tenancy agreement and move into the rejected accommodation before the authority would consider an appeal against a determination that the rejection of a property was unreasonable, was not an over-rigid policy because a review of the decision by the appeals officer "built a sufficient discretion into the system" (*per* Glidewell L.J. at 516d, thereby distinguishing *R. v. Newham L.B.C. ex p. Gentle* (1994) 26 H.L.R. 466).

[Add to text after ". . . not to institute any prosecution at all for an anti-social class of criminal offences[35]":]

nor should he fetter his discretion by treating the decision of the Director of Public Prosecutions that there was insufficient evidence to justify the prosecution of an officer, as determinative of the question of whether to dismiss for unfairness disciplinary charges against that officer based on substantially the same facts: see *R. v. Chief Constable Thames Valley Police, ex p. Police Complaints Authority* [1996] C.O.D. 324.

11–008 *[Note 38:]*

R. v. Warwickshire C.C., ex p. Colleymore is now reported at [1995] E.L.R. 217.

[Add to Note 38:]

Compare *R. v. Southwark L.B.C., ex p. Udu* (1996) 8 Admin. L.R. 25 (local authority entitled to have general policy of not funding courses at private colleges and postgraduate courses, subject to "exceptional cases").

[Add to Note 39:]

And see *R. v. Secretary of State for Education and Employment, ex p. Portsmouth Football Club Ltd* [1998] C.O.D. 142 (refusal of footballer's work permit

flawed by over-rigid adoption of policy, notwithstanding affidavit evidence
indicating that decision taken on correct basis).

[Add to Note 44 after "Schmidt v. Home Secretary [1969] 2 Ch. 149":]   **11–009**

; *cf. R. v. Secretary of State for the Home Department, ex p. Hastrup* [1996] Imm.
A.R. 616.

[Add to Note 44 after ". . .impede further enforcement action)":

R. v. National Rivers Authority, ex p. Moreton [1996] Env. L.R. 234 (NRA did
not fetter discretion in taking Welsh Water's investment budget into
account in allowing company to discharge sewage from Tenby works).

[Add to Note 52 after ". . . Asif Mahmood Khan [1984] 1 W.L.R. 1337;":]   **11–012**

Markus and Westate, "The Duty to Follow Guidance" [1977] J.R. 154;

[Note 55:]

R. v. Secretary of State for the Home Department, ex p. Fire Brigades Union is
now reported at [1995] 2 A.C. 513.

[Add to Note 58 after "Re Findlay [1985] A.C. 318":]   **11–013**

; *R. v. Gaming Board of Great Britain, ex p. Kingsley* [1996] C.O.D. 241 (there
could be no reasonable, and hence no legitimate, expectation that Gaming
Board would fetter its discretion by agreeing not to take account of certain
matters in deciding, as required to do by statute, whether the applicant was
a fit and proper person).

UNDERTAKING NOT TO EXERCISE A DISCRETION

[Add to Note 68:]   **11–014**

cf. R. v. Secretary of State for the Home Department, ex p. Fire Brigades Union
[1995] 2 A.C. 513. (Home Secretary could not disable himself from ability
to bring statutory scheme into effect by adopting alternative scheme having
consequence that statutory scheme "will not now be implemented").

[Note 77:]

replace *"Nangler"* with *"Nangle"*.

CHAPTER 12

PROCEDURAL FAIRNESS: BIAS AND INTEREST

THE TEST OF BIAS

[Add to Note 42:]

The *Gough* test has been recently followed in *R. v. Gaming Board for Great Britain, ex p. Kingsley* [1996] 10 C.L. 113 (C.A., July 4, 1996)—it was common ground that there was evidence establishing the appearance of bias, but there was no evidence of a real danger of injustice arising from it, nor could the decision lawfully be delegated to an independent tribunal; *R. v. Secretary of State for the Environment, ex p. Kirkstall Valley Campaign* [1996] 3 All E.R. 304 (*Gough* test accepted for bodies whether judicial or administrative). But *cf. David Eves v. Hambros Bank (Jersey) Ltd* [1996] 1 W.L.R. 251. (P.C.) (where the body was not asked to decide any question between the parties, the fact that a member of the court had an interest in the bank would not vitiate the proceedings on the ground of bias).

[Add to Note 42:]

In *Auckland Casino Ltd v. Casino Control Authority* [1995] 1 N.Z.L.R. 142, the New Zealand Court of Appeal noted that since *R. v. Gough* and *Webb v. R.* (1994) 122 A.L.R. 41 there was, as to the test for apparent bias, a conflict of approach between the House of Lords and the High Court of Australia, but said that once it is accepted that the hypothetical reasonable observer must be informed, the distinction between the real danger and reasonable suspicion tests becomes very thin.

[Add to Note 43:]

In the South African case *BTR Industries v. Metal & Allied Workers Union* 1992 (3) S.A. 673(A) it was held that for "judicial" situations a "reasonable suspicion" test applies while "real likelihood" of bias applies to all other cases.

DISQUALIFICATION FOR BIAS

Direct pecuniary or proprietary interests

12–012   *[Add to Note 46:]*

But in *Auckland Casino Ltd v. Casino Control Authority* [1995] 1 N.Z.L.R. 142, 148, the New Zealand Court of Appeal was prepared to accept that the *de minimis* rule could apply.

12–016   *[Add to Note 65:]*

Local Authorities (Members' Interests) (Amendment) Regulations 1996 [S.I. 1996 No. 1215] in force July 1, 1996 amend the Local Authorities (Members' Interests) Regulations 1992.

Participation in appeal against own decisions

12–017   *R. v. South Worcestershire Magistrates, ex p. Lilley* [1995] 1 W.L.R. 1595. Lay justices heard and rejected PII application and then went on to hear prosecution. The procedure was such that "a reasonable and fairminded person could reasonably have suspected the applicant could not have a fair trial". (H.L. refused leave to appeal: see [1996] 1 W.L.R. 481). *R. v. Parole Board, ex p. Watson* [1996] 1 W.L.R. 906 (C.A.) (no bias in extra-statutory practice)

Likelihood of bias because of personal attitudes and relationships

Personal hostility

12–020   *R. v. Horseferry Magistrates' Court, ex p., Bilhar Chima* [1995] C.O.D. 317 (clerk made racist remark).

12–021   *[Add after Note 91:]*

Dallaglio was applied in *R. v. Highgate Magistrate's Court ex p. Riley* [1996] C.O.D. 12.

Family relationship

12–025   *R. v. Wilson and Sprason* (1996) 8 Admin. L.R. 1. wife of prison officer on jury; *R. v. Salt* (1996) 8 Admin. L.R. 429 (son of usher on jury).

Professional and vocational relationship

[Add to Note 14:]   **12–027**

See *R. v. Legal Aid Board, ex p. Donne & Co. (a firm)* [1996] 3 All E.R. 1 (presence of territorial officer at application to Legal Aid Board for action arising out of Gulf War Syndrome).

Possibility of bias because of attitudes towards the issue

R. v. Highgate Magistrate's Court, ex p. Riley [1996] C.O.D. 12 (remark   **12–030** indicating that police officer's evidence likely to be treated more favourably than defendants).

SITUATIONS WHERE BIAS WILL NOT APPLY

Waiver

[Note 38, add:]   **12–036**

A more recent review of English, Australian and New Zealand authorities on waiver of objections for bias was undertaken by the New Zealand Court of Appeal in *Auckland Casino Ltd v. Casino Control Authority* [1995] 1 N.Z.L.R. 142. It was held that, although confronted with an agonising choice, the party ultimately complaining in that case had waived the objection by delaying until the decision was known. It was accepted, however, that displays of blatant bias, likely to undermine public confidence in the justice system, should not necessarily be capable of private waiver; while in criminal cases private waiver should not normally be possible at all.

Policy and bias

[Add to Note 81:]   **12–049**

In *R. v. Secretary of State for the Environment ex p. Kirkstall Valley Campaign Ltd* [1996] 3 All E.R. 304 Sedley J. carefully considered to what extent participation in proceedings would amount to bias. He concluded that the person need not necessarily withdraw from discussion, but it would be "wise advice" to do so. See also, *R. v. Buckinghamshire County Council ex p. Milton Keynes B.C.* (1997) 9 Admin. L.R. 159 (Conservative party members had not been "instructed" to vote, on proposals for the establishment of a grammar school, in a manner inconsistent with what was lawfully allowed in the interests of party unity as set out in *ex p. Baxter)*. And see *R. v. Bassetlaw D.C., ex p. Oxby* [1997] N.P.C. 178 (bias in grant of planning permission. Council itself, through its leader, may bring judicial review proceedings to revoke the decision).

CHAPTER 13

THE UNREASONABLE EXERCISE OF POWER

INTRODUCTION

[Add to Note 4:]   **13–002**

Recent writings setting out the scope of *Wednesbury* review include: Lord
Irvine Q.C., "Judges and Decision-Makers: the theory and practice of
Wednesbury review" [1996] P.L. 59; Martin Norris, "Ex parte Smith:
irrationality and human rights" [1996] P.L. 590; Paul Walker, "What's
Wrong with Irrationality?" [1995] P.L. 556; Deryck Beyleveld, "The
Concept of a human right and incorporation of the ECHR" [1995] P.L.
577; Sir Robert Carnwath "The reasonable limits of local authority
powers" [1966] P.L. 2440.

[Add to Note 15:]   **13–005**

But see *R. v. MAFF, ex p. First City Trading* [1997] 1 C.M.L.R. 250 where
Laws J. considers the extent to which the fundamental principles of E.C.
law as formulated by the E.C.J., such as equal treatment, non-
discrimination, proportionality and legitimate expectation may apply in
U.K. domestic law: see further, below at para. 21–030. And see J.
Schwartze (ed.) *Administrative Law under European Influence* (1996).

The balance of relevant considerations

[Note 48:]   **13–016**

Tesco Stores is now reported in [1995] 1 W.L.R. 759.

[Add to note 53:]   **13–018**

See *R. v. Secretary of State for the Home Department ex p. Zulfikar* [1996]
C.O.D. 256, where it was held that "undue weight" should not have been
given to a parole requirement that the offender "address his offending",
where the offender continued to deny the offence.

[Add the following paragraph at the end of page 558:]

   In *R. v. Secretary of State for the Home Department ex p. Venables* the House
of Lords held [1997] 3 W.L.R. 23, that, in fixing the tariffs for young

offenders and deciding the part of the sentence required for punishment and deterrence, the Home Secretary had wrongly taken into account irrelevant material derived from public petitions and via the media. Lord Steyn held that the Home Secretary's decision was also *procedurally* flawed by "the credence and weight" which he gave to the public clamour for an increase in the level of the tariff.

[Add to the end of Note 58:]

Phoenix Aviation is now reported at [1995] 3 All E.R. 37. The Divisional Court's decision in *R. v. Chief Constable of Sussex, ex p. International Trader's Ferry* is now reported at [1996] Q.B. 197. The Court of Appeal has since held that the Chief Constable's decision to provide policing on only two days a week to protect the transport of livestock where animal rights protestors were demonstrating was not unreasonable or disproportionate under domestic and E.C. law because of restraints on resources, and there being no reasonable prospects of those resources being increased: [1997] 3 W.L.R. 132. See also *R. v. Camden L.B.C., ex p. H (a minor)* [1996] E.L.R. 306 (C.A.) (committee of governors had failed to consider sufficiently what effect the reversal of the headteacher's decision to expel pupils would have on the maintenance of discipline in the school and what effect the reinstatement of X and Y would have on the victim himself). But see *R. v. Secretary of State for the Home Department, ex p. Singh (Rabhbir)* [1995] Imm. A.R. 447 (although there was no evidence to show that an appropriate balancing exercise had been carried out to ensure that the risk to the individual had been balanced against the public interest, the Secretary of State would carry out such an exercise in the course of S's asylum application). See also *Raziastaraie (Mansour Ali) v. Secretary of State for the Home Department* [1995] Imm. A.R. 459, C.A. where *R. v. Secretary of State for the Home Department, ex p. Chahal* [1995] 1 W.L.R 526 was distinguished. The House of Lords dismissed the appeal: see [1996] 2 W.L.R. 766; [1996] 2 All E.R. 865. See also *R. v. Southwark LBC ex p. Cordwell* (1995) 27 H.L.R. 594 (C.A.) (closure order under Housing Act 1985. No evidence of error in the calculation of the proper weight to be given to occupier's wishes). And see *R. v. Kensington & Chelsea RLBC ex p. Ben-el-Mabrouk* (1995) 27 H.L.R. 564 (C.A.). See also *R. v. Mid-Hertfordshire Justices ex p. Cox* (1996) 8 Admin. L.R. 409 (unreasonable failure to place weight on fact that poll tax defaulter could not afford to pay fine because destitute).

Rationality: logic, evidence and reasoning

13–019   *[Add footnote[58a] after end of first sentence:]*

"I would accordingly incline to accept the Secretary of State's argument on this point, while observing that decisions reached by him are susceptible to challenge on any *Wednesbury* ground, of which irrationality is only one". *per* Sir Thomas Bingham M.R. in *R. v. Secretary of State for the Home Department, ex p. Omibiyo* [1996] 2 All E.R. 901.

[Add to Note 59:]

R. v. Lambeth L.B.C., ex p. Ashley (1997) 29 H.L.R. 385 (points scheme for the allocation of housing was plainly "illogical and irrational"). See also *R. v. Islington L.B.C. ex p. Hassan* (1995) 27 H.L.R. 485 (finding of intentional homelessness illogical).

[Add to end of the third sentence after n.65:]   **13–021**

However, in the recent case of *Percy v. Hall* [1997] Q.B. 924, the Court of Appeal conducted an exhaustive survey of the authorities (*per* Simon Brown L.J.) and reached the conclusion that a byelaw would be treated as valid unless it was so uncertain in its language as to have no ascertainable meaning or was so unclear in its effect as to be incapable of certain application. Mere "ambiguity" would not suffice. *cf. Kruse v. Johnson* [1898] 2 Q.B. 473. See also the discussion of the test relating to byelaws and planning conditions at p. 533 *et seq.*

[Add to Note 66:]

Circular 1/85 is now Circular 11/97.

[Add to Note 70:]   **13–022**

In *R. v. Secretary of State for Home Affairs ex p. Zakrocki* [1996] C.O.D. 304, Carnwath J. held that there had been no evidential basis for the assertion that arrangements could have been made for care in the community of an immigrant and, therefore, the decision of the Home Secretary was unreasonable. And see *Methodist Church of New Zealand v. Gray* [1996] 2 N.Z.L.R. 554, 558 (successful appeal on question of law when decision based on view of facts which could not reasonably be entertained). See also *R. v. Newbury District Council v. Blackwell* [1988] C.O.D. 155 (planning committee's failure to obtain evidence of likely increase in road use on safely "unreasonable in the Wednesbury case".

[Add to Note 72:]

See *Abdi v. Secretary of State for the Home Department* [1966] 1 W.L.R. 298 (H.L.) certification that minister had knowledge of immigration policies in Spain amounted to "sufficient evidence" on which adjudicators were entitled to decide the question on asylum. But see the dissents of Lords Slynn and Mustill. *cf. R. v. Highbury Corner Magistrates, ex p. Rabhani* (unreported February 19, 1996) (Magistrates acted unreasonably on evidence before them).

[Add to Note 72:]

R. v. Epping Magistrates, ex p. Howard and Leach [1997] R.A. 258 (compensation ordered by magistrates following distraint mistakenly levied. Held, granting the application: the method used by the Magistrates, particularly their valuation of a skip, was unexplained and appeared to be a guess. The Magistrates had acted unreasonably as there was no evidence to justify the valuations. A rehearing of the claim for compensation was ordered); *R. v. Secretary of State for the Environment and Rich Investments Ltd ex p. Bexley L.B.C.* (1995) 70 P. & C.R. 522 (the Planning Inspector was wrong to conclude that the failure to arrive at a negotiated resolution of the appeal was wholly attributable to B. He ignored the fact that R had originally agreed to assume their own costs and then resiled from that agreement and thus had acted unreasonably and reached a decision which was perverse). But see *R. v. Secretary of State for the Home Department, ex p. Ellaway* [1996] C.O.D. 328; *Re Neal (Coronor: Jury)* [1996] C.O.D. 190. (Staughton J. held, refusing an application to quash an open verdict, that "it could not be said that the coroner had reached a verdict that no reasonable coroner could have reached").

13–024 *[Note 81:]*

McQuillan is now reported at [1995] 4 All E.R. 400. See also *R. v. Secretary of State for the Home Department, ex p. Adams* [1995] All E.R. (E.C.) 177. Note also that in *Chahal v. U.K.* (1997) 23 E.C.H.R. 413 it was held that the procedures before the "3 wise men" advisory review panel violated Article 5(4) of the European Convention on Human Rights. The Court held that "it was possible to employ techniques which both accommodated legitimate security concerns about the nature and sources of intelligence information and yet accorded the individual a substantial measure of procedural justice".

PRINCIPLES GOVERNING THE EXERCISE OF OFFICIAL POWER

Legal certainty and substantive legitimate expectations

13–028 *[Add to Note 99:]*

Tandridge D.C. v. Telecom Securicor Cellular Radio [1996] J.P.L. 128 refusal to grant planning permission to erect a multi-antenna mast for mobile telephone service. *Lever* [1971] 1 Q.B. 222; *Western Fish Products* [1981] 2 All E.R. 204; *Camden* (1994) 67 P. & C.R. 59 considered on question of

whether estoppel arose. (No evidence of detrimental reliance). See also, *R.
v. Criminal Injury Compensation Board ex p. Keane & Marsden* [1988] C.O.D.
128.

[Add to Note 4:]

R. v. Secretary of State for the Home Department, ex p. Alakesan, [1997] Imm.
A.R. 315 (A unsuccessfully argued that the Home Secretary was bound by
res judicata to follow the immigration adjudicator's recommendations and
that the decision was therefore unlawful. Held: provided the Home
Secretary gave reasons for departing from the recommendations of the
adjudicator and considered the recommendations fairly, there was no case
for arguing that *res judicata* bound the Minister). *R. v. Secretary of State for
Education, ex p. C* [1996] E.L.R. 93 (held: dismissing the application: it was
not irrational for the same person to reach a different decision when
reconsidering the same facts); *A & T Investments v. Secretary of State for the
Environment* (1996) 72 P. & C.R. 540; issue estoppel; *Thrasyvoulou* considered); *Hammond v. Secretary of State for the Environment* (1997) 74 P. & C.R.
134; *The Times,* February (estoppel *per rem judicatam; Thrasyvoulou* considered. A decision of a planning inspector gave rise to an estoppel and where
subsequently different inspectors reached contradictory decisions, the first
in time prevailed); *cf. R. v. South West Thames Mental Health Review Tribunal,
ex p. Demetri* [1997] C.O.D. 44; *Porter v. Secretary of State for Transport* [1996]
3 All E.R. 693. (no issue estoppel in relation to alternative development
certificate. Decision lacked the necessary element of finality. A refusal of
planning permission not determinative as a fresh application could be
made). But see *Barber v. Staffordshire County Council* [1996] 2 All E.R. 748
(issue estoppel in respect of to industrial tribunal application; *Arnold v.
National Westminster Bank plc* [1991] 2 A.C. 93 applied.

[Add to Note 7:]   13–029

P.P. Craig, "Substantive Legitimate Expectations in Domestic and Com-
munity Law" [1996] C.L.J. 289; Lester, "Government Compliance with
international human rights law: a new year's legitimate expectation" [1996]
P.L. 187—comment on *Minister for Immigration and Ethnic Affairs v. Teoh*
(1995) 69 A.L.J.R. 423. Michael Taggart, "Legitimate expectation and
Treaties in the High Court of Australia" (1996) 112 L.Q.R. 50; Ryszard
Piotrowicz, "Unincorporated treaties in Australian Law" [1996] P.L. 190;
Rabinder Singh and Karen Steyn, "Legitimate Expectation in 1996. Where
Now?" (1996) 1 Judicial Review 17; C. Himsworth, "Legitimately expect-
ing proportionality?" [1996] P.L. 46.

[Note 11:]

Browne-Wilkinson L.J. should read: Lord Browne-Wilkinson.

13-030   *[Add to Note 13:]*

R. v. IRC, ex p., Unilever plc [1996] C.O.D. 369; [1996] S.T.C. 681 (C.A.). Claim for tax relief made in similar form to that accepted in previous years and therefore unfair for the Inland Revenue Commission to resile from previous practice without notice.

[Add further to note 13:]

Note the controversial Australian Case of *Minister for Immigration and Ethnic Affairs v. Teoh* (1995) 183 C.L.R. 273, where the High Court held that the International Covenant on the Rights of the Child, which was not incorporated into Australian law, may nevertheless give rise to a legitimate expectation that executive decision-makers will comply with it, at least to the extent of giving a person affected by a decision not to act in accordance with the Convention the right to a hearing on the matter. Refer to the discussion above, in the notes to Chapter 6, paras 6–050–6–052. And see Taggart (1996) 112 L.Q.R. 50.

[Add to Note 23:]

See *R. v. Shropshire County Council, ex p. Jones* (1996) Admin. L.R. 625 (applicant for student grant given to understand he has a very good chance of securing an award does not acquire a legitimate expectation). *See also R. v. IRC, ex p. Unilever plc* [1996] C.O.D. 369; [1996] S.T.C. 681 (C.A.). And see *R. v. Gaming Board of Great Britain, ex p. Kingsley* [1996] C.O.D. 241.

13-033   "Moral objections" should read "moral obligations".

[Add to Note 33:]

Knop v. Johannesburg City Council 1995 (2) 3AJ(19).

13-035   The court of appeal resolved this difference against Sedley J. and the *Hamble* Case in *R. v. Secretary of State for the Home Department ex p. Hargreaves* [1997] 1 W.L.R. 906. The applicants contended that their expectation to eligibility for home leave was frustrated by a change in policy. It was held that the lawfulness of the change in policy was to be assessed by means of the *Wednesbury* test. The matter may not, however, rest there. See, *e.g. Pierson v. Secretary of State for the Home Department* [1997] 3 All E.R. 577 (H.L.), where it was held that the increase in sentence was unlawful for breach (Lord Steyn at least) of the "substantive principle" of the Rule of Law.

Equal treatment

13-038   *[Add to Note 45:]*

For a full account of the principle of equality in French law see Conseil D'Etat, Élvdes et Documents, *Rappart Public 1996, Sur le Principle d' égalité* (1996).

[Add to Note 47:]

See also *R. v. Secretary of State for Health ex p. Richardson* [1995] 3 C.M.L.R.
367 (E.C.J. held contrary to E.C. law free prescriptions to U.K. men when
65 and women when 60). See further para. 13–044 below. But see *Atkins v.
Wrekin D.C.* [1966] 3 C.M.L.R. 863. E.C.J. (a scheme operated by local
authority under Transport Act 1985, s. 93 which provides men over 65 and
women over 60 with travel concessions is not within the scope of Directive
79/7 on the progressive implementation of equal treatment for men and
women in matters of social security). See also *P v. S and Cornwall County
Council* [1996] 2 C.M.L.R. 247, where the E.C.J. held unlawful discrimination on the ground of gender reassignment from a man to a woman
(whose employment was then terminated as a result). See also *R. v. Ministry
of Defence, ex p. Smith* [1996] Q.B. 517. *cf. R. v. Registrar General, ex p. P and
G* [1996] 2 F.L.R. 90 (transsexuals applied for judicial review of the
Registrar's refusal to alter entries made in the register after they had
undergone gender reassignment surgery. They argued that medical
research had advanced to a stage where the biological criteria relied on to
identify their sex were no longer appropriate. Held, refusing the applications: that although recent medical research into gender identity dys-
phoria showed that a person's sex might be determined by the construction
of the brain, while uncertainties remained, the Registrar General could not
be said to have acted irrationally, nor was his decision contrary to Art. 5
E.C.H.R.)

[Add to Note 49:]

In *R. v. Ministry of Agriculture, Fisheries & Food ex p. First City Trading Ltd*
[1997] C.M.L.R. 250, Laws J. conducted an exhaustive analysis of the case
law of the E.C.J. in relation to the principle of equality as it applied to the
British beef ban. He came to the conclusion that the test under E.C. law,
requiring a substantive justification of discrimination, was different from
the *Wednesbury* test.

> "By our domestic law, if a public decision-maker were to treat
> apparently identical cases differently there would no doubt be a prima
> facie Wednesbury case against him, since on the face of it such an
> approach bears the hallmark of irrationality . . . The court would look
> for an explanation of the difference; but the justification offered would
> in the ordinary way only be rejected on the grounds of perversity".

[Add to Note 61:]   **13–041**

In *R. v. Secretary of State for the Home Department ex p. Urmaza* [1996] C.O.D.
479, Sedley J. held that where a government department publishes a policy
document, the "legal principle of consistency in the exercise of public
powers" (citing paras 13–036 to 13–045 of this work) creates a presumption

that the Minister will follow his own policy. If there is a departure from the policy, there must be good reason for it (almost certainly supported by the giving of reasons). Sedley J. added that the principle of consistency, in the eye of the law, does not extend to being consistently wrong about the proper interpretation of the policy in accordance with its objects. See also *R. v. DPP, ex p. C*; [1995] 1 Cr.App.R. 136 the Court can interfere with a decision not to prosecute where the prosecutor fails to follow the settled policy set out in the Code for Crown Prosecutions); *R. v. Commissioner of Police for the Metropolis, ex p. P* (1996) 8 Admin. L.R. 6 (police were liable to judicial review if they gave a formal caution in clear breach of the guidelines in H.O. Circular 18/1994, even if the breach was unintentional). These cases deal with consistency as an aspect of legal certainty rather than equality, for which see paras 13–029–13–035 above. See also the Canadian case *British Columbia Telephone Co. v. Shaw Cablesystems (B.C.) Ltd*, [1995] S.C.R. 739 where two administrative bodies had given inconsistent decisions and the Supreme Court of Canada held that, if each decision was in itself not unlawful, the courts have jurisdiction to declare one of the decisions inoperative. The Supreme Court based the decision on "the presumption of legislative coherence".

13–042   *[Add to Note 62:]*

But see *R. v. Aylesbury Vale D.C., ex p. Chaplin, The Times*, July 23, 1996 (noted by K. Steyn [1997] J.R. 22).

13–043   *[Add at end of Note 71:]*

And see the Northern Ireland cases of *Re Colgan, McGrane and Keleghan* (N.I.Q.B.D., unreported, November 8, 1996); *Re Wright and Fisher* (N.I.Q.B.D., unreported, December 20, 1996); and *Re Croft* (N.I.Q.B.D., unreported, January 29, 1997). In *Colgan et al.*, (which involved judicial review of a decision of the N.I. Civil Service Commission that the applicant was ineligible for appointment by reason of (Irish Nationality), Girvan J. said:

> "Apart from the Community law principle that comparable situations should be treated equally there is a principle of domestic administrative law to a similar effect . . . A decision which results in an unjustifiable inequality of treatment is open to challenge on the ground of unreasonableness since if there is no logical difference between two situations justifying a differential treatment, logic and fairness require equality of treatment".

Girvan J. applied this principle in *Wright and Fisher* (which involved the time when life sentences imposed in various cases should be considered by the Life Sentence Review Board). In *Croft*, Carswell L.C.J. said, *Re* generalisations from the present law, is that the furthest we would wish to go is to state that "administrators must be even-handed and avoid arbitrariness in the application of sets of rules such as statutes or codes to individual citizens, otherwise by committing an abuse of the power entrusted to them they may be failing lawfully to exercise that power". (The case involved RUC Reservists and length of service credited for pension purposes).

In Israel, equality, though not expressly anchored in a constitutional document, is considered by the Supreme Court to be a fundamental right, like free speech. Under the principle of equality, the Court recently held that El Al, the national airline, was obliged to offer a homosexual air steward's partner the same benefits that are offered, according to a collective labour agreement, to spouses in heterosexual relationships. See *El Al Israel Airlines Ltd v. Danilovitz* (1994) 48(5) P.D. 794. In addition, the Court held that the Israeli Air Force could not bar women soldiers from participating in a combat pilots' training course. The Court admitted that this may be costly to the Air Force and also require special arrangements and facilities. However, the Court concluded that society should be ready to pay a reasonable price in order to promote equality. See *Miller v. Minister of Defence* (1995) 49(4) P.D. 94. Recently, the Supreme Court applied a new statute which requires that in appointing members to boards of directors of Government Corporations, Ministers should strive to achieve proper representation of both sexes. The Court invalidated the appointment of three men to the boards of two such corporations, although they were fully qualified, because the Minister did not properly examine the possibility of appointing women to the vacant positions. See *Israel Women's Lobby v. Government of Israel* (1994) 48(5) P.D. 501.

In New Zealand there is a line of cases in which the concept that a local authority owes fiduciary duties to property owners when adopting rating policies has been applied with varying results. They are collected in *Lovelock v. Waitakere City Council* [1996] 3 N.Z.L.R. 310 (basis invalid for inequity upon owners of higher-valued properties).

[Add at end of Note 72:]   **13–044**

See above, para. 13–038, Note 47.

[Add at the end of Note 74:]

And recently the Aboriginal and Torres Strait Islander Commission adopted a broad policy of setting aside the bulk of the available funds for land acquisition for applications for land in the Northern Territory, because of the imminent expiry of a favourable statutory regime there. The Federal Court held that the policy was unreasonable, because it favoured Northern Territory acquisitions above those relating to other parts of the country. It could be set aside as "conduct" leading to a decision under the Administrative Decisions (Judicial Review) Act 1997 (Cth): *New South Wales Aboriginal Land Council v. ATSIC* (1995) 131 ALR 559.

13–045   *ex p. Smith* is now reported at [1995] Q.B. 351. The decision was upheld by the Court of Appeal, [1996] Q.B. 517, on the ground that the policy could not be stigmatised as irrational, being supported by Parliament and by those from whom the ministry was entitled to seek advice which had been contradicted by no evidence before the ministry. But see paragraph 13–060, Note 26 below. *R. v. Secretary of State for Social Security, ex p. Armstrong* (1996) 8 Admin. L.R. 626 (the test in section 72 Social Security Contributions and Benefits Act 1992 for entitlement to the care component of disability living allowance which was whether a disabled person could prepare a cooked meal, was not necessarily discriminatory against women, as it was not to be applied only to those who could already cook. Those applicants who could not cook must be assumed to be ready to learn); *Hughes v. Secretary of State for the Environment and New Forest D.C.* (1996) 71 P. & C.R. 168. (application for judicial review from planning inspector's decisions refused. The inspector refused to grant planning permission for a mobile home to house a gypsy family. H argued unsuccessfully that: there was a blanket policy against the provision of gypsy sites which was the policy was partial, unequal and discriminatory against a national minority and destructive of a traditional way of life and therefore *ultra vires* and it was contrary to the common law and Article 8 E.C.H.R.); *R. v. Secretary of State for Foreign and Commonwealth Affairs, ex p. Manelfi* [1996] 12 C.L. 65 (judicial review of decision that M was ineligible for employment at GCHQ because of the foreign nationalities of his parents—M claimed application of the rules without waiver were *Wednesbury* unreasonable and contrary to the common law and the International Covenant on Civil and Political Rights 1996, Article 26. Held, dismissing the application: the decision in the making of the rules and their application were made in the interests of national security and were non-justiciable). For a full statement of the extent to which equality is considered "a general axiom cf rational behaviour", see the recent Privy Council case *Matadeen v. Pointu* and *The Minister of Education and Science* (Mauritius), February 18, 1998. *Compare Hugo v. President of the Republic of South Africa* 1996 (4) SA 1012 (D).

OPPRESSIVE DECISIONS

13–051   *[Add to Note 88:]*

In *R. v. Mid-Hertfordshire Justices, ex p. Cox* (1996) Admin. L.R. 409, it was held perverse for Magistrates to have imposed the same sanction on a poll tax defaulter who could not afford to pay because destitute as one who simply refused to pay. But see *R. v. Secretary of State for the Home Department ex p. Zulfikar* [1996] C.O.D. 256 (policy of strip-searching prisoners not unreasonable).

[Add to Note 91:]

But see *R. v. Investors Compensation Scheme Ltd ex p. Bowden* [1996] 1 A.C. 261 (H.L.) where the refusal to provide full compensation was held not unreasonable.

THE INTENSITY OF REVIEW

Managerial and policy decisions

[Notes 6 and 7:]   **13–056**

Bridge L.J. should read Lord Bridge.

[Add to Note 8:]   **13–057**

R. v. Lord Chancellor, ex p. Maxwell [1997] 1 W.L.R. 104 (substitution of trial judge for another judge not irrational act of Lord Chancellor. Deployment of judicial resources justiciable, but the decision, involving allocation of resources between different courts, is almost always for Lord Chancellor alone). See also *R. v. Lord Chancellor ex p. Stockler* (1996) 8 Admin. L.R. 590; *R. v. Radio Authority ex p. Bull* [1997] 3 W.L.R. 1094 (authority's ban on Amnesty International's broadcasts should only be interfered with where "manifest breach" of principles). *cf. R. v. Coventry City Council, ex p. Phoenix Aviation* [1995] 3 All E.R. 37 and *R. v. Chief Constable of Sussex ex p. International Traders' Ferry Ltd* [1997] 3 W.L.R. 132. In *Phoenix* it was held that the public authorities operating air and sea ports were not entitled, in the absence of an emergency, to ban the flights or shipments of livestock by animal exporters so as to avoid the disruptive consequences of unlawful protesters. To do so would infringe the rule of law. Nor (*per* Simon Brown L.J.) were the legitimate interests of the exporters sufficiently considered. In *International Traders' Ferry* the Court of Appeal held that it was not unreasonable for the Chief Constable to reduce effective policing of the export traders to two days per week in the face of lack of sufficient resources.

Decisions infringing fundamental rights

[Add to Note 20:]   **13–059**

cf. Brind with the approach of the Israel Supreme Court in *Kahane v. Broadcasting Authority*—media coverage of PLO. See I. Zamir & I. Zysblat, *Public Law in Israel* (1996), p. 74.

[Add a new footnote 20a at end of second paragraph:]

For an excellent account of the extent of the use of human rights in English courts see Murray Hunt, *Using Human Rights Law in English Courts*

(1997). And see M. Beloff and H. Mountfield, "Unconventional Behaviour? Judicial Uses of the European Convention on Human Rights in England and Wales" 1996 E.H.R.L.R. 467.

13–060   *[Add to Note 26:]*

R. v. Ministry of Defence ex p. Smith was upheld by the Court of Appeal: see [1996] Q.B. 517, but Bingham M.R. accepted that, in relation to an unreasonable decision, "the more substantial the interference with human rights, the more the court will require by justification before it is satisfied that the decision is reasonable." Note the reversal of the usual *Wednesbury* burden of proof. See also *Tan Te Lam v. Superintendent of Tai A Chav Detention Centre* [1997] A.C. 97 (P.C) where it was accepted that in respect of the lawfulness of the detention of a migrant in Hong Kong "very clear words" would be needed to authorise continued detention; *R. v. Secretary of State for the Home Department, ex p. Launder* [1997] 1 W.L.R. 839 (it was normally open to the Court to review the exercise of the Home Secretary's discretion under the Extradition Act 1989, s. 12. The fact that a decision was taken on policy grounds of an important or sensitive nature and involving delicate relations between foreign states did not affect the court's duty to ensure the applicant was afforded proper protection, although the court would be mindful of both the limitations of its constitutional role and the need in such a case for "anxious scrutiny"; *R. v. Secretary of State for the Home Department, ex p. Norney* (1995) 7 Admin. L.R. 861 (unlawful to delay referring cases of discretionary life prisoners to parole board until the end of tariff period. This policy was unreasonable in the *Wednesbury* sense. It flouted the principles of common law and the European Convention on Human Rights). But see: *R. v. Parole Board, ex p. Martin* [1996] C.O.D. 236 (decision not to release mandatory life prisoner on licence was not perverse).

[Add at end of paragraph (1):]

The approach in *Leech* was expressly followed by Laws J. in *R. v. Lord Chancellor, ex p. Witham* [1997] 2 All E.R. 779 (court fees deprived citizen of his constitutional right of access to the courts. Such rights not "the consequence of the democratic political process but would be logically prior to it"). Leech was also followed in *R. v. Secretary of State for the Home Department, ex p. Simms, O'Brien, The Times* [1997] C.O.D. 217 (prohibition on use by a journalist of material gathered on a visit to a prisoner violated prisoners' right to free speech and the restriction not necessary or justified), but the Court of Appeal overruled this judgment, holding no right of a prisoner to communicate with a journalist. See *ex p. Simms* (1998) 95 L.S.G. 23. *cf. R. v. Secretary of State for the Home Department ex p Maby* C.L.D. June 1996. *Leech* was taken a step further in *R. v. Secretary of State for Social Security ex p. Joint Council for the Welfare of Immigrants* [1997]

112

W.L.R. 275 where it was held that regulations excluding from income support entitlement those who sought asylum otherwise than on immediate arrival in the United Kingdom or whose claims were rejected and awaiting appeal, both conflicted with and rendered rights in other legislation nugatory and were so Draconian to an extent that "no civilised nation can tolerate." *per* Simon Brown L.J. citing Lord Ellenborough C.J. in *R. v. Eastbourne (Inhabitants)* (1803) 4 East. 103 at 107, 102 E.R. 769 at 770 "the law of humanity, which is anterior to all positive laws obliges us to afford (poor foreigners) them relief, to save them from starving". And see also Lord Steyn's acceptance of the concept of "substantive fairness" in *Pierson v. Secretary of State for the Home Department* [1997] 3 W.L.R. 492.

[Add the following to the end of the paragraph:]   **13–063**

At the time of writing the Human Rights Bill is proceeding with its passage through the Parliament. If enacted, it would permit courts directly to enforce provisions of the European Convention on Human Rights in respect of the exercise of public functions. In respect of legislation, however, courts would only be permitted to issue a "declaration of incompatibility" with the Convention and it would thus lie with Parliament whether to remedy the incompatibility (which it could do through a "fast track" procedure, by means of a statutory instrument).

PROPORTIONALITY

Proportionality in English law?

[Add to Note 91:]   **13–085**

See, *e.g. R. v. Admiralty Board of the Defence Council ex p. Coupland* [1996] C.O.D. 147 (sentence of dismissal from service wholly disproportionate to offence); *R. v. Highbury Corner Magistrates, ex p. Rabhani* [1996] 7 C.L. (magistrates acted *Wednesbury* unreasonably and made a decision that no reasonable magistrates properly directing themselves could have reached on the evidence before them in refusing a downward variation of maintenance order). But see *R. v. Secretary of State for the Home Department, ex p. Tremayne,* May 2, 1996 (unreported). (Home Secretary's decision to introduce random urine sampling of prisoners was not irrational. The approach balanced the interests of prisoners against the need to address the problem of drug taking). See further, *R. v. Secretary of State for the Home Department ex p. Singh (Manvinder)* [1996] Imm. A.R. 41; *Kalunga v. Secretary of State for the Home Department* [1994] Imm. A.R. 585; *Whitchelo v. Secretary of State for the Home Department,* unreported, April 2, 1996.

[Add to Note 3:]

See cases discussed above at para. 13–018. In *R. v. Chief Constable of Sussex, ex p. International Trader's Ferry* [1997] 3 W.L.R. 132, Kennedy L.J. said that in that case proportionality and irrationality would "in practice yield the same result". And see the cases cited under 13–060 above. See also *R. v. Secretary of State for Health, ex p. R.P. Scherer Ltd* See Rt Hon. Lord Hoffmann "A Sense of Proportion", (1997) The Irish Jurist, 49. [1996] 32 BMLR 12 (decision by the Secretary of State to place gel-filled Temazepam capsules on the list of drugs which were not allowed to be prescribed to N.H.S. patients not disproportionate).

[Add to Note 12 after reference to Zamir:]

Recently, proportionality has been formally recognised by the Supreme Court of Israel as a separate ground (different from unreasonableness) for the review of administrative action. The Court held that the proportionality test consists of three elements. First, the means adopted by the authority in exercising its power should rationally fit the legislative purpose. Secondly, the authority should adopt such means that do not injure the individual more than necessary. And third, the injury caused to the individual by the exercise of the power should not be disproportional to the benefit which accrues to the general public. Under this test the Court recently invalidated some administrative decisions. See, for example *Ben-Atiya v. Minister of Education* (1995) 49 (5) P.D.1. And see I. Zamir and Z. Zysblat, *Public Law in Israel* (1996), especially Sections 2, 3 and 11.

PART IV

PROCEDURES AND REMEDIES

CHAPTER 14

THE HISTORICAL DEVELOPMENT OF JUDICIAL REVIEW REMEDIES AND PROCEDURES

There are no additions to Chapter 14

CHAPTER 15

JUDICIAL REVIEW PROCEDURES

INTRODUCTION

[Add to Note 1:]   15–001

See now *Access to Justice* (1996), Final Report to the Lord Chancellor on the Civil Justice System in England and Wales.

The nominated judges

By June 1996 three Lord Justices and 24 puisne had been nominated to determine applications for judicial review.   15–006

Legal aid

[Add:]   15–007

In 1996 the Bar Pro Bono Unit was established. It holds a register of barristers who will offer up to three days of their time for cases, including applications for judicial review, in which justice may otherwise be denied. The address is Second Floor West, 7 Gray's Inn Square, Gray's Inn, London WC1R 5A7.

[Add to Note 16:]   15–008

For further discussion of legal aid for applications for judicial review, see L. Bridges *et al.*, *An Applicant's Guide to Judicial Review* (1995), Chap. 7.

Obtaining the leave of the court[24]

Criteria on which leave is granted or refused

[Add to Note 32:]   15–014

cf. R. v. Secretary of State for Trade and Industry, ex p. Greenpeace Ltd [1998] C.O.D. 59, where a hearing of an application for leave, in which the only issue was delay, took more than two days. Laws J. commented that

". . . cases occasionally arise where the question whether leave should be granted involves substantial issues of principle, even though the applicant would pass Lord Diplock's test as to the potential merits of his application. Most cases where the prospective respondent asserts delay as a basis for refusing leave will not fall into this category; but in my judgment the present case is exceptional".

[Add to Note 33:]

In *R. v. Somerset County Council and ARC Southern Ltd, ex p. Dixon* [1997] C.O.D. 323 at 327, Sedley J. re-emphasised that at the "threshold at the point of the application for leave is set only at the height necessary to prevent abuse", "to have 'no interest whatsoever' is not the same as having no pecuniary interest. It is to interfere in something with which one has no legitimate concern at all; to be, in other words, a busybody" and "beyond this point, the question of standing has no materiality at the leave stage".

[Add to Note 35 after ". . . [1994] C.O.D. 325":]

In *R. v. Traffic Commissioner for the North Western Traffic Area, ex p. BRAKE* [1996] C.O.D. 248, Turner J. disagreed with the approach in *Association of Darlington Taxi Owners* and refused to set aside leave to move for judicial review which had been granted to an unincorporated association the aim of which was to promote greater safety in the use of lorries on public roads. See also para. 2–038, above.

15–015   *[Add new Note 37a after "(4) "unarguable" or "groundless" ":]*

See *Re Cookstown District Council* (unreported, June 10, 1996, Northern Ireland Q.B.D.) in which Kerr J. held that "the requirement to raise an arguable case is a modest one. It need only be shown that if the assertions made by the applicant prove to be correct, it would be tenable to claim that he may be entitled to judicial review of the decision challenged. See also *Re Gary Jones* (unreported, July 10, 1996, Northern Ireland Q.B.D.) where Campbell J. said that test for the grant of leave was whether the judge is satisfied "that there is a case fit for further investigation at a full *inter partes* hearing of the substantive application for judicial review". This was quoted with approval by Higgins J. in *Re Bignell* (unreported, July 28, 1996, Northern Ireland Q.B.D.).

[Add at the end of paragraph 15–015:]

Doubts have arisen as to the power of the court to grant leave in respect of only one or some of the applicant's grounds—leave to apply on the other grounds being either refused or not expressly granted. As the Court of Appeal pointed out in *R. v. Criminal Injuries Compensation Board, ex p. A*

[1997] 3 W.L.R. 776, "there is no provision in the rules for a conditional grant of leave (save only as to costs and security under Order 53, r. 3(9)". (Note that the House of Lords has granted leave to appeal in this case: [1998] 1 W.L.R. 277). Strong calls have been made for Order 53 to be amended to give the judge at the leave stage express power to grant leave to apply for judicial review on only some of the applicant's grounds: see Laws J. in *R. v. Secretary of State for Transport, ex p. Richmond L.B.C.* [1994] 1 W.L.R. 74, 97–98 and Law Com. No. 226, paragraph 5.15. Even in the absence of such an express power, the court has however on occasion invoked its inherent jurisdiction (on which see generally M.S. Dockray, "The Inherent Jurisdiction to Regulate Civil Proceedings" (1997) 113 L.Q.R. 120) to indicate that only one or more of the grounds are fit to be argued at the full hearing. If leave has not expressly been refused for such "weak" grounds (but leave has merely not been granted), it appears that those apparently weak grounds may nevertheless be raised at the full hearing, since the original application in its ambit is still alive, provided the respondent has been put on notice that such grounds will be advanced at the full hearing: *R. v. Bow Street Metropolitan Stipendiary Magistrate, ex p. Roberts* [1990] 1 W.L.R. 1317. Where, however, a judge has invoked the inherent jurisdiction of the court expressly to refuse leave in respect of one or more grounds the position may be somewhat different: it is unlikely that such grounds will be entertained at the full hearing, though in exceptional cases they may be. In *R. v. Staffordshire County Council, ex p. Ashworth* (1997) 9 Admin. L.R. 373 Turner J. adopted a robust approach, holding that the court "should not be afraid to exercise its inherent power to control its own processes" in order to decide whether or not to entertain submissions on the grounds not granted leave.

[Add to Note 40:]

It must be shown that the misrepresentation had been material and had an effect on the judge's decision: *R. v. Secretary of State for the Home Department, ex p. Beecham (Grazyna)* [1996] Imm. A.R. 97. See also *R. v. Liverpool City Council, ex p. Filla* [1996] C.O.D. 24 and *R. v. Wealden D.C., ex p. Pinnegar* [1996] C.O.D. 64.

[Add to Note 41:]

See also *R. v. Lord Chancellor, ex p. Maxwell* [1997] 1 W.L.R. 104 at 112–113. Henry L.J. stated that

> "we wish to do all we can to discourage any comparable application relating to the deployment of judicial manpower . . . the realistic assumption must be that the vast preponderance of such applications are doomed to failure and so should be critically examined at the leave stage. If the exceptional case comes along, it will be clearly just that, and that will be so clear that these words will not deter either the applicant's advisors or the single judge."

Applying for leave

15–016   *[Add to Note 44:]*

A person who decides to oppose an *ex parte* application for leave to apply for judicial review is not a "party to the proceedings" for the purposes of costs; accordingly the High Court has no power to entertain a wasted costs application following the withdrawal of the application for judicial review: *R. v. Camden L.B.C., ex p. Martin* [1997] 1 W.L.R. 359. Leave may be set aside (on which see para. 15–024, below) despite having been granted *inter partes*: *R. v. Secretary of State for the Home Department, ex p. Vafi (Sita) (No. 2)* [1995] Imm. A.R. 528.

15–017   *[Add to Note 49:]*

A challenge to the refusal of the Home Secretary to refer a case back to the Court of Appeal (Criminal Division) under Criminal Appeal Act 1968, s. 17 is a criminal cause or matter: *R. v. Secretary of State for the Home Department, ex p. Ogilvy* [1996] C.O.D. 497 (C.A.).

The timing of an application for leave

15–019   *[Add to Note 54:]*

See further Alistair Lindsay, "Delay in Judicial Review Cases: A Conundrum Solved?" [1995] P.L. 417.

[Add to Note 57:]

In *R. v. D.P.P., ex p. Camelot Group plc* [1997] 7 C.L. 9, Ognall J. refused leave in February 1997 (*obiter*) on the ground that the applicants had known since early 1996 of the existence of a scheme identical to the one they sought to challenge—though it was potentially less financially harmful— and had done nothing about it. On a renewed application (see [1998] C.O.D. 54), the Divisional Court granted leave but refused the substantive application. See also *R. v. Secretary of State for Trade and Industry, ex p. Greenpeace Ltd* [1998] C.O.D. 59, considered in n. 59 below.

[Add to Note 59:]

See also *R. v. Commissioners of Customs and Excise, ex p. Eurotunnel plc* [1995] C.O.D. 291 where the Divisional Court held that a challenge to "continuing practices" and a "continuing failure" were disingenuous attempts to disguise the fact that the applicant's real attack was on the validity of certain E.C. Directives and statutory instruments based on them. In *R. v. Secretary* of State for Trade and Industry, ex p. Greenpeace Ltd [1998] C.O.D. 59, Laws J. held that Order 53, r. 4(1) was to be construed so that time began to run from the date on which the *grounds* of the application first arose. In most cases this would be the same date as the specific decision impugned on the application, but there were instances (as in the present case) where the real substance of the case consisted in something done before the date of the decision which the applicant choose to assault. Laws J. also held that the requirement of promptness was to be applied with particular strictness where the applicant was a pressure group bringing a public interest challenge.

[Add to Note 60:]

And R. v. Bath City Council, ex p. Crombie [1995] C.O.D. 283.

[Add to the end of the paragraph:]

At the full hearing, however, the applicant's delay is a factor to be taken into account by the court only if to grant relief would be likely to cause hardship, prejudice or detriment to the respondent or a third party within the meaning of section 31(6)(b) of the Supreme Court Act 1981: see *R. v. Criminal Injuries Compensation Board, ex p. A* [1997] 3 W.L.R. 776 (in which the Court of Appeal overruled *R. v. Tavistock General Commissioners, ex p. Worth* [1985] S.T.C. 564; leave to appeal to the House of Lords has been granted: see [1998] 1 W.L.R. 277). A Court may take the view that it is self-evident that a delay would cause prejudice to good administration without requiring specific proof of this: see *R. v. Newbury District Council and Another, ex p. Chievely Parish Council* [1997] J.P.L. 1137 (unexplained delay in applying out of time for judicial review of a major planning proposal).

[Add to Note 65:]   **15–021**

cf. R. v. Knightsbridge Crown Court, ex p. Brookner (July 29, 1997, CO/881/95, unreported) where the Divisional Court stated:] "The explanation for the delay is said to be the difficulty in the applicant obtaining legal aid. That, as it seems to me, is not a satisfactory explanation" (*per* Rose L.J.).

[Add to Note 66:]

And R. v. Collins, ex p. M.S. [1998] C.O.D. 52.

[Add to end of paragraph:]

In *R. v. BBC, ex p. Referendum Party* (1997) 9 Admin. L.R. 553, the court held that the applicant had not been guilty of lack of promptness in waiting for both the BBC and, some weeks later, the Independent Television Commission to make decisions relating to party election broadcasts before seeking leave.

15–023   *[Add:]*

It is important to write a "letter before action" before making an application for leave to apply for judicial review: see L. Bridges *et al., An Applicant's Guide to Judicial Review* (1995), pages 99–101; *R. v. Housing Benefits Review Board of Milton Keynes B.C., ex p. Macklen* [1996] 8 C.L. 637; *R. v. Liverpool City Council, ex p. Connolly* [1996] 7 C.L. 584.

15–024   *[Add to Note 77:]*

And see L. Bridges, G. Meszaros and M. Sunkin, *Judicial Review in Perspective* (2nd ed., 1995), Chap. 7.

Challenging the grant or refusal of leave

15–025   *[Add:]*

It is highly undesirable that an application to set aside leave should be made at a late stage of the proceedings and after the lodging of evidence. It would, however, be wrong for the court to refuse to consider such an application, albeit late, as this might save the costs of a full hearing: *R. v. Eurotunnel Developments Ltd, ex p. Stephens* [1996] C.O.D. 151. Leave may be set aside despite having been granted *inter partes* (*i.e.* "ex parte on notice"): *R. v. Secretary of State for the Home Department, ex p. Vafi (Sita) (No. 2)* [1995] Imm. A.R. 528.

[Add to Note 80:]

See n. 40, above.

Interlocutory stage

Service

15–028   *[Add to Note 85:]*

Order 53, r. 5 requires the substantive application to be begun within 14 days of the grant of leave. Time is unlikely to be extended by the Court, even if the tardiness is that of an applicant's lawyer rather than that of an applicant personally: *R. v. Institute of Chartered Accountants in England and*

Wales, ex p. Andreou (1996) 8 Admin. L.R. 557 (C.A.). *cf. R. v. Secretary of State for the Environment, ex p. Parry* [1998] C.O.D. 17. See also *R. v. Law Society, ex p. First National Commercial Bank plc* [1996] C.O.D. 22.

[Delete Note 86 and replace with:]

Order 53, r. 5(3). The meaning of "persons directly affected" was considered by the House of Lords in *R. v. Rent Officer Service, ex p. Muldoon; R. v. Rent Officer Service, ex p. Kelly* [1996] 1 W.L.R. 1103. Lord Keith held "that a person is directly affected by something connotes that he is affected without the intervention of any intermediate agency". In the instant case the Secretary of State for Social Security, who applied to be joined as a respondent to applications for judicial review challenging a failure to determine claims for housing benefit, was only indirectly affected (his department ultimately paid 95 per cent of the cost of this benefit by way of subsidy to the local authority) as it was the local authority which would have to pay the applicants directly if the applications for judicial review were successful.

[Add to Note 88:]

See further JUSTICE/Public Law Project, *A Matter of Public Interest* (1996) and Sir Konrad Schiemann, "Interventions in Public Interest Cases" [1996] P.L. 240.

Discovery

[Add to Note 4:]   15–032

In the context of judicial review challenges to extradition proceedings, see *In the matter of Ewan Quayle Launder* [1996] C.O.D. 369.

[Add to text after Note 5:]

Only in exceptional cases will an appellant in judicial review proceedings be entitled to discovery of material which was not before the Court below; there has to be new evidence which could not have been made available at first instance by reasonable diligence: *R. v. Secretary of State for the Home Department, ex p. Gardian* [1996] Imm. A.R. 6. In *R. v. Chief Constable of Sussex, ex p. International Trader's Ferry Ltd* [1997] 3 W.L.R. 132 at 143, the parties served further affidavit evidence after the Divisional Court's judgment and requested the Court of Appeal to consider it on an appeal. The Court did so with reluctance in so far as the material related to pre-trial matters, stressing the principle that there must be finality in litigation and citing *Ali v. Secretary of State for the Home Department* [1984] 1 W.L.R.

663 and *Ladd v. Marshall* [1954] 1 W.L.R. 1489. (In July 1997 the House of Lords granted leave to appeal: see [1997] 1 W.L.R. 1092).

[Add new paragraph 15–032a:]

Withdrawal

Approximately half of all applications for judicial review granted leave are withdrawn before the full hearing. For a recent study, see M. Sunkin, "Withdrawing: A Problem in Judicial Review? in P. Leyland and T. Woods, *Administrative Law Facing the Future* (1997). A new practice direction was issued in May 1997: *Practice Direction (Crown Office List: Court Orders)* [1997] 1 W.L.R. 825. Where, after the grant of leave, the respondent undertaken to reconsider the impugned decision, an applicant may in certain circumstances quite properly refuse to withdraw the proceedings from the Crown Office List: see *R. v. Secretary of State for the Home Department, ex p. Alabi* [1998] C.O.D. 103.

Appeals

15–035   *[Add to Note 11:]*

Refusing the applicant leave to appeal from his decision in *R. v. Secretary of State for the Environment, ex p. Kirkstall Valley Campaign Ltd* [1996] 3 All E.R. 304, Sedley J. commented (see [1996] C.O.D. 343): "It is not yet known by what principles Parliament has in mind that the court should apply on an application for leave to appeal. The way the court approaches it, for better or for worse at the moment, is that there needs to be an issue of legal principle upon which the applicant has lost and would like to appeal". The unsuccessful applicant in the instant case was in the unusual position of having won all the issues of legal principle. The Court of Appeal has since given general guidance in *Smith v. Cosworth Casting Processes Ltd* [1997] 1 W.L.R. 1538. A Court may grant leave to appeal even if it is not satisfied that the appeal has any realistic prospect of succeeding where, for example, the issue is one which should in the public interest be examined by the Court of Appeal or that the appeal raised an issue where the law required clarifying.

APPLICATIONS FOR THE WRIT OF HABEAS CORPUS[14]

15–036   *[Add to Note 14:]*

Sir William Wade, "Habeas Corpus and Judicial Review" (1997) 113 L.Q.R. 55.

[Add to Note 15:]

See now, however, Lord Woolf, *Access to Justice—final report* (1995), p. 257. Under the new procedural regime it is proposed that although habeas corpus should not be entirely subsumed into judicial review it should be possible to seek a writ of habeas corpus on a claim for judicial review. It is also recommended that English names (writ of release, writ to give evidence, writ to answer a charge and writ of transfer) replace the various Latin names of the four forms of writ.

[Add to Note 23:]   **15–037**

In 1995, the Crown Office received 90 applications for habeas corpus, of which 12 were allowed: see Lord Chancellor's Department, *Judicial Statistics for England and Wales for the Year 1996* (Cm. 3290, 1995), p. 17.

Procedure: R.S.C. Order 54

The inter partes hearing

[Add to Note 42:]   **15–044**

Hearsay and double hearsay evidence may be contained in the affidavit evidence; it is implicit from *R. v. Secretary of State for the Home Department, ex p. Khawaja* [1984] A.C. 74 that the court may take into account all relevant material in determining the lawfulness of detention, though certain evidence may of course be disregarded if it is not worthy of any weight: *Re Rahman* [1997] 3 W.L.R. 990.

Appeals

[Add to Note 51:]   **15–048**

In *Cuoghi v. Governor of Brixton Prison and Another* [1997] 1 W.L.R. 1346 the Court of Appeal held that an order relating to the obtaining of evidence for the purposes of an application for habeas corpus was a "criminal cause or matter" within the meaning of section 18(1)(a) of the Supreme Court Act 1981; the Court of Appeal therefore had no jurisdiction to entertain an appeal against such an order.

Scope of review

[Add to Note 58:]   **15–050**

See also Law Com. No. 226, Part XI and Sir William Wade, "Habeas Corpus and Judicial Review" (1997) 113 L.Q.R. 55. In *R. v. Secretary of State for the Home Department, ex p. Rahman* [1996] 4 All E.R. 945 at 950, Collins

J., holding that hearsay and double hearsay evidence contained in affidavit evidence was admissible, stated: "If that were not so, then there would be a distinction, and an artificial distinction, between the remedies available on judicial review and habeas corpus. One of the things *Khawaja* makes clear is the distinction is not one of substance and merely one of form." An appeal against the decision of Collins J. was dismissed: see *Re Rahman* [1997] 3 W.L.R. 990.

[Add to Note 60:]

For a recent example of a challenge to a decision-maker's jurisdiction to detain (rather than an underlying administrative decision), see *Re S.-C. (Mental Patient: Habeas Corpus)* [1996] Q.B. 599 (C.A.). See also *Tan Te Lam and others v. Superintendent of Tai A Chau Detention Centre and another* [1997] A.C. 97 (P.C.) where it was held that the determination of the facts relevant to the question whether the applicants were being detained "pending removal" (a condition imposed by legislation) went to the jurisdiction of the director of the detention centre to detain. In *R. v. Bedwellty Justices, ex p. Williams* [1997] A.C. 225 at 235, considering the use of the term "jurisdiction" in judicial review more generally, Lord Cooke of Thorndon stated *obiter*: "All in all, the habeas corpus cases contain some difficult dicta and are best treated, in my respectful opinion, as a separate tract of law". See also *R. v. Oldham Justices, ex p. Cawley* [1997] Q.B. 1.

15–051   *[Add to Note 62:]*

See also Sir William Wade, "Habeas Corpus and Judicial Review" (1997) 113 L.Q.R. 55.

15–053   *[Add to Note 65:]*

See also *R. v. Secretary of State for the Home Department, ex p. Rahman* [1996] 4 All E.R. 945 (Collins J.), affirmed by C.A. *sub nom. Re Rahman* [1997] 3 W.L.R. 990.

The need for reform

15–057   *[Add to Note 74:]*

But see now, however, Lord Woolf, *Access to Justice—final report* (1995), p. 257 discussed in para. 15–036 above.

STATUTORY APPLICATIONS TO QUASH

Procedure

15–061   *[Add to Note 82:]*

The term "six weeks" means 42 days and the corresponding date rule does

not apply: see *Okolo v. Secretary of State for the Environment and another* [1997]
4 All E.R. 424 (C.A.).

THE INTERRELATIONSHIP BETWEEN THE PROCEDURES

Order 53 and statutory applications to quash

[Add to Note 22:]   **15–078**

See also *R. v. Dacorum D.C., ex p. Cannon* [1996] 2 P.L.R. 45.

[Add new paragraph:]

Appeal on point of law and appeal by case stated

Where there exists a statutory right of appeal against a decision, leave to   **15–081**
apply for judicial review is unlikely to be granted: see further paragraph
20–018. Thus in *R. v. Special Educational Needs Tribunal, ex p. F* [1996]
E.L.R. 213 leave to apply for judicial review was set aside because the
applicant ought to have appealed under the provisions of the Tribunal and
Inquiries Act 1992, s. 11 (which laid down a time limit of 28 days). In *R. v.
Peterborough Magistrates' Court, ex p. Dowler* [1997] Q.B. 911 it was held that
it would defeat Parliament's intention if the more leisurely timetable of
judicial review were permitted to delay challenge to Magistrates' decisions
by way of appeal.

    In exceptional circumstances, however, an applicant who fails to exercise
a right to appeal within a prescribed time limit may be permitted to make
an application for judicial review; the court has residual power to consider
an application for judicial review where an appeal has not been pursued
whenever it is just and convenient to do so: see, for example *R. v. Oxford
Social Security Appeal Tribunal, ex p. Wolke* [1996] C.O.D. 418. There will be
a strong case for allowing an application for judicial review to proceed in
such circumstances where the court is satisfied that there had been a
genuine oversight by the applicant and no prejudice will be caused to third
parties: see, for example *R. v. East Sussex Valuation Tribunal, ex p. Silverstone*
[1996] C.O.D. 402; and *R. v. Highbury Corner Magistrates, ex p. Rabhani*
[1996] 6 C.L. 84 (failure to appeal was the fault of the applicant's legal
advisors and personal liberty was at stake). See also *Harley Development Inc.
v. I.R.C.* [1996] 1 W.L.R. 727 (P.C.). Where a dispute involves pure issues
of law, judicial review may be regarded as more appropriate than an appeal
by way of case stated: *R. v. Tunbridge Wells Justices, ex p. Tunbridge Wells B.C.*
(1996) 8 Admin L.R. 453. The existence of a right of appeal to the Crown
Court does not preclude a person convicted of offences by Magistrates'
Court from seeking relief by way of judicial review where the complaint

raised is of procedural impropriety, unfairness or bias: *R. v. Hereford Magistrates' Court, ex p. Rowlands* [1998] Q.B. 110, discussed further below at paragraph 20–019, n.41.

CHAPTER 16

PREROGATIVE ORDERS

INTRODUCTION

[Add to Note 7:]   16–002

In *Access to Justice—final report* (1996), p. 257 Lord Woolf, although an enthusiast for adopting modern English, did not support this proposal: "The Latin names are used throughout the common law world and have become synonymous with the duty of superior courts to protect the public against the abuse of power. I am not sure that the proposed alternatives are that much easier to comprehend."

Applicants and respondents

[Add to Note 22:]   16–005

See also *R. v. Secretary of State for the Home Department, ex p. Fire Brigades Union* [1995] 2 A.C. 513 in which it was held the terms of Criminal Justice Act 1988, s. 171(1), providing that an Act of Parliament "shall come into force on such day as the Secretary of State may by order made by statutory instrument appoint", were not apt to create any duty owed to members of the public.

MANDAMUS[38]

[Add to Note 41:]   16–010

See further para. 6–091, Note 34, above.

Demand and refusal

[Add to Note 47:]   16–012

Whatever the formal position now on demand and refusal, the matter may be rather academic as an applicant who fails to write an appropriate "letter before action" before seeking leave to move for judicial review is unlikely to be granted leave: see para. 15–023, above.

Interrelationship between mandamus and other remedies

16–016   *[Add:]*

In *R. v. Secretary of State for Trade and Industry, ex p. Duddridge* (1996) 8 Admin. L.R. 269 the applicants unsuccessfully sought an order of mandamus to compel the minister to issue regulations, guidelines or some other directive under the Electricity Act 1989. The Court of Appeal held that the minister was under no legal duty to do so; the question whether mandamus would issue to compel such a duty did not therefore arise.

CERTIORARI AND PROHIBITION

16–019   *[Note 65:]*

See now P. Cane, *An Introduction to Administrative Law* (3rd ed., 1996), pp. 62–63.

CHAPTER 17

INJUNCTIONS IN JUDICIAL REVIEW PROCEEDINGS

NATURE OF INJUNCTIVE RELIEF[1]

Procedural considerations

[Add to Note 9:]   17–004

See, *e.g. The Great House at Sonning Ltd v. Berkshire C.C., The Times*, March
25, 1996 (Court of Appeal strikes out proceedings begun by general
endorsed writ for an injunction for nuisance caused by allegedly wrongful
obstruction of a public highway. The local authority had made a closure
order under Road Traffic Regulation Act 1984, s. 14. The only remedy was
by way of judicial review.)

[Add to Note 16:]   17–006

In *The Great House at Sonning Ltd v. Berkshire C.C., The Times*, March 25,
1996 (see Note 9, above), the Court of Appeal was divided as to whether
the plaintiffs had any private law rights. The majority (Hutchison and
Norse L.JJ.) held that so long as the closure order stood, there was no
private law right protected by the tort of public nuisance. Saville L.J.,
dissenting, held that it was trite and ancient law that a person who could
prove particular loss and damage over and above that sustained by the
public at large for an obstruction of the highway had a private right to
recover that loss from the tortfeasor. The plaintiffs' claim did not depend
upon them proving that the local authority was not authorised by statute to
block the road, merely that the authority was threatening to obstruct the
highway so as to cause them special damage.

INTERLOCUTORY ORDERS

[Add to Note 21:]   17–007

Lord Woolf in *Access to Justice—final report* (1996), p. 253 recommended that,
in the proposed new civil procedures, the court should be able to grant
interim relief before the preliminary consideration of the claim, although

interim relief on an *ex parte* basis would only be granted in a very clear and urgent case.

[Add to Note 22:]

In *Access to Justice—final report*, p. 253, Lord Woolf recommends that the court should be given power to make interim declarations.

Interlocutory injunction

17–011   *[Note 35:]*

The correct citation to the *British Telecommunications* Case is [1995] C.O.D. 56.

[Add:]

cf. R. v. Secretary of State for Health, ex p. Generics (U.K.) Ltd [1997] C.O.D. 294, February 25, 1997 where the Court of Appeal held that the balance of convenience test was not an apt concept when considering the exercise of the court's discretion in the "highly unusual" circumstances of that case.

17–013   *[Add to Note 39:]*

For the E.C.J.'s ruling in that particular case, see *R. v. H.M. Treasury, ex p. British Telecommunications plc*, Case C-392/93 [1996] Q.B. 615.

[Add to Note 40:]

cf. R. v. Advertising Standards Authority, ex p. Direct Line Financial Services Ltd [1998] C.O.D. 20 (interim injunction granted restraining ASA from publishing adjudication).

17–015   *[Add to Note 43:]*

See also *Coventry City Council v. Finnie* (1997) 29 H.L.R. 658 (where a local authority had taken out an injunction to restrain defendants for the purposes of law enforcement under Local Government Act 1972, s. 222 there was no obligation in law for cross-undertakings in damages to be given, unless justified by special circumstances subject to the court's discretion.

CONSIDERATIONS PARTICULARLY AFFECTING PUBLIC AUTHORITIES

Attachment and committal for contempt

17–031   *[Add:]*

Where an interim injunction has been granted, it was not open to the party in whose favour it was made to disregard it, to seek to negotiate away its effect and give permission to the other party to act in breach of it: *R. v. Inland Revenue Commissioners, ex p. Kingston Smith* [1996] S.T.C. 1210 (court on its own motion initiated contempt proceedings against officers of the Inland Revenue).

INJUNCTIONS IN SPECIFIC CONTEXTS

Injunctions and subordinate legislation

[Add to Note 33:]   **17–046**

See also *R. v. Secretary of State for Trade and Industry, ex p. Duddridge* (1996) 8 Admin L.R. 269 in which the applicants sought an order compelling the Secretary of State to issue regulations, guidelines or some other directive to licence holders under the Electricity Act 1989 requiring restrictions on the electromagnetic fields from cables laid as part of the national grid. The Court of Appeal held that the Secretary of State was under no legal duty to do so.

Injunctions and judicial proceedings

[Add to Note 40:]   **17–048**

See also *R. v. Leominster Magistrates' Court, ex p. Aston Manor Brewery, The Times*, January 8, 1997. A permanent stay of proceedings was ordered on a prosecution brought against the applicant by a local authority under Natural Mineral Waters Regulations 1985, reg. 13(4). It was an abuse of process for these criminal proceedings to continue when a company suing the applicant in civil proceedings was in effective control of the prosecution and the local authority was unable to exercise independently its duties as prosecutor.

[Add to Note 41:]   **17–049**

See also *R. v. Executive Council Joint Disciplinary Scheme, ex p. Hipps* [1996] 9 C.L. 1. Dyson J. refused an application for judicial review brought against an inquisitorial body appointed by the Institute of Chartered Accountants to investigate the applicant's auditing of accounts of Polly Peck International. The applicant argued that this inquiry ought to be suspended until the outcome of civil action brought against it by Polly Peck's administrator. Dyson J. held that the relevant principles of law were:

"(a) that the court was not concerned with the notion of *Wednesbury* unreasonableness but had to exercise jurisdiction and decide whether to grant a stay of proceedings;

(b) such jurisdiction should not be over-used;

(c) a stay had to be refused unless a real risk of serious prejudice could be demonstrated by the party seeking the stay;

(d) in a case where the court decided that there was a real risk of prejudice, the risk had to be weighed against other considerations including the strong public interest in pursuing the disciplinary process;

(e) the court ultimately decided what was fair when balancing these considerations although much weight would be given to opinion of the disciplinary body in relation to what factors militated against the stay; and

(f) the facts of similar cases were not of much use as each case had to be considered on its own facts."

CHAPTER 18

DECLARATIONS

The Nature of the Declaratory Judgment[1]

[Note 2:]   **18–001**

In relation to the views of Sir William Wade on *Webster v. Southwark L.B.C.*
[1983] Q.B. 698 see now H.R.W. Wade and C.F. Forsyth, *Administrative
Law* (7th ed., 1994), p. 592, n. 67 to similar effect.

[Note 9:]   **18–005**

Airedale N.H.S. Trust v. Bland is now reported at [1993] A.C. 789.

Jurisdiction

The supervisory jurisdiction of a court in private law proceedings

[Note 22:]   **18–009**

Airedale N.H.S. Trust v. Bland is now reported at [1993] A.C. 789.

Non-justiciable issues

[Note 33:]   **18–012**

R. v. Inland Revenue Commissioners, ex p. Woolwich Equitable Building Society is
reported at [1990] 1 W.L.R. 1400; the correct citation in Simons Tax Cases
is [1990] S.T.C. 682. For recent cases in which delegated legislation
approved by Parliament has been held *ultra vires*, see *R. v. Lord Chancellor,
ex p. Witham* [1997] 2 All E.R. 779 and *R. v. Secretary of State for Social
Security, ex p. Joint Council for the Welfare of Immigrants* [1997] 1 W.L.R. 275.

Interlocutory and interim declarations

[Add to Note 37:]   **18–015**

In *Access to Justice—Final Report to the Lord Chancellor* (1996) at para. 18.15,
Lord Woolf also recommends that there be express provision for the grant

of interim declarations. See also *Newport Association Football Club Ltd v. Football Association of Wales Ltd* [1997] 2 All E.R. 87 (the grant of an interim injunction in support of a claim for a declaration is not a decision on the merits of the claim and is therefore not tantamount to an interim declaration).

DISCRETION

Whether the issue is theoretical

18–020   This paragraph was considered in *R. v. Head Teacher and Governors of Fairfield Primary School and Hampshire County Council, ex p. W* [1998] C.O.D. 106.

18–021   *[Add to Note 55:]*

In *Access to Justice—Final Report to the Lord Chancellor* (1996) at para. 18.10, Lord Woolf also recommends that there be a power to grant advisory declarations in cases where the issue is of public importance and is defined in sufficiently precise terms, and where the appropriate parties are before the court.

Utility[56]

18–023   *[Note 57:]*

Reported *sub nom. R. v. Southampton Crown Court, ex p. Roddie; Re Roddie and Rose* [1991] 1 W.L.R. 303; the correct citation in the All England Reports is [1991] 2 All E.R. 931.

Where the declaration could interfere with criminal proceedings

18–031   *[Add new Note 78A to the end of the paragraph:]*

In *R. v. Medicines Control Agency, ex p. Pharma Nord Ltd* [1997] C.O.D. 439, a company which marketed a product which had been classified as "medicinal" by the Medicines Control Agency applied for judicial review, seeking a declaration that it was not unlawful for them to market the product without a licence; they asserted it was merely a non-medicinal food supplement. Collins J. held that the issue was a factual one which should be left to be decided in the forum contemplated by the E.C. Directive and national legislation on the marketing of medicinal products, namely the criminal court. There the applicants would have the advantage that in that forum the prosecution would have to prove to the criminal standard that the product was a medical product. Collins J. applied the principles laid down by the Divisional Court in *R. v. Director of Public Prosecutions, ex p. Camelot Group plc* [1998] C.O.D. 54 where it was said that, other things being equal, criminal disputes, even upon pure issues of law, are best decided: (a) in criminal courts; and (b) between the parties most directly affected by the outcome. The civil courts should, moreover, be the warier of embarking upon this jurisdiction: (i) otherwise than at the suit of the Attorney-General (not least where he has refused his *fiat* for relator proceedings); (ii) when it involves existing, and not merely prospective future conduct; (iii) when what is sought is a declaration of criminality rather than of non-criminality; and (iv) when the facts are in issue.

CHAPTER 19

PECUNIARY REMEDIES IN JUDICIAL REVIEW

INTRODUCTION

The general approach

[Note 4a:]   19–003

X (Minors) v. Bedfordshire C.C. is now reported at [1995] 2 A.C. 633.

Statutory and discretionary compensation and restitution

[Add to Note 21:]   19–007

Criminal Justice Act 1988, s. 133 places a statutory duty upon the Secretary of State for the Home Department to pay compensation to a person who suffers punishment as the result of a conviction where there has been a miscarriage of justice. In *R. v. Secretary of State for the Home Department, ex p. Atlantic Commercial (U.K.) Ltd* [1997] C.O.D. 381 Popplewell J. held that it was abundantly clear that such compensation was only payable to a natural person, not to a company.

Relationships between the grounds of judicial review and rights to a pecuniary remedy

[Note 21a:]   19–008

See now *X (Minors) v. Bedfordshire C.C.* [1995] 2 A.C. 633, 736F.

[Add to Note 33:]   19–009

Lambert v. West Devon B.C. [1997] J.P.L. 735 (defendant in breach of duty of care under *Hedley Byrne v. Heller* principles when planning officer told plaintiff to go ahead with development when officer knew, or ought to have known, that planning permission issue was unresolved). *cf. Tidman v. Reading B.C.* [1994] 3 P.L.R. 72 (in giving general advice on planning matters, planning authorities held not to be in a duty of care situation). See further para. 19–043 below.

PROCEDURAL CONSIDERATIONS IN MAKING PECUNIARY CLAIMS

19–013 *[Add to Note 48:]*

See further para. 3–021, above.

19–014 *[Note 49:]*

R. v. Ministry of Agriculture, Fisheries and Food, ex p. Live Sheep Traders Ltd is now reported at [1995] C.O.D. 297.

[Add:]

R. v. Secretary of State for the Home Department, ex p. Vafi (Sita) (No. 2) [1995] Imm. A.R. 528; and *R. v. Secretary of State for Social Security, ex p. Armstrong* (1996) 8 Admin L.R. 626 (Court of Appeal refuses leave to apply for judicial review where "only purpose of pursuing the application was to obtain a declaration which might in its turn found a claim form some damages for breach of European law". No facts were alleged to support any such claim).

[Add to Note 50:]

The Court of Appeal subsequently held that the applicant had no claim for damages:] see *R. v. Northavon D.C., ex p. Palmer* (1996) 8 Admin. L.R. 16.

DEFENDANTS IN MONETARY CLAIMS RELATING TO JUDICIAL REVIEW

19–015 *[Add to Note 54:]*

See further the discussion by the House of Lords of direct and vicarious liability in *X (Minors) v. Bedfordshire C.C.* [1995] 2 A.C. 633.

[Note 56:]

Police Act 1964, s. 48 has been repealed; see now Police Act 1996, s. 88. The Court of Appeal has held that a chief constable is not vicariously liable for police officers who raped and buggered a fellow woman police constable in the section house where she was living: see *W v. Commissioner of Police of the Metropolis* [1997] I.C.R. 1073. See also Police Act 1997, s. 42 which makes the Director-General of the National Criminal Intelligence Service liable in respect of torts committed by constables under his direction and control.

[Add to Note 58:]   **19–016**

See also *Percy v. Hall* [1997] Q.B. 924 (plaintiffs bought actions for false imprisonment and wrongful arrest against Ministry of Defence police after byelaws under which the plaintiffs had been arrested were held *ultra vires*. The Court of Appeal held that the fact that the byelaws were subsequently held to be void for uncertainty did not render tortious the actions of the police officers who, at the relevant time, reasonably believed the byelaw offences were being committed). See also *R. v. Bow Street Magistrates' Court and Another, ex p. McDonald (No. 2), The Times*, July 11, 1997 (council officers acting under authority of a warrant not liable in tort for seizing busker's guitar, even though the warrant later held to have been wrongly issued; the issue of the warrant was a judicial decision and as such effective unless and until set aside by a superior court).

[Note 60:]

National Health Service Act 1977, s. 125 is amended by National Health Service and Community Care Act 1990, Schedule 2. *cf. Capital & Counties plc v. Hampshire C.C.* [1997] Q.B. 1004 where the Court of Appeal held that the language of the Fire Services Act 1947, s. 30 was not apt to establish an implied immunity from proceedings in negligence or breach of statutory duty for fire fighters involved in extinguishing a fire.

[Note 67:]   **19–017**

Criminal Justice Act 1991, s. 85 is amended by Criminal Justice and Public Order Act 1994, ss 97 and 101.

The Crown as a defendant[69]

[Add to Note 76:]   **19–020**

See *Mulcahy v. Ministry of Defence* [1996] Q.B. 732 (Court of Appeal holds that it was not fair, just or reasonable to impose duty of care in battle situations on the ministry; nor was the ministry obliged to maintain a safe system of work in battle situations); *Barrett v. Ministry of Defence* [1995] 1 W.L.R. 1217 (Court of Appeal holds that ministry owed duty of care to naval airman who collapsed due to drink and asphyxiated on his own vomit; the ministry's care of the serviceman after his collapse had been inadequate).

Magistrates

19–026   The position of magistrates and their clerks is now regulated by Part V of the Justices of the Peace Act 1997; the provisions in the Justices of the Peace Act 1979 are repealed. There is immunity from civil actions in respect of acts or omissions which are within a justice or justices' clerk's jurisdiction: section 51. Actions may be brought with respect to a matter not within their jurisdiction if, but only if, it is proved that the justice or clerk acted in bad faith: section 52. Section 53 of the 1997 Act provides that if any action is brought in circumstances where no action is to lie, a judge in the court where the action is brought may, on the defendant's application, set aside the proceedings in the action with or without costs.

19–027   *[Note 7:]*

For provisions as to indemnification of justices and justices' clerks for damages and costs, see now Justices of the Peace Act 1997, s. 54.

LIABILITY AND DAMAGES IN TORT IN RELATION TO JUDICIAL REVIEW

General difficulties

19–031   *[Add to Note 20:]*

See also *X (Minors) v. Bedfordshire C.C.* [1995] 2 A.C. 633 at 751G *per* Lord Browne-Wilkinson: "In my judgment, the courts should proceed with great care before holding liable in negligence those who have been charged by Parliament with the task of protecting society from the wrongdoings of others".

19–032   *[Note 23:]*

The *East Rivers* case has recently been considered by the House of Lords in *Stovin v. Wise and Norfolk County Council* [1996] A.C. 923 and the Court of Appeal in *Capital & Counties plc v. Hampshire C.C.* [1997] Q.B. 1004 at 346–348.

[Add to Note 24:]

Murphy v. Brentwood D.C. has not been followed in New Zealand: see *Invercargill City Council v. Hamlin* [1996] A.C. 624 (P.C.). See further I. Duncan-Wallace (1996) 112 L.Q.R. 369.

Liability for unlawful administrative action in the case of different torts

19–035   *[Add new Note 38A after "nuisance":]*

See *The Great House at Sonning Ltd v. Berkshire C.C.*, *The Times*, March 25 1996 (C.A., Saville L.J. dissenting) in which it was held, striking out a writ for an action in public nuisance, that a person affected by a road closure order made under Road Traffic Regulation Act 1984, s. 14 had no private right to assert; the only remedy lay in public law proceedings.

Negligence[39]

[Add to Note 43:]   **19–036**

See also *X (Minors) v. Bedfordshire C.C.* [1995] 2 A.C. 633 at 735D *per* Lord Browne-Wilkinson that "no one principle is capable of being formulated applicable to all cases" for determining the circumstances in which the law would impose a common law duty of care arising from the exercise of statutory powers and duties.

[Add to Note 46:]   **19–038**

See also *X (Minors) v. Bedfordshire C.C.* [1995] 2 A.C. 633 at 737H-738.

[Add to Note 51:]   **19–040**

In *Barrett v. Enfield L.B.C.* [1997] 3 W.L.R. 628 the Court of Appeal declined to impose a duty of care on a local authority in respect of decisions taken about the future of a child in care that would normally have been made by a parent. There were, however, circumstances in which social workers and other members of staff could be negligent in an "operational manner", *e.g.* listing property belonging to the child, or in reporting what they had observed for the purposes of an interdisciplinary assessment of what action should be taken in relation to a child, or in failing to carry out instructions properly. Leave to appeal to the House of Lords has been granted: see [1998] 1 W.L.R. 277. In *X (Minors) v. Bedfordshire C.C.* [1995] 2 A.C. 633 at 748H Lord Browne-Wilkinson gave as examples of breach of duties which will not involve unjusticiable policy questions: "to remove the children, to allocate a suitable social worker to make proper investigations". He contrasted these with "other allegations the investigation of which by a court might require the weighing of policy factors, *e.g.* allegations that the County Council failed to provide a level of service appropriate to the plaintiffs' needs. If the case were to go to trial, the trial judge might have to rule out these issues as not being justiciable" (749A).

[Add new Note 55a after "In Murphy nothing was said, however, about the policy/operational approach,":]   **19–041**

In *X (Minors) v. Bedfordshire C.C.* [1995] 2 A.C. 633 at 736C Lord Browne-Wilkinson said that this part of the decision in *Anns* had largely escaped criticism in later cases.

[Add to Note 58:]

In *Stovin v. Wise and Norfolk County Council* [1996] A.C. 923, Lord Hoffmann described the distinction between policy and operation as "inadequate": it was often elusive—and even if the distinction were clear cut, so leaving no element of discretion in the sense that it would be irrational (in the public law meaning of that word) for a public authority not to exercise its power, it did not follow that the law should superimpose a common law duty of care.

19–042   *[Add to Note 60:]*

In *X (Minors) v. Bedfordshire C.C.* [1995] 2 A.C. 633 at 738G Lord Browne-Wilkinson said:

> "Where Parliament has conferred a statutory discretion on a public authority, it is for that authority, not for the courts, to exercise the discretion: nothing which the authority does within the ambit of the discretion can be actionable at common law. If the decision complained of falls outside the statutory discretion, it *can* (but not necessarily will) give rise to common law liability".

[Add new Note 62a after "It is unfortunate that the term "unreasonable" is used both in judicial review and negligence; it usually means different things in each context.":]

In *X (Minors) v. Bedfordshire C.C.* [1995] 2 A.C. 633, Lord Browne-Wilkinson addressed this point, though his dicta have not helped to clarify this area of law. His Lordship stated at 736F that:

> "For myself, I do not believe that it is either helpful or necessary to introduce public law concepts as to the validity of a decision into the question of liability at common law for negligence. In public law a decision can be ultra vires for reasons other than *Wednesbury* unreasonableness (e.g. breach of the rules of natural justice) which have no relevance to the question of negligence".

As Cane points out in "Suing Public Authorities in Tort" (1996) 112 L.Q.R. 13, it is unclear why *Wednesbury* unreasonableness has been singled out as the only form of *ultra vires* which can give rise to liability in tort for negligence.

[Add to Note 64:]

See now *X (Minors) v. Bedfordshire C.C.* [1995] 2 A.C. 633 where Lord Browne-Wilkinson stated that "a common law duty of care cannot be imposed on a statutory duty if the observance of such a common law duty of care would be inconsistent with, or have a tendency to discourage, the due performance by the local authority of its statutory duties" (at 739D–E)

In the context of a local authority's statutory duties to protect children, his Lordship held (at 749H) that "a common law duty of care would cut across the whole statutory system set up for the protection of children at risk" and

> "if liability in damages were to be imposed, it might well be that local authorities would adopt a more cautious and defensive approach to their duties. . . . If the authority is to be made liable in damages for a negligent decision to remove a child (such negligence lying in the failure properly first to investigate the allegations) there would be a substantial temptation to postpone making such a decision until further inquires have been made in the hope of getting more concrete facts. Not only would the child in fact being abused be prejudiced by such delay; the increased workload inherent in making such investigations would reduce the time available to deal with other cases and other children" (750F–G)

[Add to Note 65:]

And see *X (Minors) v. Bedfordshire C.C.* [1995] 2 A.C. 633 at 739C: "the question whether there is such a common law duty and if so its ambit, must be profoundly influenced by the statutory framework within which the acts complained of were done" (*per* Lord Browne-Wilkinson). In *Stovin v. Wise and Norfolk County Council* [1996] A.C. 923 Lord Hoffmann stated:

> "Whether a statutory duty gives rise to a private cause of action is a question of construction. It requires an examination of the policy of the statute to decide whether it was intended to confer a right to compensation for breach. Whether it can be relied upon to support the existence of a common law duty of care is not exactly a question of construction, because the cause of action does not arise out of the statute itself. But the policy of the statute is nevertheless a crucial factor in the decision."

[Add to Note 68:]

In *X (Minors) v. Bedfordshire C.C.* [1995] 2 A.C. 633 Lord Browne-Wilkinson stated in relation to social workers investigating child abuse that

> "If there were no other remedy for maladministration of the statutory system for the protection of children, it would provide a substantial argument for imposing a duty of care. But the statutory complaints procedure contained in s. 76 of the [Child Care Act 1980] and the much fuller procedures now available under the [Children Act 1989] provide a means to have grievances investigated, though not to recover compensation. Further, it was submitted (and not controverted) that the local authorities' ombudsman would have power to investigate cases such as these" (751A–B).

See also *Barrett v. Enfield L.B.C.* [1997] 3 W.L.R. 628 where the Court of Appeal, holding that it was contrary to public policy to impose a duty of care on a local authority in relation to those decisions about a child in its care which would normally be made by a parent, stated that if complaint was to be made, then an investigation by an ombudsman was more likely to result in a satisfactory conclusion than the investigation by the courts. The ombudsman could, in appropriate cases, award compensation for maladministration. (Leave to appeal to the House of Lords has been granted: see [1998] 1 W.L.R. 277).

Negligent misstatement[71]

19–043   *[Add to Note 77:]*

See also *Welton v. North Cornwall D.C* [1997] 1 W.L.R. 570 (Court of Appeal accepts plaintiff guesthouse-owner's pleaded case that there was a special relationship between her and the council's environmental health officer which gave rise to a duty to take reasonable care in the statements he made as to the extent of the alterations required to comply with the law). There is uncertainty as to whether, in giving general advice, a local planning authority owes a duty of care under *Hedley Byrne v. Heller* principles. In *Lambert v. West Devon B.C.*[1997] J.P.L. 735 (considered at para. 19–008, n. 33 above) the judge accepted that a duty could arise. *cf. Tidman v. Reading B.C.* [1994] 3 P.L.R. 72 (although the council had published a document encouraging persons involved in planning matters to seek guidance and advice from planning officers, a person who sought such guidance or advice did not thereby necessarily place the council in a position where it owed him a duty under *Hedley Byrne*) and *R. v. Hounslow L.B.C., ex p. Williamson* [1996] E.G.C.S. 27 (no duty of care in respect of expressions of opinion by planning officer).

Misfeasance in public office[78]

19–045   *[Add to Note 80:]*

See also *Dunlop v. Woollahra M.C.* [1982] A.C. 158 (Privy Council) and *Northern Territory v. Mengel* (1995) 60 A.L.J.R. 527 (High Court of Australia). The Indian Supreme Court has recognised misfeasance in public office as a species of tortious liability and held that if a public functionary does not use power for a bona fide purpose and in a transparent manner and makes arbitrary allotments of petrol pump dealerships of public corporations or of governmental accommodation, he would be liable in damages even though there may be no injury to any third party. See *Common Cause v. Union of India*, 1996 (6) SCC 530; and *Shivsagar Tiwari v. Union of India*, 1996 (6) SCC 558.

[Add to Note 83:]   **19–046**

The necessary mental element in the tort was considered by Clarke J. in
Three Rivers D.C. v. Bank of England (No. 2) [1996] 3 All E.R. 558 where it
was confirmed that the tort could be established in two alternative ways.

[Add to Note 85:]

In relation to the second limb, in *Three Rivers D.C. v. Bank of England
(No. 2)* [1996] 3 All E.R. 558 it was held, following the majority in *Northern
Territory v. Mengel*, that it was not sufficient to prove simply knowledge of
the unlawful nature of the act and that the act caused the plaintiff's loss. *Per*
Clarke J. at 582:

> "For the purposes of the requirement that the officer knows that he
> has no power to do the act complained of, it is sufficient that the
> officer has actual knowledge that the act was unlawful or, in circum-
> stances in which he believes or suspects that the act is beyond his
> powers, that he does not ascertain whether or not that is so, or fails to
> take such steps as would be taken by an honest and reasonable man to
> ascertain the true position. For the purposes of the requirement that
> the officer knows that his act will probably injure the plaintiff or a
> person in a class of which the plaintiff is a member it is sufficient that
> the officer has actual knowledge that this act will probably damage the
> plaintiff or such a person, if he does not ascertain whether or not that
> is so, or he fails to make such inquiries as an honest and reasonable
> man would make as to the probability of such damage."

[Add to Note 93:]   **19–049**

In such situations today, liability may arise independently of the tort of
misfeasance in public office: see *Brasserie du Pêcheur S.A. v. Germany; R. v.
Secretary of State for Transport, ex p. Factortame (No. 4)*, Joined Cases C-46 &
48/93 [1996] Q.B. 404, discussed below at para. 21–191A.

Breach of statutory duty[96]

[Note 98:]   **19–051**

A.B. and Others v. South West Water Services Ltd is reported at [1993] Q.B.
507.

[Note 2a:]   **19–053**

X (Minors) v. Bedfordshire C.C. is now reported at [1995] 2 A.C. 633.

[Note 3:]

R. v. Inner London Education Authority, ex p. Ali is reported at (1990) 2
Admin. L.R. 822.

19–054   *[Note 5a:]*

X (Minors) v. Bedfordshire C.C. is now reported at [1995] 2 A.C. 633.

19–055   *[Add:]*

In 1997 the House of Lords in *O'Rourke v. Camden L.B.C.* [1997] 3 W.L.R. 86 held, overruling *Thornton v. Kirklees M.D.C.* [1979] Q.B. 626, that a breach of the duty to provide temporary accommodation under Part III of the Housing Act 1985 pending a decision as to whether a person was homeless, did not create a private law right to claim damages. On the housing duties of local authorities generally, see further Chapter 26 below.

Recent cases in which it has been held that no action for damages lie for breaches of statutory duty include the following. In *Capital & Counties plc v. Hampshire C.C.* [1997] Q.B. 1004 the Court of Appeal held that the Fire Services Act 1947, s. 13 ("A fire authority shall take all reasonable measures for ensuring the provision of an adequate supply of water, and for securing that it will be available for use, in case of fire") did not confer a right of private action upon a member of the public injured by its breach. In *Issa and Another v. Hackney L.B.C.* [1997] 1 W.L.R. 956 the Court of Appeal held that Part III of the Public Health Act 1936, creating a right for a local authority to make complaints to the justices of the peace in respect of statutory nuisances, was a self-contained code and it could not be construed to create a civil cause of action—even though this meant there was a class of case were serious wrongs continued to be without an effective remedy. In *Oluto v. Home Office and Another* [1997] 1 W.L.R. 328 the Court of Appeal held there to be no right to damages for detention in custody contrary to the time limits set by the Prosecution of Offences Act 1985, s. 22 and the regulations made thereunder: applying *Elguzouli-Daf v. Commissioner of Police for the Metropolis* [1995] Q.B. 335, no claim for breach of statutory duty lay against the Crown Prosecution Service for its failure to ensure that the plaintiff did not spend longer in prison than permitted by the custody time limit.

[Note 11:]

Thornton v. Kirklees M.D.C. [1979] Q.B. 626 has now been overruled (see above). *X (Minors) v. Bedfordshire C.C.* is now reported at [1995] 2 A.C. 633.

False imprisonment

19–058   *[Add:]*

In *Olutu v. Home Office and Another* [1997] 1 W.L.R. 328 the Court of Appeal held that a prison governor was not liable for false imprisonment where he detained a person after the custody time limit set by the Prosecution of Offenders Act 1985 had expired. Such a person was detained unlawfully. The prisoner governor was not, however, either entitled or bound to release the person in view of the direction to him in the warrant and the fact that the person was in the custody of the Crown Court; only an order of the court could end that period of custody.

Measure of damages

[Add to Note 21:]   **19–060**

The Law Commission has since issued a supplementary Consultation Paper. In *Thompson v. Commissioner of Police for the Metropolis* [1997] 3 W.L.R. 403 the Court of Appeal issued guidelines to juries on damages in actions against the police. It was held that an award of £50,000 was the absolute maximum appropriate for exemplary damages; such a sum should be awarded only where officers of at least the rank of superintendent had been involved in the unlawful conduct.

Reform and the impact of liability

[Note 49a:]   **19–066**

Northern Territory v. Mengel is now reported at (1995) 60 A.L.J.R. 527.

DAMAGES IN RELATION TO CONTRACTS[67]

Contracts made in breach of public law duties and discretions

[Paragraph number 10–074 should read 19–074].   **19–074**

[Add to Note 75:]

On June 2, 1997 the Department of the Environment announced that the government is to review the operation of compulsory competitive tendering with a view to replacing it with a "better value" regime. Extensive consultation will take place.

[Add to Note 76:]

See further G. Lindrup, *Butterworth's Public Procurement and CCT Handbook*. See also Public Supply Contracts Regulations 1995 (S.I. 1995 No. 201) and Public Services Contracts Regulations 1993 (S.I. 1993 No. 3328).

RESTITUTIONARY CLAIMS[97]

Recovery of money paid under an ultra vires demand

[Add to Note 1:]

See further J. Beatson, "Mistakes of law and Ultra Vires public authority receipts: the Law Commission report" [1995] R.L.R 280.

[Add to Note 7:]

See also *British Steel plc v. Customs and Excise Commissioners* [1997] 2 All E.R 366 in which the Court of Appeal applied the reasoning of *Woolwich* to hold that a demand for duty on hydrocarbon oil following an unlawful refusal to grant relief from that duty was an "unlawful demand". British Steel could continue with the writ action as it might be able to prove that it was an "approved person" within the meaning of the relevant legislation; if it could do so, it would have a restitutionary claim.

Restitution of money paid to a public authority under an ultra vires contract

19–086 *[Add to Note 17:]*

Islington L.B.C. appealed against the Court of Appeal's judgment only in respect of the award of compound interest on the repayments which had to be made in relation of the *ultra vires* swap agreements. In *Westdeutsche Landesbank Girozentrale v. Islington L.B.C.* [1996] A.C. 669, the House of Lords held, by a majority, that simple interest only could be awarded; In *A. G. v. Blake* [1998] 1 All E.R. 833, the Court of Appeal suggested *obiter* that restitution might be available in relation to money which was payable in consequence of the commission of a criminal offence.

CHAPTER 20

THE DISCRETION OF THE COURT

VARIED ROLE

The prima facie approach

Add to Note 9:]   20–007

See also *R. v. Lincolnshire C.C. and Wealden D.C., ex p. Atkinson, Wales and Stratford* (1996) 8 Admin L.R. 529 at 550, *per* Sedley J.: "To refuse relief where an error of law by a public authority has been demonstrated is an unusual and strong thing; but there is no doubt that it can be done." And see *R. v. Secretary of State for the Environment, ex p. Walters* [1998] C.O.D. 121 and *R. v. Islington L.B.C., ex p. Degnan* [1998] C.O.D. 46. (Noted at para. 10–19, Note 72).

Delay

Add to Note 11:]   20–008

And see further Alistair Lindsay, "Delay in Judicial Review Cases: A Conundrum Solved?" [1995] P.L. 417.

Add:]   20–009

At the full hearing, the applicant's delay in applying for leave is a factor to be taken into account in the exercise of discretion to withhold relief only if to grant a remedy would be likely to cause hardship, prejudice or detriment to the respondent or a third party within the meaning of section 31(6)(b) of the Supreme Court Act 1981: see *R. v. Criminal Injuries Compensation Board, ex p. A* [1997] W.L.R. 776. (Note that leave to appeal to the House of Lords has been granted in this case: [1998] 1 W.L.R. 277). The Court may take the view that such hardship, prejudice or detriment is self-evident without the respondent adducing specific evidence of it: see *R. v. Newbury District Council and Another, ex p. Chievely Parish Council* [1997] J.P.L. 1137 (explained delay in applying for leave to move for judicial review of a major planning proposal).

The significance of the requirements of good administration

20–011   *[Add to Note 17:]*

R. v. Cambridgeshire C.C., ex p. Darnell [1995] C.O.D. 434 ("inimical to good administration" to bind local authority to a statement, that it would consider the applicant for contract work, while outcome of police investigation into alleged corruption in the authority's property department was awaited). *cf. R. v. Dr Fagin and Dr Travers, ex p. Mountstephen* [1996] C.O.D. 416 where, despite being "rather uneasy about the practical implications of the conclusions I have felt bound to reach which may have widespread ramifications", Brooke J. held that psychiatric illness was an injury received in execution of duty for the purposes of the Police Pensions Regulations 1987.

Utility

20–012   *[Add new Note 18a after "It will not provide a remedy if it will serve no purpose.":]*

See *e.g. R. v. Secretary of State for Employment, ex p. Seymour-Smith* [1997] 1 W.L.R. 473 in which the House of Lords discharged a declaration to the effect that the Unfair Dismissal (Variation of Qualifying Period) Order 1985 was incompatible with the principle of equal treatment, which had been granted by the Court of Appeal, on the ground that the declaration would serve no useful purpose: it neither enabled employees to sue for unfair dismissal in the industrial tribunal nor told the Government of the United Kingdom that legislation needed to be changed.

[Add to Note 19:]

See also *R. v. H.M. Inspectorate of Pollution, ex p. Chapman* [1996] C.O.D. 154 (court refused to adjudicate upon an academic question of law where National Power plc had withdrawn its objections to a disclosure of certain documents after the grant of leave to apply for judicial review); *R. v. Ministry of Agriculture, Fisheries and Food, ex p. Live Sheep Traders Ltd* [1995] C.O.D. 297 (delegated legislation under challenge had been repealed and replaced more than two months before the applicants sought judicial review); *R. v. Secretary of State for Home Department, ex p. Adams (No. 2)* [1995] C.O.D. 426 (exclusion order made under Prevention of Terrorism (Temporary Provisions) Act 1989, s. 5 revoked after Article 177 reference to European Court of Justice; court therefore withdrew reference and refused underlying application for judicial review. The court had been concerned with a specific legal issue which no longer existed). *cf. R. v. Kensington and Chelsea R.L.B.C., ex p. Ben-el-Mabrouk* [1995] C.O.D. 278 in which the Court of Appeal did not take the view that the rehousing of the applicant before the hearing of the application for judicial review rendered the question academic; the point at issue was one of considerable public importance to local authorities.

[Add to Note 22:]   **20–014**

In *R. v. Lincolnshire C.C. and Wealden D.C., ex p. Atkinson, Wales and Stratford* (1996) 8 Admin. L.R. 529 the court refused to grant *certiorari* (but did grant a declaration) in the unusual circumstances that it could "say with confidence what the outcome of due process would have been". In that case there had been a belated inquiry by the local authority into the relevant matters which established that there was nothing which would have made a difference to the decision affecting the applicant even if the right things had been done at the right time.

Theoretical issues and advisory declarations[25]

[Add to Note 26:]   **20–016**

In *Access to Justice—Final Report to the Lord Chancellor* (1996), p. 252, Lord Woolf recommended that the court should have an express power to grant advisory declarations when it is in the public interest to do so. The power should be limited to cases where the issue was of public importance and was defined in sufficiently precise terms and where appropriate parties were before the court.

Alternative remedies[32]

[Add new Note 35a after "For the court to require the alternative procedure to be **20–019** *exhausted prior to resorting to judicial review is in accord with judicial review being very properly regarded as being a remedy of last resort.":]*

See, *e.g. R. v. Council of Legal Education, ex p. Eddis* (1995) 7 Admin. L.R. 357 (visitor enjoyed exclusive jurisdiction over educational matters and therefore judicial review not possible before the appeal to the visitor had been completed); *R. v. Law Society, ex p. Kingsley* [1996] C.O.D. 59 (leave to move for judicial review of decisions of Law Society set aside because of existence of alternative remedy in the form of an appeal to the Master of the Rolls); *R. v. Ministry of Agriculture, Fisheries and Food, ex p. Dairy Trade Federation Ltd* [1995] C.O.D. 3 (the European Commission and the Monopolies and Mergers Commission were better equipped to handle the complex questions of fact and law raised by a complaint about the Milk Marque scheme; such recourse would not necessarily take longer than judicial review); *R. v. Birmingham C.C., ex p. A (a Minor)* [1997] 2 F.L.R.

The Discretion of the Court

841 (where neither facts nor law were in dispute and the chief ground for complaint was that a local authority had failed, through delay, to carry out its duties towards a child in need in its area, the appropriate form of redress was the complaints procedure established by Children Act 1989, s. 26); *R. v. Secretary of State for the Home Department , ex p. Watts* [1997] C.O.D. 152 (leave to move for judicial review set aside because applicant had statutory right of appeal to Secretary of State under Town and Country Planning Act 1990, s. 78 against a grant of planning permission subject to conditions); *R. v. Secretary of State for the Home Department, ex p. Capti-Mehmet* [1997] C.O.D. 61 (leave to apply for judicial review refused where asylum seeker failed, in part through the error or incompetence of his legal representatives, to appeal within time limit from Special Adjudicator to Immigration Appeal Tribunal); *R. v. Director of Public Prosecutions, ex p. Camelot Group plc* [1998] C.O.D. 54 (leave to apply for judicial review of D.P.P.'s decision not to prosecute initially refused given the existence of an alternative remedy, namely a private prosecution).

[Add to Note 37:]

In *R. v. East Sussex Valuation Tribunal, ex p. Silverstone* [1996] C.O.D. 402 delegated legislation provided for a statutory appeal on point of law against Council Tax valuations. The applicant, adopting the wrong procedure, applied for judicial review. Carnwath J. held that it would not, however, be right to refuse the application for that reason only: a residual jurisdiction was available under judicial review; the applicant, who appeared in person, had made a genuine mistake; the letter from the valuation tribunal informing the applicant of his rights of appeal was not as clear as it might have been; and no prejudice had been caused to other parties.

20–020 *[Add to Note 38:]*

In *R. v. Lambeth L.B.C., ex p. Crookes* (1997) 29 H.L.R. 28 the issue arose whether complaints about delays and improper actions by a local authority in determining claims for housing benefit should more appropriately be directed to the Local Commissioner for Administration (on which, see above at para. 1–092 *et seq.*) rather than brought by way of application for judicial review. It was held that relief on the basis of this alternative remedy would be limited to the judicial review equivalent of maladministration and would not encompass any of the other grounds of illegality, proportionality and irrationality—every procedural irregularity would be likely to exhibit maladministration, although not every act of maladministration would be encompassed by procedural irregularity. See also *R. v. Lambeth London Borough Council, ex p. Ogunmayiwa, The Times,* April 17, 1998 (application for judicial review not barred on ground that other remedies had not been exhausted where a local authority had raised an expectation of an internal review of case but had not carried out that review).

[Add to Note 39:]

R. v. East Yorkshire Borough of Beverley Housing Benefits Review Board, ex p. Hare (1995) 27 W.L.R. 637 (Housing Benefit (General) Regulations 1987, reg. 86(1)(c)), whereby board could set aside its own decisions where "the interests of justice so require", did not cover complaints such as those in the present case, which did not relate to breaches of natural justice).

[Add to Note 40:]

R. v. Tower Hamlets London Borough Council, ex p. Bradford (1997) 29 H.L.R. 756 (applicants had failed to avail themselves of the statutory complaints procedure for alleged failures in service provision under the Chronically Sick and Disabled Persons Act 1970, s. 2, Children Act 1989, s. 17 and National Health and Community Care Act 1990, s. 47. Refusing relief would, however, have resulted in an unacceptable delay in an assessment of a child's needs in relation to rehousing).

[Add to Note 41:]

In R. v. Hereford Magistrates' Court, ex p. Rowlands [1997] Q.B. 110 the Divisional Court held that the existence of a right of appeal from decisions of magistrates to the Crown Court (in respect of matters of pure fact and matters of mixed fact and law) and appeal by way of case stated to the High Court (in respect of matters of pure law) did not preclude either the grant of leave to apply for judicial review or the grant of substantive relief where there were proper grounds of procedural unfairness or bias on the part of magistrates. To hold otherwise "would be to emasculate the long-established supervisory jurisdiction of this court over magistrates' courts, which has over the years proved an invaluable guarantee of the integrity of proceedings in those courts" (*per* Lord Bingham of Cornhill C.J.).

[Add to Note 57:]   **20–032**

But see the suggestion in A.G. v. Blake (Jonathan Cape Ltd, third party) [1998] 1 All E.R. 833 (C.A.) (Court's power to grant injunctive relief in support of the criminal law extended to enforcing public policy—in this case restraining receipt by the criminal of further benefit resulting from the crime).

PART V

E.C. LAW IN ENGLISH ADMINISTRATIVE LAW

CHAPTER 21

E.C. LAW IN ENGLISH ADMINISTRATIVE LAW

INTRODUCTION

Treaties to which the Community is a party

[Add to Note 31:] **21–013**

For the status of the WTO Agreement in national laws, see P. Eeckhout, "The Domestic Legal Status of the WTO Agreement: Interconnecting Legal Systems" (1997) 32 C.M.L.Rev. 11.

Circumstances in which directives have direct effect

[Add:] **21–027**

A right granted by a directive against the State, however, may be pleaded not only in proceedings against the State but also in proceedings between individuals. See Case C–194/94 *CIA Security v. Signalson and Securitel SPRL* [1996] E.C.R. I–2001.

[Add to Note 52:]

Case C–192/94 *El Carte Inglés* [1996] E.C.R. I–1281.

[Add to Note 54:] **21–028**

In *Griffin v. South West Water Services Ltd* [1995] I.R.L.R. 15, Blackburn J. held, applying *Foster*, that a privatised water company is a State authority against which directives can be enforced directly. He stated that the material criterion for the purposes of direct effect is not whether the body in question is under the control of the State but whether the public service which it performs is under State control.

General principles of law

[Add:] **21–030**

The application of the general principles of Community law as a ground of review of national measures was examined by Laws J. in *R. v. Ministry of*

Agriculture, Fisheries and Food, ex p. First City Trading Ltd [1997] 1 C.M.L.R. 250. Following the BSE crisis and the imposition of a world-wide ban on the export of British beef by the Commission, the Government adopted the Beef Stock Transfer Scheme granting emergency aid to undertakings operating slaughterhouses and cutting premises. The applicants were exporters of beef who did not operate their own slaughterhouses or cutting premises and were therefore not entitled to aid. They argued that the aid scheme infringed the general principle of equal treatment as recognised in Community law because it favoured exporters who had their own slaughtering and cutting facilities *vis-à-vis* those who did not. Laws J. held that the aid scheme was not reviewable on grounds of compatibility with the general principles of law recognised by the European Court. He drew a distinction between, on the one hand, national measures adopted pursuant to Community law and, on the other hand, national measures adopted solely by virtue of domestic law. Although the first type of measure must comply with the general principles of law recognised by the case law of the European Court, the second type of measure need to comply only with the Treaty and written Community law. Laws J. rejected recourse to the principle of equality as a ground of review on the basis that the Beef Stock Transfer Scheme was not adopted pursuant to Community law. It was neither required by Community law nor did the Government have to rely upon any Community law permission in order to implement it. In any event, Laws J. considered that the scheme did not breach the general principle of equality as recognised in Community law.

Jurisdiction of the European Court of Justice

21–032 *[Add to Note 68:]*

For a recent example, see Case C–42/94 *Heidemij Advies BV v. Parliament* [1995] E.C.R. I–1417.

Interpretation by national courts

21–038 *[Add to Note 74 after "in the field of criminal law.":]*

The judgment in *Kolpinghuis* was followed in Case C–168/95 *Arcaro* [1996] E.C.R. I–4705.

Preliminary rulings by the European Court[78]

21–041 *[Add to Note 81:]*

Case C–111/94 *Job Centre* [1995] E.C.R. I–3361; Joined Cases C–74 and C–129/95 *Criminal proceedings against X* [1996] E.C.R. I–6609.

[Note 85:]

Case C–458/93 *Saddik* is now reported at [1995] E.C.R. I–511; Case
C–167/94 *Grau Gomis and others* is now reported at [1995] E.C.R. I–1023.

[Add to Note 85:]

The order for reference need not contain an exhaustive account of the
factual and legal context in which the questions are raised but it must
contain sufficient information to enable the Court of Justice to provide the
national court with a helpful answer to the questions referred: Case
C–125/94 *Aprile v. Amministrazione delle Finanze dello Stato* [1995] E.C.R.
I–2919. For examples of cases where the reference was rejected as inadmissible see Case C–307/95 *Max Mara* [1995] E.C.R. I–5083; C–101/96 *Italia
Testa* [1996] E.C.R. I–3081; Case C–191/96 *Modesti* [1996] E.C.R. I–3937.

[Add to paragraph 21–041:]

Where a national court makes a reference for a preliminary ruling to the
European Court, only the questions referred are addressed to the European
Court. The case itself is not transferred to it and is still pending before the
national court. If, after a preliminary reference has been made, the
defendant acquiesces to the plaintiff's claims, the national court is not
precluded from accepting the acquiescence and terminating the proceedings on the ground that the case has been referred to the European Court
and is no longer pending before it. See Joined Cases C–422, 423 & 424/93
Zabala Erasun and Others [1995] E.C.R. I–1567.

Scope of preliminary rulings

[Add:]   21–043

A preliminary reference on the interpretation of a Community provision
may be admissible even where on the circumstances of the case that
provision applies by virtue of national law and not by virtue of Community
law: see Case C–130/95 *Giloy v. Hauptzollamt Frankfurt am Main-Ost*,
judgment of July 17, 1997; Case C–28/95 *Leur-Bloem v. Inspecteur des
Belastingdienst/Ondernemingen Amsterdam 2*, judgment of July 17, 1997.

Direct effect and primacy in the United Kingdom

[Add New Note 4a after "by means of subordinate legislation.":]   21–052

For the interpretation of section 2(2), see *R. v. Secretary of State for Trade and
Industry, ex p. Unison* [1997] 1 C.M.L.R. 459.

JUDICIAL REVIEW OF COMMUNITY MEASURES

Inherent judisdiction?

21–064 *[Add to Note 33:]*

See also T. Tridimas, "The European Court of Justice and Judicial Activism" (1996) 21 E.L.Rev. 199.

Challenge to validity via Article 177; standing and time-limits

21–066 *[Add to Note 36:]*

TWD was applied in Case C–178/95 *Wiljo NV v. Belgian State* [1997] E.C.R. I–585 but distinguished in Case C–241/95 *R. v. Intervention Board for Agricultural Produce, ex p. Accrington Beef Co. and Others* [1996] E.C.R. I–6699.

Grounds of review

21–070 *[Add to Note 47:]*

Case C–417/93 *Parliament v. Council* [1995] E.C.R. I–1185; Case C–21/94 *Parliament v. Council* [1995] E.C.R. I–1827; C–156/93 *Parliament v. Commission* [1995] E.C.R. I–2019. In Case C–392/95 *Parliament v. Council* [1997] E.C.R. I–3213, the Court annulled the Visa Regulation (No. 2317/95, [1995] O.J. L234, p. 1) on the ground that the European Parliament had not been consulted properly.

General principles of law[57]

Equality

21–074 *[Add to Note 59:]*

See T. Tridimas, "The Application of the Principle of Equality to Community Measures" in A.A. Dashwood (ed.), *The Principle of Equal Treatment in Community Law* (1997) pp. 215–242.

21–075 *[Add to Note 66:]*

For an unsuccessful claim that the principle of equality was breached in the allocation of quotas, see Case C–241/95 *R. v. Intervention Board for Agricultural Produce, ex p. Accrington Beef Co. and Others* [1996] E.C.R. I–6699

Differential treatment among economic operators established in different
Member States may be the inevitable consequence of the fact that
Community harmonisation measures provide only for minimum requirements: Case C–128/94 *Hönig v. Stadt Stockach* [1995] E.C.R. I–3389. Also,
in adopting harmonisation measures, the Community institutions enjoy
wide discretionary powers. Since haromonisation has to be pursued in
stages, a harmonisation measure may lead to differences in treatment
between comparable groups of persons, where one group becomes subject
to Community law and another remains subject to national law. Such
differences are not prohibited provided that they are based on objective
criteria: Case C–479/93 *Francovich v. Italian Republic (Francovich II)* [1995]
E.C.R. I–3843.

Add to Note 71:]   21–077

See also Case C–396/93 P *Henrichs v. Commission* [1995] E.C.R. I–2611,
para. 43.

Proportionality

Add to Note 72:]   21–078

N. Emiliou, *The Principle of Proportionality in European Law* (1996), T.
Tridimas, "The Principle of Proportionality in Community Law: From the
Rule of Law to Market Integration" (1996) XXXI *The Irish Jurist* 83.

Add to Note 75:]

f. Case C–104/94 *Cereol Italia v. Azienda Agricola Castello* [1995] E.C.R.
I–2983. In that case the Court found that penalties which went as far as
forfeiture of entitlement to aid for two marketing years, where a producer
deliberately or by reason of serious negligence failed to notify the
Commission of changes in the area sown, were proportionate in view of
the importance of the obligation of notification for the operation of the aid
system. By contrast, in Case C–296/94 *Pietsch v. Hauptzollamt Hamburg-
Valtershof* [1996] E.C.R. I–3409 the Court annulled a Commission regulation which imposed a charge on the import of mushrooms from third
countries equal to 90 per cent of their value, on the ground that the level of
the charges was disproportionate and amounted effectively to a prohibition
of imports. Also, in Case C–295/94 *Hüpeden & Co KG v. Hauptzollamt
Hamburg-Jonas* [1996] E.C.R. I–3375 the Court annulled a Council regulation holding that a flat-rate charge set at a very high level (150 per cent of
the value of the goods) and levied on all traders who exceeded the import
quota regardless of whether they did so inadvertently of fraudulently was
excessive.

21–080   *[Add to Note 77:]*

Case C–103/96 *Directeur Général des Douanes et Droits Indirects v. Eridania Beghin-Say SA* [1997] E.C.R. I–1453.

21–081   *[Add new Note 79a at end of paragraph:]*

Claims based on infringement of the principle of proportionality were rejected in Case C–84/94 *United Kingdom v. Council (Working Time Directive Case)* [1997] I.C.R. 443; Case C–426/93 *Commission v. Germany* [1995] E.C.R. I–3723; Case C–233/94 *Germany v. Parliament and Council* [1997] E.C.R. I–2405.

Legal certainty and legitimate expectations

21–082   *[Add Note 79b after "must be clear" (second line of paragraph):]*

In Case C–143/93 *Van Es Douane Agenten v. Inspecteur der Invoerrechten en Accijnzen* [1996] E.C.R. I–431 the Court held that a Commission regulation concerning the classification of goods under the Common Customs Tariff was inapplicable for lack of clarity. *cf.* Case C–103/96 *Directeur Général des Douanes et Droits Indirects v. Eridania Beghin-Say SA* [1997] E.C.R. I–1453.

21–083   *[Add to Note 85:]*

For a recent case concerning the retroactive revocation of administrative acts, see Case C–90/95–P *Henri de Compte v. Parliament* [1997] E.C.R. I–1999.

[Add to Note 86:]

Sofrimport was distinguished in Case C–51/95 P *Unifruit Hellas EPE v. Commission* [1997] E.C.R. I–727.

Human rights[92]

21–090   *[Add to Note 11:]*

Reference to the objective of protecting human rights is made in the provisions of the Treaty on the Community development policy. See Article 130u(2) of the Treaty and Case C–268/94 *Portugal v. Council* [1996] E.C.R. I–6177.

166

[Add new paragraph 21-090A:]   **21-090A**

Opinion on the accession of the Community to the ECHR

In 1994 the Council sought the Opinion of the Court pursuant to Article
228(6) of the Treaty on whether the accession of the Community to the
European Convention for the Protection of Human Rights would be
compatible with the Treaty. In March 1996 the Court delivered its
Opinion (Opinion 2/94 [1996] E.C.R. I–1759). The Court considered that
the question of compatibility with the Treaty was not admissible because
no specific arrangements had been made at that stage concerning the way
in which the Community would become subject to the machinery of
judicial control established by the Convention. The Court examined
however whether the Community had competence to accede to the
Convention and came to a negative conclusion. The Court started by
referring to Article 3b of the Treaty which provides that the Community
may act only within the limits of the powers conferred upon it by the
Treaty and of the objectives assigned to it therein. It stated that no Treaty
provision confers on the Community institutions any general power to
enact rules on human rights or to conclude international conventions in
this field. In the absence of express or implied powers for this purpose, the
Court turned to examine whether Article 235 of the Treaty may constitute
a legal basis for accession. Article 235 provides that if, in the course of the
operation of the common market, action by the Community proves
necessary to attain one of the objectives of the Community and the Treaty
has not provided the necessary powers, the Council may, acting unanimously on a proposal from the Commission and after consulting the
European Parliament, take the appropriate measures. The Court stated that
Article 235 cannot serve as the basis for widening the scope of Community
powers beyond the general framework created by the provisions of the
Treaty as a whole. It pointed out that, under the case law, respect for
human rights is a condition of the lawfulness of Community acts. It stated
however that accession to the Convention would entail a substantial change
in the present Community system for the protection of human rights. It
would entail the entry of the Community into a distinct international
institutional system as well as integration of all the provisions of the
Convention into the Community legal order. The Court rejected by
implication the core argument in favour of competence submitted by the
Commission and by several Member States that respect for fundamental
rights is a component of all Community policies or, as the Commission
put it, a transverse objective forming an integral part of the Community's
objectives. It is notable that the Opinion contains scant discussion of that
argument which, it is submitted, is not unmeritorious. In view of the case
law of the Court, which emphasises that the Community is bound by
fundamental rights, and the references to human rights in the founding
Treaties, it is difficult not to regard the protection of such rights as part of

the Community objectives. Clearly, Article 235 may not be used to grant the Community institutions powers in areas which fall beyond the competence of the Community. Thus, it is not possible for the Council to legislate on the basis of that provision on fundamental rights in fields which do not otherwise fall within the scope of the Treaty. That does not mean however, that the Community does not have competence to accede to the Convention and be bound by it within the scope of application of Community law. Whether accession is compatible with Community law will depend on the specific arrangements concerning the relationship between the European Court of Human Rights and the European Court of Justice. For further comments on Opinion 2/94, see P. Allott, [1996] C.L.J. 409.

The right to be heard

21–091   *[Add to Note 13:]*

In principle, the Court of First Instance will not raise of its own motion a plea that the rights of the defence have been violated: Case T–106/95 *Fédération Française des Sociétés d' Assurances and others v. Commission*, [1997] E.C.R. II–229.

[Add to Note 14:]

By contrast, the rights of defence do not entitle a person to bring a direct action at the Court of First Instance without legal representation: C–174/96 P *Lopes v. Court of Justice* [1996] E.C.R. I–6401; Case C–175/96P *Lopes v. Court of Justice* [1996] E.C.R. I–6409.

Staff cases

21–092   *[Add at the end of the paragraph:]*

In *Ojha v. Commission* (Case C–294/95 P [1996] E.C.R. I–5863), the Court of Justice held, reversing the decision of the Court of First Instance, that where a Commission official is redeployed in the interests of the service, although redeployment is not a disciplinary offence, it may not take place on the basis of documents which concern the official's conduct in the service and which are not communicated to him. That would be contrary to Article 26 of the Staff Regulations which provide that documents contained in the personal file of an official may not be used by the institution against the official unless they have been communicated to him before they were filed. The purpose of that provision is to safeguard the official's rights of defence.

Other proceedings

[Add at the end of the paragraph:]   **21–098**

In *Lisrestal v. Commission* Case T–450/93 [1994] E.C.R. II–1177 the Court
of First Instance annulled a Commission decision reducing financial
assistance granted to the applicants from the European Social Fund to
support a vocational training scheme on the ground that the rights of
defence had been infringed. The Court of First Instance found that the
applicants were directly and adversely affected by the decision reducing
the assistance since they bore primary responsibility for the overpaid
sums. It concluded that the Commission could not adopt the contested
decision without first giving the applicants the possibility of setting forth
their views on the proposed reduction in assistance. On appeal, the Court
of Justice upheld the decision of the Court of First Instance (Case C–
32/95 P *Commission v. Lisrestal and Others* [1996] E.C.R. I–5373. The
Court dismissed the argument of the Commission that the respondents
were not concerned by the procedure leading up to the adoption of the
contested decision which was addressed to the competent authortiy of
the Member State concerned as interlocutor of the Fund. It held that the
contested decision, although not addressed to the respondents, was
"initiated against" them for the purposes of the rights of defence. See
further Case T–346/94 *France-Aviation v. Commission* [1995] E.C.R. II–
2841.

[Add new paragraph after 21–098a:]

Access to official documents

On December 6, 1993, the Council and the Commission adopted a Code
of Conduct concerning public access to documents in their possession
(93/730, [1993] O.J. L340, p. 41). The Council also adopted a decision on
public access to Council documents (93/731, [1993] O.J. L340. p. 43) and
by a separate decision made consequential amendments to its rules of
procedure (Decision 93/662 of December 6, 1993, [1993] O.J. L304, p. 1).
In Case C–58/94 *Netherlands v. Council* [1996] E.C.R. I–2169 the Court
dismissed an application for the annulment of those measures. It held that
the action against the Code of Conduct was inadmissible because the Code
was not intended to produce legal effects in itself but merely to set general
guidelines for furture specific measures. The Court rejected the action
against the other two measures as unfounded. The Dutch Government
argued that the Council could not adopt rules concerning the public's right
of access to information, which is a fundamental right, on the basis of
provisions relating to its internal organisation. The Court pointed out that
the public's rights of access to documents held by public authorities have

received "progressive affirmation" in the laws of the Member States. It held that, so long as the Community legislature has not adopted general rules on the right of public access to documents held by the Community institutions, it falls to the institutions themselves to take measures within their powers of internal organisations to enable them to respond to and to process such requests for access in a manner commensurate with the interests of good administration. In Case T–194/94 *Carvel and Guardian Newspapers v. Council* [1995] E.C.R. II–2765, the Court of First Instance held that it was unlawful for the Council to refuse access to certain documents pursuant to Article 4(2) of Decision 93/731, which enables the Council to refuse access in order to protect the confidentiality of its deliberations. The Court of First Instance held that, in exercising its discretion to refuse access, the Council must genuinely balance the interests of citizens in gaining access to its documents against any interest of its own in maintaining the confidentiality of its deliberations. In Case T–105/95 *World Wide Fund for Nature v. Commission* [1997] E.C.R. II–315 (see *The Times*, March 26, 1997), the Court of First Instance annulled the Decision of the Commission to refuse the applicant access to documents relating to its investigations into a possible breach of environmental law by Ireland, on the ground that the refusal was inadequately reasoned. The Court pointed out that exceptions to the right of public access to documents held by the Community institutions must be interpreted restrictively. Referring to its judgment in *Carvel*, it stated that where an institution relies on the exception of confidentiality of its proceedings, it must strike a genuine balance between the interests of the citizen in obtaining access to information and its own interest in protecting the confidentiality of its deliberations. It also held that the Commission may refuse on grounds of public interest access to documents relating to an investigation into a possible breach of Community law by a Member State. The Commission however may not merely invoke the possible opening of an infringement procedure against the Member State as justification. It is required to indicate, at the very least by reference to categories of documents, the reasons for which it considers that the documents requested are related to a possible opening of an infringement procedure. It should indicate to which subject-matter the documents requested relate and particularly whether they involve inspections or investigations relating to a possible procedure for infringement.

The requirement to state reasons

21–099   *[Add new Note 34a after "essential procedural requirement":]*

The Parliament may not bring an action for annulment on the ground that the contested act is insufficiently reasoned, as failure to state reasons does not in itself impair its prerogatives: Case C–156/93 *Parliament v. Commission*

[1995] E.C.R. I–2019; Case C–303/94 *Parliament v. Council* [1996] E.C.R. I–2943.

[Add to text:]

Since the purpose of the requirement to state reasons is to enable the Court to exercise its power of review, the plea that a statement of reasons is lacking or is inadequate may be raised by the Court on its own motion: Case C–166/95 P *Commission v. Daffix* [1997] E.C.R. I–983 however the Court is not under a duty to so and, depending on the circumstances of the case, it may reject as inadmissible a plea that the contested act is insufficiently reasoned if it is not submitted in time: Case T–106/95 *Fédération Française des Sociétés d' Assurances and others v. Commission* [1997] E.C.R. II–229.

[Add to Note 41:]   **21–100**

For a recent case where the Court annulled a Commission Decision on State aid, see Joined Cases C–329/93, 62/95 63/95 *Germany, Hanseatische Industrie-Beteiligungen GmbH and Bremer Vulkan Verbund AG v. Commission* [1996] E.C.R. I–5151. See also Case T–95/94 *Sytraval and Brink's France S.A.R.L. v. Commission* [1995] E.C.R. II–2651. By contrast, in Case C–166/95 P *Commission v. Daffix* [1997] E.C.R. I–983, the Court of Justice found that on the circumstances of the case the decision of the Commission to remove an official from office on grounds of misconduct was sufficiently reasoned and quashed the judgment of the CFI (Case T–12/94 [1995] E.C.R.–SC II–233). Similarly, in *Parliament v. Innamorati*, the Court held that in a competition for recruitment of Community officials, the criteria for marking adopted by the selection board are secret so that failure to communicate those criteria to an unsuccessful candidate does not breach the requirement to give reasons. Case C–254/95 P *Parliament v. Innamorati* [1996] E.C.R. I–3423, reversing the decision of the Court of First Instance in Case T–289/94 [1995] E.C.R.–SC II–393.

[Add to Note 47:]   **21–102**

For a politically sensitive case concerning the legal basis and the statement of reasons of a measure, see Case C–84/94 *United Kingdom v. Council (Working Time Directive Case)* [1997] I.C.R. 443.

JUDICIAL REVIEW OF NATIONAL MEASURES

Grounds of review

Fundamental rights

[Add: new Note 94a after "in the U.K. courts":]   **21–126**

For a recent decision of the Value Added Tax and Duties Tribunal applying

Article 6(1) of the European Convention on Human Rights in the context of Community rights see *Hodgson v. Commissioners of Customs and Exercise* [1997] Eu.L.R. 116, discussed below. See also in relation to Article 8: *U v. W* [1997] 2 C.M.L.R. 431.

21–126A   *[Add new paragraph 21–126A:]*

Issues pertaining to the protection of human rights arose in a number of cases concerning sanctions imposed by the Community to the Federal Republic of Yugoslavia. In Case C–84/95 *Bosphorus Hava Yollari Turizm ve Ticaret AS v. Minister for Transport and the Attorney-General* [1996] E.C.R. I–3953 in issue was Article 8 of Regulation No. 990/93 concerning trade between the Community and the Federal Republic of Yugoslavia ([1993] O.J. L102, p. 14). Article 8 required Member States to impound all vessels, freight vehicles and aircraft "in which a majority or controlling interest is held by a person or undertaking in or operating from the Federal Republic of Yugoslavia." Pursuant to that provision, the Irish authorities impounded an aircraft which Bosphorus Airways, a Turkish company, had leased from the Yugoslav national airline. The Court interpreted Article 8 as applying to an aircraft based in or operating from the Federal Republic of Yugoslavia even though the owner had leased it to another undertaking, which was neither based nor operating from there, and which was not controlled by Yugoslavian interests. The Court dismissed the argument of the Turkish company that such a broad interpretation of Article 8 infringed its fundamental right to property and its freedom to pursue a commercial activity. It held that any measure imposing sanctions has, by definition, consequences which affect the right to property and commercial freedom, thereby causing loss to innocent third parties. The importance of the aims pursued by the regulation was such as to justify negative consequences, even of a substantial nature. In Case C–177/95 *Ebony Maritime SA v. Prefetto della Provincia di Brindisi and Others* [1997] E.C.R. I–1111, the Court held that Regulation No. 990/93 did not preclude an Italian law which provided for confiscation of the cargo where a vessel infringed the provisions of the regulation even though the penalty of confiscation was provided without any proof of fault on the part of the owner of the cargo. The Court dismissed the argument that the Italian law violated the principle *nulla poena sine culpa* and that it was contrary to the principle of proportionality. It stated that a system of strict criminal liability is not in itself incompatible with Community law. Where it is for the Member States to provide sanctions for breach of Community measures, such sanctions must be analogous to those applicable to infringements of national law of a similar nature and also, in any event, they must be effective, proportionate and dissuasive. It is for the national court to determine whether the penalty of confiscation complies with those requirements. The Court however stated that, in making that determination, the national court had to take into account that the objective pursued by Regulation No. 990/93, which was to

bring to an end the state of war in the region concerned and the massive
violation of human rights, was one of fundamental general interest for the
international Community. For another case arising from the sanctions
against Yugoslavia, see Case C–124/95 *R. v. H.M. Treasury and Another, ex p.
Centro-Com S.r.l.* [1997] 3 W.L.R. 239.

The principle of proportionality

[Add new Note 97a after "under the Treaty":]　　　　　　**21–128**

For the application of the principle of proportionality to national measures
affecting the common commercial policy, see Case C–83/94 *Leifer and
Others* [1995] E.C.R. I–323; Case C–124/95 *R. v. H.M. Treasury and Another,
ex p. Centro-Com S.r.l.* [1997] 3 W.L.R. 239. In two recent cases, the Court
found that national provisions requiring security for costs in judicial
proceedings infringed Article 6 of the Treaty because they were disproportionate. See *Hayes v. Kronenberger GmbH* (Case C–323/95 [1997] E.C.R.
I–171); Case C–29/95 *Pastoors and Trans-Cap v. Belgian State* (Case C–29/95
[1997] E.C.R. I–285, discussed below at 21–142A.

[Add to Note 99:]　　　　　　**21–129**

For an example of the application of the principle of proportionality on
national consumer protection legislation restricting the free movement of
goods, see Case C–51/94 *Commission v. Germany* [1995] E.C.R. I–3599.

[Add to Note 4:]　　　　　　**21–131**

On confiscation, see also *Leifer* [1995] E.C.R. I–3231; Case C–84/95
*Bosphorus Hava Yollari Turizm ve Ticaret AS v. Minister for Transport and the
Attorney-General* [1996] E.C.R. I–3953, 1996; Case C–177/95 *Ebony Maritime SA v. Prefetto della Provincia di Brindisi and Others* [1997] E.C.R. I–1111,
discussed in para. 21–126A above.

21–132

[Add to Note 5:]

See also Case C–139/95 *Balestra v. Istituto Nazionale della Previdenza Sociale
(INPS)* [1997] E.C.R. I–549.

[Add new Note 6a after "but impossible, to answer":]　　　　　　**21–133**

Although in order to determine whether a national measure complies with
the principle of proportionality the Court will take into account whether
other less restrictive measures exists, a restriction imposed by a Member

State on a fundamental freedom will not necessarily fail the test of proportionality merely because another Member State imposes a less severe restriction. If that were so, Member States would need to align their legislation with the Member State which imposes the least onerous requirements. See Case C–384/93 *Alpine Investments* [1995] E.C.R. I–1141; Case C–3/95 *Reisebüro Broede v. Gerd Sandker* [1996] E.C.R. I–6511.

21–134   *[Add to Note 7:]*

De Peijper was followed in Case C–201/94 *R. v. Medicines Control Agency, ex p. Smith and Nephew Pharmaceuticals Ltd* [1996] E.C.R. I–5819.

[Add new Note 7a after "operating in a normal manner":]

For cases where the Court of Justice left ample discretion to the national court to apply the principle of proportionality, see C–83/94 *Leifer and Others* [1995] E.C.R. I–3231; Case C–85/94 *Piageme and Others v. Peeters* [1995] E.C.R. I–2955.

21–137   *[Add to Note 10:]*

see also Case C–101/94 *Commission v. Italy* [1996] E.C.R. I–2691; Case C–55/94 *Gebbard v. Consiglio dell'Ordine degli Avvocati e Procuratori di Milano* [1995] E.C.R. I–4165. In *Reisebüro Broede v. Gerd Sandker* (Case C–3/95, [1996] E.C.R. I–6511) the Court held that the provisions of the Treaty on the freedom to provide services do not preclude a national rule which reserves to persons who are qualified lawyers the professional recovery of debts by way of judicial proceedings. Such a restriction is not disproportionate to the aim of protecting the consumers of legal services and the sound administration of justice.

21–138   *[Add new Note 10a after "with different situations":]*

For the application of the principle of proportionality by English courts in cases involving claims based on Community law, see *R. v. Chief Constable of Sussex, ex p. International Trader's Ferry Ltd* [1997] 3 W.L.R. 132, discussed below; *Wilander and Another v. Tobin and Another* [1997] 2 C.M.L.R. 346; *U v. W* [1997] 2 C.M.L.R. 431.

Equality

21–140   *[Add at the end of the paragraph:]*

In Case C–237/94 *O'Flynn v. Adjudication Officer* [1996] E.C.R. I–2617, a preliminary reference was made concerning the Social Fund (Maternity and Funeral Expenses) Regulations 1987. The regulations provide for the granting of a funeral payment, a means-tested social benefit, to cover the costs associated with a person's funeral. The benefit covers the costs associated with burial or cremation but does not cover the cost of transporting the coffin at a place of burial which is distant from the deceased's home. Under the regulations, a funeral payment is made only if the funeral takes place in the United Kingdom. Mr Flynn, an Irish national resident in the United Kingdom as a former migrant worker, applied for a funeral payment in connection with his son's burial but his application was refused on the ground that the burial took place in Ireland. The Court held that the funeral payment is a social advantage within the meaning of Article 7(2) of Regulation No. 1612/68 on freedom of movement of workers within the Community and therefore migrant workers must enjoy it under the same conditions as national workers. It stated that conditions imposed by national law must be regarded as indirectly discriminatory where, although applicable irrespective of nationality, they affect essentially migrant workers or the great majority of those affected are migrant workers; where they are indistinctly applicable but can more easily be satisfied by national workers than by migrant workers; or where there is a risk that they may operate to the particular detriment of migrant workers. On that basis, the Court found the condition that the burial or cremation must take place in the United Kingdom indirectly discriminatory. It held that that condition was not justified by objective reasons such as the cost or practical difficulties of paying the benefit where the burial takes place outside the United Kingdom. The Court added that there was nothing to prevent the United Kingdom from limiting the allowance to a lump sum or reasonable amount fixed by reference to the normal cost of burial within the national territory. Following the judgment of the European Court, the Social Security Commissioner awarded to the claimant a funeral payment: Decision of June 19, 1997 by Mr J. Messher.

[Add new Note 15a after the new text:]

For indirect discrimination on grounds of sex, see: Case C–457/93 *Kuratorium für Dialyse und Nierentransplantation v. Lewark* [1996] E.C.R. I–243; C–278/93 *Freers and Speckmann v. Deutsche Bundespost* [1996] E.C.R. I–1165; *cf.* Case C–317/93 *Nolte v. Landesversicherungsanstalt Hannover* [1995] E.C.R. I–4625; and Case 444/93 *Megner and Scheffel v. Innungskrankenkasse Rheinhessen-Pfalz* [1995] E.C.R. I–4743 where the Court found that the exclusion of persons working less than 15 hours a week from the statutory sickness and old-age insurance schemes did not amount to indirect discrimination on grounds of sex as it was necessary to achieve social policy aims. See also C–400/93 *Royal Copenhagen* [1995] E.C.R. I–1275.

[Add new paragraph:]   **21–142A**

In two recent cases the Court considered the application of Article 6 of the Treaty, which prohibits discrimination on grounds of nationality, or national procedural rules. In *Data Delecta and Forsberg* Case C–43/95 [1996 E.C.R. I–4661 it held that Article 6 prohibits a Member State from requiring a person established in another Member State, who has brough before one of its own courts an action against one of its own nationals, tc lodge security for the costs of those proceedings where no such require ment is imposed on persons established in the first Member State and where the action is concerned with the exercise of fundamental freedoms guaranteed by Community law. In *Hayes v. Kronenberger GmbH* Case C–323/95, judgment of March 20, 1997, it was argued that the requirement that the plaintiff must lodge security for judicial costs is justified where ar order for judicial costs cannot be enforced in the country of the plaintiff' domicile. In such a case, the requirement to lodge security is designed tc avoid a foreign plaintiff being able to bring proceedings without running any financial risk should he lose his case. The Court pointed out that not all Member States are parties to the Brussels and to the Lugano Conventions and that, as a result, as between some Member States, it will be more difficult to enforce an order for costs made in a Member State against non residents. The Court held, however, that it was not necessary for the purposes of the proceedings in issue to consider whether that situatior might warrant the imposition of security for costs on non-residents where such risk existed. It focused on the German rule of procedure in issue. I held that, in so far as that rule imposed different treatment depending or the plaintiff's nationality, it ran counter to the principle of proportionality On the one hand, it could not secure payment of judicial costs in every trans-frontier case since security could not be required from a German plaintiff not residing in Germany and having no assets there. On the other hand, it was excessive because a non-German plaintiff who resided and had assets in Germany could also be required to furnish security. In *Chequepoin. S.A.R.L. v. McClelland and Another* [1997] Q.B. 51 the Court of Appeal held that a court order requiring an impecunious foreign company ordinarily resident in another Member State to provide security for costs was not discriminatory contrary to Community law since an English company in a similar position would be treated in the same manner and might be required to provide security for costs under the Companies Act 1985. For the obligation to lodge deposit in criminal proceedings, see Case C–29/95 *Pastoors and Trans-Cap v. Belgian State* (Case C–29/95 [1997] E.C.R. I–285

21–143A   *[Add new paragraph:]*

There is a close affinity between the principle of equal treatment and the protection of fundamental rights. In *P v. S and Cornwall County Counci* Case C–13/91 [1996] E.C.R. I–2143 the applicant in the main proceedings was dismissed from his employment following his decision to undergo general reassignment by surgical operation. The question was referred to the Court whether the Equal Treatment Directive (see below at 21–173,

. 61) precludes dismissal of a transexual for reasons related to a gender
reassignment. The Court held that, in view of sex equality as a fundamen-
al human right, the scope of the directive cannot be confined to
iscrimination based on the fact that a person is of one or other sex. It
tated that discrimination arising from gender reassignment is based
ssentially, if not exclusively, on the sex of the person concerned. Where a
erson is dismissed on the ground that he or she has undergone gender
reassignment, he or she is treated unfavourably by comparison with
ersons of the sex to which he or she was deemed to belong before
ndergoing gender reassignment. The Court concluded (at para. 22) that:

> "To tolerate such discrimination would be tantamount, as regards
> such a person, to a failure to respect the dignity and freedom to which
> he or she is entitled, and which the Court has a duty to safeguard".

The case provides a prime example of the way the Court views the
rinciple of equality as a general principle of Community law transcending
he provisions of Community legislation. In effect, the Court applied a
eneral principle of unwritten Community human rights law, according to
vhich discrimination on arbitrary criteria is prohibited, rather than the
rovisions of the Equal Treatment Directive, a literal interpretation of
vhich does not seem to support the Court's finding. By contrast, in Case
C-450/93 *Kalanke v. Freir Hansestadt Bremen* [1995] E.C.R. I–3051, the
Court found that the Bremen Law on Equal Treatment which provided for
ositive discrimination in favour of women was imcompatible with Article
(4) of the Equal Treatment Directive. For other issues concerning
iscrimination on grounds of sex, see Case C–137/94 *R. v. Secretary of State
r Health, ex p. Richardson* [1995] E.C.R. I–3407.

Protection of legitimate expectations

Add:]   21–145

The application of the principle of protection of legitimate expectations was
xamined recently in two cases concerning the recovery of unlawful State
ids. In Case C–169/95 *Spain v. Commission* [1997] E.C.R. I–135 the Court
dopted a decision finding that certain aid granted by Spain to a steel
oundry in Aragon was compatible with the common market. Following an
ction by an English company, the Court annulled the Commission
lecision (Case C–198/91 *Cooke v. Commission* [1993] E.C.R. I–2487). In
ompliance with the Court's judgment, the Commission initiated the
rocedure under Article 93(2) of the Treaty in order to assess the
ompatibility of the aid with the common market. By a new decision the
Commission declared the aid to be unlawful and ordered its recovery. The
Spanish Government argued that the decision ordering recovery frustrated
he legitimate expectations of the recipient undertaking. The Court held

that undertakings to which aid has been granted cannot, in principle entertain a legitimate expectation that the aid is lawful unless it has been granted in compliance with the procedure laid down in Article 93. A diligent operator should normally be able to determine whether that procedure has been followed. The fact that the Commission initially decided not to raise any objections to the aid in issue could not be regarded as capable of having caused the recipient undertaking to entertain any legitimate expectation since that decision was challenged in due time before the Court which annulled it. However regrettable it might have been, the Commission's error could not erase the consequences of the unlawful conduct of the Spanish authorities.

In Case C–24/95 *Land Rheinland-Pfalz v. Alcan Deutschland GmbH*, [1997] E.C.R. I–1591, the Court held that the competent national authority must revoke a decision granting unlawful aid even if the time-limit laid down under national law for the revocation of unlawful administrative acts has elapsed. Where State aid is found to be incompatible with the common market by the Commission, the national authorities do not have any discretion. Their role is merely to give effect to the Commission's decision. Since the national authorities have no discretion, the recipient of unlawfully granted State aid ceases to be in a state of uncertainty once the Commission has adopted a decision finding the aid incompatible with the common market and requiring recovery. The principle of legal certainty cannot therefore preclude repayment of the aid on the ground that the national authorities were late in complying with the decision requiring repayment. The Court also held that the competent authority must revoke a decision granting unlawful aid even if the competent authority is responsible for the illegality of the decision to such a degree that revocation appears to be a breach of good faith towards the recipient. The obligation to recover exists even where such recovery is excluded by national law because the gain no longer exists.

ENFORCEMENT OF COMMUNITY RIGHTS IN NATIONAL COURTS

The procedural rules applicable and the remedies available

21–148   *[Add to Note 27:]*

See further M. Hoskins, "Tilting the Balance: Supremacy and National Procedural Rules" (1996) 21 E.L.Rev. 365; A. Ward, "Effective Sanctions in EC Law: A Moving Boundary in the Division of Competence" (1995) 1 E.L.J. 205.

Procedural obstacles to the exercise of Community rights

Limitation periods

[Add to beginning of Note 36:]   **21–154**

See, *e.g.* Case C–435/93 *Dietz v. Stichting Thuiszorg Rotterdam*, [1996] E.C.R.
I–5223.

[Add new Note 36a after ". . . of a purely internal character":]

See further Case C–312/93 *Peterbroeck, van Campenhout & Cie SCS v.
Belgian State* [1995] E.C.R. I–4599, discussed below 21–172; Opinion of the
Advocate-General in Case C–90/94 *Haahr Petroleum*, Joined Cases C–114
115/95 *Texaco A/S* and Case C–242/95 *GT-Link A/S* delivered on February
27, 1997.

[Add to Note 40:]   **21–157**

On time-limits see also *Peterbroeck.* discussed below, 21–172 and see further
the Opinion of the Advocate-General in Case C–2/94 *Denkavit International
v. Kamer van Koophandel en Fabrieken voor Midden-Gelderland* [1996] E.C.R.
I–2827; and in Case C–90/94 *Haar Petroleum*, Joined Cases C–114 115/95
Texaco A/S and Case C–242/95 *GT-Link A/S* delivered on February 27,
1997.

Other obstacles in national law to the exercise of Community rights

Defence on passing-on qualified

[Add at the end of the paragraph:]   **21–163**

The Court re-examined the defence of passing on in Joined Cases C–192
to C–218/95 *Société Comateb and Others v. Directeur Général des Douanes et
Droits Indirects*, [1997] E.C.R. I–165. The dispute arose from the imposition
by French law of dock dues (*octroi de mer*) on the importation of goods
from other Member States to the French overseas departments. In
Administration des Douanes et Droits Indirects v. Legros and Others (Case
C–163/90 [1992] E.C.R. I–4625) the Court had found that dock dues were
charges having equivalent effect to customs duties and therefore incompatible with Community law. The Court however limited the temporal effect
of its judgment so that claims for refund could not be brought in relation
to dock dues paid before the date of the Court's judgment except by
claimants who has initiated proceedings before that date. In *Comateb*, the

applicants sought the recovery of dock dues paid on the importation of goods into Guadeloupe in the period between July 17, 1992, the day after the judgment in *Legros* was delivered, and December 31, 1992. Their claim however encountered an obstacle posed by national law. French law required a person liable to pay dock dues to incorporate them in the cost price of the goods sold. The applicants therefore were unable to obtain recovery since, under the French Customs Code, a person may obtain reimbursement of unlawfully paid duties only where they have not been passed on to the purchaser. The Court first pointed out that, in principle, a Member State is required to reimburse charges levied in breach of Community law. Referring to *San Giorgio*, it stated that repayment is not required where it is established that the person required to pay the charges has actually passed them on to other persons. The fact however that there is an obligation under national law to incorporate the charge in the cost price of goods does not mean there is a presumption that the entire charge has been passed on, even when failure to comply with that obligation carries a penalty. Accordingly, a Member State may resist repayment to the trader only where it is established that the charge has been borne in its entirety by someone other than the trader and that reimbursement would constitute unjust enrichment. If the burden of the charge has been passed on only in part, it is for the national authorities to repay the trader the amount not passed on. The Court also held that, even where the charge has been passed on, repayment to the trader of the amount thus passed on does not necessarily entail his unjust enrichment. The trader may claim that, although the charge has been passed on to the purchaser, its inclusion in the cost price has, by increasing the price of goods and reducing sales, caused him damage which excludes, in whole or in part, any unjust enrichment. Where domestic law permits the trader to plead such damage in the main proceedings, it is for the national court to give such effect to the claim as may be appropriate. Furthermore, traders may not be prevented from applying to the courts having jurisdiction, in accordance with the conditions laid down in *Brasserie du Pêcheur and Factortame* for reparation of loss caused by the levying of charges not due, irrespective of whether those charges have been passed on.

The duty of national courts not to apply national measures which obstruct the exercise of Community rights

21–172   *[Note 57:]*

Delete from "See further . . ." to end of note.

21–172A   *[Add new paragraphs after 21–172:]*

The duty of national courts to provide effective protection of Community rights does not extend so far as to require them to raise of their

own motion a point of Community law in all cases. That issue arose in
Case C–312/93 *Peterbroeck v. Belgian State* [1995] E.C.R. I–4599 and in
Joined Cases C–430 and C–431/93 *Van Schijndel and Van Veen v. SPF*
[1995] E.C.R. I–4705. *Peterbroeck* concerned the compatibility with Community law of certain provisions of the Belgian Income Tax Code. Under
the Code, a taxable person may contest the imposition of a tax before the
Regional Director of direct contributions. If his complaint fails, he may
appeal to the Court of Appeal against the decision of the Director. The
taxable person may submit to the Court of Appeal new arguments, namely
arguments other than those examined by the Director, within a period of
60 days. Arguments presented after that period are rejected as inadmissible.
In *Peterbroeck* the Belgian authorities imposed on a Dutch company tax at a
rate higher than that applicable to Belgian companies. Peterbroeck contested the tax, *inter alia*, on grounds of incompatibility with Community
law but raised the arguments based on Community law for the first time
before the Court of Appeal after the expiry of the 60 day time-limit. The
national court considered that the provisions of the Income Tax Code
prevented it from raising on its own motion a point which a taxpayer could
no longer raise before it but referred to the Court of Justice the question
whether those provisions were compatible with Community law. The
Court gave a negative reply. After recalling its case law that a national
procedural provision must not render the application of Community law
excessively difficult, the Court stated (at page 14) that in order to establish
whether that is the case, the following enquiry should be pursued;

> "... a national procedural provision ... must be analysed by
> reference to the role of that provision in the procedure, its progress
> and its special features, viewed as a whole before the various national
> instances. In the light of that analysis the basic principles of the
> domestic judicial system, such as protection of the rights of the
> defence, the principle of legal certainty and the proper conduct of
> procedure, must, where appropriate, be taken into consideration."

The Court held that although a 60 day time-limit is not objectionable *per
se*, the time-limit provided by the Belgian Code was incompatible with
Community law in the light of the special features of the applicable
procedure. The Court relied on four arguments. First, it pointed out that
the Court of Appeal was the first Court capable of making a reference for a
preliminary ruling as the Director of direct contributions was an administrative authority and as such not a court or tribunal within the meaning of
Article 177. Secondly, it stated that the 60 day time-limit started to run
from the time when the Director lodged a certified copy of the contested
decision. That meant that the period during which new pleas could be
raised by the appellant had expired by the time the Court of Appeal held its
hearing so that the Court of Appeal was denied the possibility of
considering the question of compatibility with Community law. Thirdly,
the Court stated that no other national court in subsequent proceedings

181

could consider of its own motion the question of compatibility. Fourthly, it held that the impossibility for national courts to raise points of Community law on their own motion does not appear to be reasonably justifiable by principles such as the requirement of legal certainty or the proper conduct of procedure.

21–172B   In *Van Schijndel* the Court was asked ro rule, on a preliminary reference by the Hoge Raad, on whether a national court is required to raise on its own motion a point of Community law in civil proceedings pending before it. Applying the *Rewe* case law (see above, paragraph 21–153), the Court held that where, by virtue of domestic law, national courts must raise on their own motion points of law based on binding domestic rules which have not been raised by the parties, such an obligation also exists in relation to binding rules of Community law. The Court went a step further holding that national courts must raise on their own motion points based on binding rules of Community law, where domestic law does not require but confers discretion on them to apply on their own motion binding rules of national law. That obligation is based on Article 5 E.C. and the duty to ensure the legal protection which persons derive from the direct effect of Community law. The Court held, however, that a national court is not required to raise on its own motion an issue concerning the breach of provisions of Community law where examination of that issue would oblige the national court to abandon the passive role assigned to it by going beyond the ambit of the dispute defined by the parties themselves and relying on facts other than those on which the party with an interest in application of those provisions bases his claim. That limitation should be considered in principle as correct. As the Court pointed out, it is justified by the principle that, in a civil suit, it is for the parties to take the initiative, the Court being able to act on its own motion only in exceptional cases where the public interest requires its intervention. That principle reflects conceptions prevailing in most of the Member States as to the relation between the State and the individual. It also safeguards the rights of defence and ensures proper conduct of the proceedings.

21–172C   The judgments in *Peterbroeck* and *Van Schijndel* are finely balanced. On the one hand, the Court recognises that in principle the protection of Community rights remains subject to the procedural rules of the national jurisdictions. On the other hand, *Peterbroeck* illustrates that the Court is prepared to take a broad view of what constitutes a national provision which makes the protection of Community rights "virtually impossible or excessively difficult". The judgments reflect the need to establish a balance between the procedural autonomy of the Member States and the effective protection of Community rights, and indicate that the Court prefers to follow a case-by-case approach rather than precipitate a major change in the procedural systems of the Member States.

The principle of effective judicial review

Add to Note 63:]   **21–175**

See also the Opinion of the Advocate-General in Joined Cases *R. v. Secretary of State for the Home Department, ex p. Mann Singh Shingara and Abbas Radiom,* discussed below, 21–177B.

Add to Note 64:]   **21–176**

The obligation to state reasons, however, applies only to individual decisions of the national authorities which have adverse legal effects on individuals and not to national rules of general application: Case C–70/95 *Sodemare SA and Others v. Fédération de Maisons de Repos Privées de Belgique (Femarbel) ASBL and Regione Lombardia,* [1997] E.C.R. I–3395.

Add to Note 65:]   **21–177**

On the right to a judicial remedy against action or inaction by the Community institutions, see Case C–282/95 P *Guérin Automobiles v. Commission,* [1997] E.C.R. I–1503.

Add new paragraphs:]   **21–177A**

Recently, the obligation to provide effective remedies has given rise to interesting case law both at national and at Community level. In *Hodgson v. Commissioners of Customs and Excise* [1997] Eu.L.R. 116, the Value Added Tax and Duties Tribunal held that judicial review was not a sufficient remedy capable of securing the effective protection of Community rights in the case of a person required to pay a penalty for failure to pay excise duties. The case concerned Article 5(3) of the Excise Duties (Personal Reliefs) Order 1992 which establishes a presusmption to the effect that where a person, upon entering the United Kingdom, imports from another Member State goods in excess of certain specified quantities he is presumed to have done so for a commercial purpose, and is therefore subject to a penalty if he has failed to pay excise duties, unless he satisfies the Commissioners to the contrary. In an earlier case (*Customs amd Excise Commissioners v. Carrier* [1995] 4 All E.R. 38) the Divisional Court had held that, according to Article 5(3), it was for the Commissioners to decide whether a person imported goods for a commercial purpose and that the magistrates were bound by that decision which was only subject to judicial review. In *Hodgson,* the Tribunal found that Article 5(3) did not properly implement Article 9(2) of Directive 92/12 on excise duties (see Council Directive 92/12 on the general arrangements for products subject to excise duty and on the holding, movement and monitoring of such products, 1991] O.J. L76, p. 1). It held that Article 9(2) provides for certain criteria

which Member States must take into account in order to establish whethe;
goods are imported for a commercial purpose but does not authoris(
Member States to adopt a provision such as that of Article 5(3) which, a;
interpreted by the Divisional Court, lays down an irrebuttable presump·
tion. The Tribunal took the view that the restriction of the availabl(
remedies to judicial review did not satisfy the two limbs of the *Rewe* test
namely the requirement of non-discrimination and the requirement o·
minimum protection. It concluded that an individual's Community lav·
rights include the procedural right to have any interference with hi
primary right (namely, in that case, the right to import tobacco for hi
personal use) effectively justiciable by the courts. (See further *Wilander an(
Another v. Tobin and Another* [1972] 2 C.M.L.R. 346.

21–177B   In Joined Cases C–65/95 and C–111/95 *R. v. Secretary of State for the Hom(
Department, ex p. Shingara and Radiom* ([1997] E.C.R. I–3343; see *The Times*
June 23, 1997) on a reference by the Queen's Bench Division, the Cour
had the opportunity to examine the legal remedies available to Communit)
nationals who are refused entry in the territory of a Member State or
grounds of public security. Mr Shingara, a French national, was refuse(
leave to enter the United Kingdom on grounds of national security. M
Radiom, who has both Iranian and Irish nationality, applied for a residenc(
permit but his application was rejected on grounds of national security
Under section 13(5) of the Immigration Act 1971, where a foreign nationa
is refused leave to enter on such grounds, he has no right of appea
although he may seek leave to apply for judicial review. One of the issue
referred for a preliminary ruling was whether the applicants had as a matte·
of Community law a right to appeal to an immigration adjudicator agains
the decisions refusing them entry. Article 8 of Directive 64/221 provide
that a Community national shall have the same remedies in respect of an·
decision concerning entry, or refusing the issue or renewal of a residenc(
permit, or ordering expulsion of the territory. "as are available to national
of the State concerned in respect of acts of the administration". Th(
applicants and the Commission argued that where nationals of a Membe
State have a specific right of appeal against any refusal of recognition o·
their right to entry, nationals of other Member States must have the sam(
right of appeal in respect of a similar refusal even if the reasons for th
refusal differ. The fact that both their cases concern the right of entry int(
the national territory provides a sufficient degree of similarity to requir
that judicial remedies of appeal must be available. The Court did not accep
that argument. It stated at paragraphs 30–31:

> "the two situations are . . . in no way comparable: whereas in the cas
> of nationals the right of entry is a consequence of the status o·
> national, so that there can be no margin of discretion for the State a
> regards the exercise of that right, the special circumstances which ma·
> justify reliance on the concept of public policy as against nationals o·
> other Member States may vary over time and from one country t(

another, and it is therefore necessary to allow the competent national authorities a margin of discretion (Case 41/71 *Van Duyn v. Home Office* [1974] E.C.R. 1337, paragraph 18).

Consequently, the reply to the . . . question is that on a proper construction of Article 8 of the directive, where under the national legislation of a Member State remedies are available in respect of acts of the administration generally and different remedies are available in respect of decisions concerning entry by nationals of that Member State, the obligation imposed on the Member State by that provision is satisfied if nationals of other Member States enjoy the same remedies as those available againt acts of the administration generally in that Member State."

It follows from the judgment that it is permissible for a Member State to   **21–177C**
reat nationals of other Member States less favourably than its own ationals with regard to the remedies available against decisions refusing ntry or ordering explusion from the national territory. The obligation ncumbent on the Member State is to make available to nationals of other Member States the same remedies as those provided against acts of the dministration generally in that Member State. The Court did not express view as to what the minimum content of such remedies must be. Two oints must be made however in this context. First, it follows from the ase law of the Court as a whole that such remedies must provide full and ffective protection. Secondly, Article 9 of Directive 64/221 provides for ninimum procedural guarantees for the persons concerned. The Advocate-General stated that a Community national is entitled to challenge a ecision refusing him leave to enter or ordering his explusion on grounds f public security or public policy by means of an effective remedy which nsures that "the entire administrative decision, including its substantive rounds, is subjected to judicial scrutiny." He stated that, in English law, he requirements of Article 8 are in principle satisfied by allowing the erson concerned to apply for judicial review. He added however the *caveat* hat if judical review of decisions concerning the entry or expulsion of oreign nationals did not allow the courts to undertake complete and ffective examination of such decisions, including review of their sub-tance, Community law would require such restrictions to be set aside.

In *Shingara and Radiom* the Court also examined Article 9 of Directive   **21–177D**
4/221. It held that, under Article 9(2), a decision refusing the issue of a irst residence permit or ordering expulsion of the person concerned before he issue of the permit must be referred for consideration to an indepen-lent authority as provided by Article 9(1) only where there is no right of ppeal to a court of law against that decision, or where such appeal may be mly in respect of the legal validity of the decision, or where the appeal annot have suspensory effect. Notably, the Advocate-General took the iew that the first two cases provided for by Article 9(1), namely, where here is no right of appeal to a court of law, or where such appeal may only

be in respect of the legal validity of the decision, are contrary to the genera
principles of Community law which guarantees individuals full and
effective judicial protection. The Court did not endorse that view
Referring to its previous case law, it stated that the purpose of Article 9 is
to provide minimum procedural guarantees for the persons concerned. I
pointed out that, where the right of appeal is restricted to the legality of the
decision, the purpose of the intervention of the independent authority is to
enable an exhaustive examination of all the facts and circumstances
including the expediency of the proposed measure, to be carried out before
the decision is finally taken.

Finally, in *Shingara and Radiom* the Court held that a national of a
Member State against whom an initial decision refusing entry into another
Member State has been made on grounds of public order or public security
has a right of appeal under Article 8 of the Directive and, if appropriate, a
right to obtain the opinion of an independent competent authority in
accordance with Article 9, with respect to a fresh decision taken by the
administrative authorities on an application made by him after a reasonable
period has elapsed since the last decision prohibiting him from entering the
country.

Compensation and damages

21–183   *[Add new Note 73a after "the chosen solution":]*

Contrast Case C–66/95 *R. v. Secretary of State for Social Security, ex p. Sutton*
judgment of April 22, 1997; [1997] E.C.R. I–2163 (see *The Times*, April 25
1997). See further Case C–180/95 *Draehmpaehl v. Urania Immobilienservic
ohG*, [1997] E.C.R. I–2195.

The liability of Member States in damages for breach of Community law

21–191A   *[Add new paragraphs:]*

In a series of important judgments the Court extended and clarified the
principle of Member State liability in damages.

Breach of Community law as a result of action by the national legislature

In *Brasserie du Pêcheur S.A. v. Germany; R. v. Secretary of State for Transport
ex p. Factortame Ltd (No. 4)* Joined Cases C–46 and C–48/93 [1996] Q.B
404 the Court held that liability in damages may arise not only where a
Member State fails to take implementing measures in order to transpose a

directive into national law but also where the national legislature by
positive action infringes a provision of the Treaty. The Court established
that Member State liability in damages is a universal principle. It held that
since the principle of State liability is inherent in the system of the Treaty,
it "holds goods for any case in which a Member State breaches Community law, whatever be the organ of the State whose act or omission was
responsible for the breach". It follows that a Member State is liable
irrespective of whether the breach which gave rise to the damage is
attributable to the legislature, the judiciary or the executive. Also liability is
not confined to breach of provisions which are not directly effective, the
right of reparation being "the necessary corollary" of, rather than a
substitute for, direct effect. The conditions which must be fulfilled in order
for State liability in damages to arise differ depending on the nature of the
breach of Community law. Where the breach emanates from the national
legislature in circumstances where the legislature has wide discretion
comparable to that of the Community institutions in implementing
Community policies, Community law confers a right of reparation where
three conditions are fulfilled:

(1) the rule of law infringed must be intended to confer rights on
    individuals;
(2) the breach must be sufficiently serious; and
(3) there must be a direct causal link between the breach of the
    obligation resting on the State and the damage sustained by the
    injured parties.

The second condition was not specified in *Francovich* but, as confirmed by
Dillenkofer (see below), failure to transpose a directive is in itself a serious
breach. In *Brasserie du Pêcheur* the Court listed the following factors as being
material in determining whether an infringement passes the threshold of
seriousness:

(i) the clarity and precision of the rule breached;
(ii) the measure of discretion left by that rule to the national
     authorities;
(iii) whether the infringement and the damage caused was intentional
      or involuntary;
(iv) whether any error of law was excusable or inexcusable;
(v) the fact that the position taken by a Community institution may
    have contributed towards the omission;
(vi) the adoption or retention of national measures or practices
     contrary to Community law.

In any event, a breach of Community law will be sufficiently serious if it **21–191B**
has persisted despite a judgment of the Court of Justice which establishes
the infringement in question. In *Brasserie du Pêcheur*, the Court drew a
distinction between the provisions of German law prohibiting the marketing of beer which did not conform to the requirements of German law on

the purity of beer and those prohibiting the import of beers containing additives. With regard to the first, the Court held that it would be difficul to regard the breach of Article 30 as an excusable error, since the incompatibility of the purity requirements with Article 30 was manifest in the light of earlier case law. By contrast, in the light of the existing case law, the criteria available to the national legislature to determine whether the prohibition of the use of additives was contrary to Community law wa significantly less conclusive until the judgment in the *Beer Case* (Case 178/84 *Commission v. Germany* [1987] E.C.R. 1227). The Court also gave guidelines with regard to the situation in *Factortame*. It stated that different considerations apply to the provisions of the Merchant Shipping Act 198 making registration of fishing vessels subject to the requirement of nationality and those imposing residence and domicile requirements for vessel owners and operators. The requirement of nationality constitute direct discrimination manifestly contrary to Community law. The breach committed therefore by imposing that requirement is sufficiently serious In assessing whether the requirements imposing residence and domicile are sufficiently serious the national court may take into account, *inter alia*, the particular features of the common fisheries policy, the attitude of the Commission, which made its position known to the United Kingdom in good time, and the assessments as to the state of certainty of Community law made by the national courts in the interim proceedings brought by individuals affected by the Merchant Shipping Act. A further consideration to be taken into account is whether the United Kingdom failed to adopt immediately the measures needed to comply with the Order of the President of the Court of Justice made in proceedings for interim measures requested by the Commission: see Case 178/84 *Commission v. Germany* [1987] E.C.R. 1227. If the United Kingdom failed to do so, that must be regarded by the national court as constituting in itself a serious breach.

21–191C   With regard to the third condition of liability, the Court held that it is for the national courts to determine whether there is a direct causal link between the breach of the obligation borne by the State and the damage suffered by the injured parties. The Court held that, subject to the right to reparation which flows directly from Community law, where the conditions of liability are satisfied the State must make reparation for the consequences of the loss caused in accordance with the domestic rules on liability, provided that the conditions for reparation laid down by national law are not less favourable than those relating to similar domestic claims and that they are not such as in practice to make it impossible or excessively difficult to obtain reparation. The Court held that the requirement of English law of proof of misfeasance in public office would make it in practice impossible to obtain reparation and is thus incompatible with Community law. It is therefore now patently clear that the judgment in *Bourgoin* is no longer a reliable authority. Under German law, where a legislative act is in breach of a higher-ranking national law, for example the

Constitution, a right of reparation ensues only where the applicant can be regarded as the beneficiary of the obligation breached. The Court held that such a restriction would also make it in practice impossible or extremely difficult to obtain effective reparation for loss or damage resulting from a breach of Community law.

In determining the conditions of State liability in damages the Court drew comparisons with the conditions governing the liability of the Community institutions under Article 215(2) of the Treaty. The Court held that the conditions under which the State may incur liability for damage caused to individuals by a breach of Community law cannot, in the absence of particular justification, differ from those governing the liability of the Community in like circumstances. It is submitted however that the comparison drawn by the Court is not necessarily reflected in the case law. It follows from the case law of the Court under Article 215(2) that, in determining whether a Community institution has manifestly and gravely disregarded its discretionary powers, the Court refers to two elements: (a) the effect of the measure on individuals, in other words, the degree of harm suffered by them as a result of the measure; and (b) the extent to which the law has been violated. The first element refers to the nature of the damage suffered rather than to the infringement *per se*. Under the case law, however, it is a necessary condition for the establishment of unlawfulness. In particular, a requirement which consistently appears in the case law is that, in order for liability to ensue, the damage alleged by the applicants must go beyond the bounds of the economic risks inherent in the activities in the sector concerned (see, *e.g.* Joined Cases C–104/89 and C–37/90 *Mulder v. Council and Commission* [1992] E.C.R. I–3061, paragraph 13). That element, however, is absent in the case of Member State liability in damages.

21–191D

With regard to the extent of reparation, the Court held in *Brasserie du Pêcheur* that it must be commensurate with the loss or damage sustained. Total exclusion of loss of profit as a head of damage for which reparation may be awarded cannot be accepted. Also, it must be possible to award specific damages, such as exemplary damages provided for by English law, pursuant to claims or actions founded on Community law, if such damages may be awarded pursuant to similar claims or actions founded on domestic law.

21–191E

Liability will be easier to establish where a Member State commits a breach of Community law in circumstances where it has limited discretion or no discretion at all. In *R. v. Ministry of Agriculture, Fisheries and Food, ex p. Hedley Lomas (Ireland) Ltd*, Case C–5/94, [1997] Q.B. 139 the United Kingdom imposed a general ban on the export of live animals to Spain for slaughter on the ground that their treatment in Spanish slaughterhouses was contrary to Directive 74/577 on stunning of animals before slaughter ([1974] O.J. L316, p. 10). The Directive seeks to avoid the unnecessary suffering of animals while being slaughtered. It does not provide for any procedures for monitoring compliance with its provisions. In accordance with the general ban, Hedley Lomas was refused an export licence for a quantity of sheep intended for slaughter in a Spanish slaughterhouse. The licence was refused even though, according to the information obtained by Hedley Lomas, the slaughterhouse in question had been approved since 1986 and was complying with Community directives on animal welfare and even though the United Kingdom authorities had no evidence to the contrary. Hedley Lomas applied to the referring court for a declaration that the refusal to issue an export licence ran counter to Article 34 and for damages. The United Kingdom authorities conceded that the refusal to issue an export licence was contrary to Article 34 but claimed that it was justified under Article 36. The Court held that recourse to Article 36 is not possible where Community directives provide for harmonisation of the measures necessary to achieve the specific objective which would be furthered by reliance upon that provision. The fact that Directive 74/577 did not lay down any Community procedure for monitoring compliance with its provisions made no difference. The Court added that a Member State may not unilaterally adopt, on its own authority, corrective or protective measures to obviate any breach by another Member State of Community rules. On the issue of damages, the Court found that the conditions of liability laid down in *Brasserie du Pêcheur* were fulfilled. With regard to the first condition, the Court recalled that Article 34 creates rights for individuals which national courts must protect. With regard to the seriousness of the breach, the Court held that where, at the time when it committed the infringement, the Member State in issue was not called upon to make any legislative choices and had only considerably reduced discretion, or even no discretion, the mere infringement of Community law may be sufficient to establish the existence of a sufficiently serious breach. The Court noted that on the circumstances of the case, the United Kingdom authorities were not even in a position to produce any proof of non-compliance with the Directive by the slaughterhouse to which the animals for which the export licence was sought were destined.

Failure to transpose a directive into national law

21–191F The judgment in *Francovich* was reiterated and extended in Joined Cases C–178, C–179, C–188–190/94 *Dillenkofer et al. v. Germany* [1997] Q.B. 259. The case arose from Germany's failure to implement the Package Travel Directive (Directive 90/314/EEC on package travel, package holidays and package tours, [1990] O.J. L158, p. 59) which seeks to protect the purchaser of package travel in the event of the insolvency of the travel operator. Article 7 provides that the organiser or retailer of package travel must provide the consumer with "sufficient evidence of security for the refund of money paid over and for the repatriation of the consumer in the event of insolvency". The Directive required implementation by December 31, 1992 but it was not implemented in Germany until 1994. The applicants were purchasers of package tours who, following the insolvency of their tour operators in 1993, either never left for their destination or incurred expenses to return home. Having failed to obtain reimbursement of the sums paid to the operators or the repatriation expenses, they sought compensation from the German State on the ground that, if Germany had implemented the Directive within the prescribed time-limit, they would have been protected against the insolvency of the tour operators.

In *Dillenkofer* it was argued by several governments that a State may incur liability for late transposition of a Directive only where there has been a serious breach of Community law. The Court declined to accept that argument. It stated that failure of a Member State to implement a Directive within the prescribed period is *per se* a serious breach of Community law and, consequently, it gives rise to a right of reparation for individuals subject to the conditions of liability provided for in *Francovich*. No other condition need be taken into consideration. In particular, liability does not depend on the circumstances which caused the period of transposition to be exceeded. The Court stated expressly that liability in damages does not depend on the prior finding by the Court of an infringement of Community law attributable to the State; nor on the existence of intentional fault or negligence on the part of the State. The Court proceeded to examine whether the first two conditions of liability provided for in *Francovich* were fulfilled in relation to the Package Travel Directive and held that Article 7 of the Directive intended to grant rights to individuals whose content was sufficiently indentifiable.

Incorrect transposition of a directive

In *R. v. H.M. Treasury, ex p. British Telecommunications plc*, Case C–392/93 **21–191G** [1996] Q.B. 615 the Court held that the conditions provided for in *Brasserie du Pêcheur* must also be fulfilled in order for liability to arise where a Member State incorrectly transposes a directive into national law. In issue was Article 8(1) of Directive 90/531 on the procurement procedures of entities operating in the water, energy, transport and telecommunications sector. The Court found that the United Kingdom had interpreted the directive erroneously and, as a result, it had implemented it incorrectly but held that the incorrect implementation did not amount to a serious breach. The Court stated that Article 8(1) was imprecisely worded and was reasonably capable of bearing the interpretation given to it by the United Kingdom in good faith. That interpretation was shared by other Member States and was not manifestly contrary to the wording of the directive and the objectives pursued by it. Also, no guidance was available to the United Kingdom from the case law of the Court with regard to the interpretation of Article 8. Finally, the Commission did not raise the matter when the

191

implementing legislation was adopted. It is submitted that the last proposition should be treated with caution. The fact that the Commission
considers that the interpretation which a Member State has given to a
directive is incorrect is a factor of lesser importance. The most important
factor seems to be the existence of case law which can offer guidance on
the issue whether the interpretation given by the Member State is tenable.

Interim measures

*Interim relief in the English courts to suspend national measures implementing
Community regulations*

21–197A *[Add new paragraphs:]*

The power of national courts to provide interim relief was extended in
Atlanta. (Case C–465/93 *Atlanta Fruchthandelsgesellschaft (I) v. Bundesamt für
Ernährung und Forstwirtschaft* [1995] E.C.R. I–3761; see also Case C–334/95
Krüger GmbH & Co. KG v. Hauptzollamt Hamburg-Jonas, judgment of July
17, 1997; and *R. v. Licensing Authority* established by the Medicines Act
1968, *ex p. Generics (U.K.) Ltd and E.R. Squibb & Sons* [1997] 2 C.M.L.R.
201). The difference between *Zuckerfabrik* and *Atlanta* is that whereas in the
first interim protection was sought to preserve the status quo, in the
second it was sought to establish a new situation. The applicants were
importers of bananas from third countries who, in proceedings before a
German court, challenged the validity of the Bananas Regulation (Council
Regulation No. 404/93, [1993] O.J. L47, p. 1 examined by the Court in
Case C–280/93 *Germany v. Council* [1994] E.C.R. I–4973) and by way of
interim relief requested import licences in addition to those which they
had been granted pursuant to that regulation. The Court held that the
interim protection which national courts must afford to individuals must
be the same whether they seek suspension of enforcement of a national
measure adopted on the basis of a Community regulation or the grant of
interim measures settling or regulating the disputed legal positions or
relationships for their benefit. The Court dismissed the argument that the
grant of such interim relief has more radical consequences for the
Community legal order. It held that the consequences of the interim
measure, whatever they may be, for the Community legal order must be
assessed as part of the balancing exercise performed by the national court
between the Community interest and the interests of the individual. In
Atlanta the Court also clarified the conditions for granting interim relief
laid down in *Zuckerfabrik* providing, among others, the following
guidelines:

> (a) When making the interim order, the national court must set out
> the reasons for which it considers that, in the preliminary
> reference proceedings, the Court of Justice should find the
> regulation invalid.

(b) In assessing whether the regulation may be declared invalid by the Court of Justice, the national court must take into account the discretion enjoyed by the Community institutions in the sector concerned. Thus in the field of the common agricultural policy, regard must be had to the established case law of the Court according to which the Community institutions enjoy a wide margin of discretion which reflects their political responsibilities.

(c) In considering the damage which may be caused to the regime established by the regulation if interim measures are ordered, the national court must take into account, on the one hand, the cumulative effect which would arise if a large number of courts were also to adopt interim measures for similar reasons and, on the other hand, the special features of the applicant's situation which distinguish him from all other operators concerned.

(d) In accordance with Article 5 of the Treaty, the national court must respect the case law of the Community courts. Thus if the Court of Justice has dismissed on the merits an action for annulment of the regulation in issue, the national court can no longer order interim measures or must revoke existing ones unless the grounds of illegality submitted to it differ from those rejected by the Court in its judgment. The same applies if the Court of First Instance has dismissed on the merits an action for annulment of the regulation by a final judgment.

With regard to the Bananas Regulation, the Court pointed out in *Atlanta* that in previous proceedings challenging the validity of the regulation brought by the German Government under Article 173, the Court had dismissed the application for interim measures (Case C–280/93 R *Germany v. Council* [1993] E.C.R. I–3667) The national court was bound to accept the findings made by the Court of Justice in the context of that application concerning the serious and irreparable nature of the damage, unless the applicant before the national court was able to show a specific situation which distinguished him from other operators ins the relevant sector. The Court therefore left open the possibility of a national court granting interim measures even in a case where the Court of Justice has refused to grant interim measures against the same regulation in proceedings before it brought by a Member State. This is understandable given that the type of damage which an interim order seeks to avoid differs in the two cases. Where a Member State brings annulment proceedings against a regulation and seeks interim measures in the context of that action, it acts in the national public interest and is entitled to invoke damage suffered by a whole sector of the economy. Where an individual trader brings proceedings and seeks interim protection, he invokes the damage suffered by him in his private capacity.

National courts do not have the power to order interim protection where, **21–197B** by virtue of a Community regulation, the existence and scope of individual rights must be established by another Community measure implementing the regulation and that measure has not yet been adopted. In *Port GmbH v. Bundesanstalt für Landwirtschaft und Ernährung*, [1996] E.C.R. 6065 Case C–68/95, (judgment of November 26, 1996) an undertaking importing bananas claimed on grounds of hardship import licences in addition to those it was entitled under the Bananas Regulation. On a reference for a preliminary ruling by the Higher Administrative Court of Hesse, the Court held that Article 30 of the Bananas Regulation enables and, depending on the circumstances, even requires the Commission to lay down transitional rules providing for the allocation of additional import licences in cases of hardship. However, the Court held that the national court did not have power to grant additional import licences to the undertaking concerned by way of interim measure in the context of national proceedings in which the validity of the Bananas Regulation was contested. The Court distinguished the case in issue from *Zuckerfabrik* and *Atlanta*. The case in issue concerned granting traders interim protection in a situation where, by virtue of a Community regulation, the existence and scope of traders' rights was to be established by a Commission measure which the Commission had not yet adopted. The Court pointed out that the Treaty makes no provision for a preliminary reference by which a national court may ask the Court of Justice to rule that an institution has failed to act. Consequently, national courts have no jurisdiction to order interim measures pending action on the part of the institution. Judicial review of alleged failure to act can be exercised only by the Community judicature.

Conclusions

21–204A *[Add new paragraphs:]*

It is not accidental that the most important developments in the sphere of Community public law in the last two years concern the enforcement of Community rights in national courts. The more the Community legal system develops, the greater the role national courts are called upon to play in the protection of Community rights. Undoubtedly, the judgments of the Court of Justice on Member State liability in damages mark a new stage in the evolution of the law of remedies. Overall, it can be said that those judgments are balanced and do not result in an unwarranted extension of State liability (see further T. Tridimas, "Member State Liability in Damages" [1996] C.L.J. 412). Liability is easy to establish where a Member State fails to take implementing measures in order to transpose a directive into national law, but much more difficult to establish in any other case. The response of English courts to the incoming tide of Community law continues to be a positive one. In the overwhelming majority of cases concerning Community law, domestic courts have assimilated and applied the principles laid down in the case law of the Court of Justice. In areas not affected by the Community legal order, however, domestic courts have been reluctant to import the methodology and the approach of the Community judicature. (See, *e.g.* in relation to the principle of legitimate expectations, the judgment of the Court of Appeal in *R. v. Secretary of State for the Home Department, ex p. Hargreaves* [1997] 1 W.L.R. 906; *cf. R. v. Ministry for Agriculture, Fisheries and Food, ex p. Hamble (Offshore) Fisheries Ltd* [1995] 2 All E.R. 714; and *R. v. Secretary of State for Transport, ex p. Richmond-upon-Thames L.B.C.* [1994] 1 W.L.R. 74).

In the last two years, English courts were called upon to apply Community **21–204B** law in a number of cases. Although most cases before English courts where Community rights are in issue pertain to employment and social law, a number of important cases have arisen concerning free movement (see, *e.g.* on the free movement of persons *R. v. Secretary of State for the Home Department, ex p. Gallagher* [1996] 1 C.M.L.R. 543; *Sahota v.Secretary of State for the Home Department; Zeghraba v. Secretary of State for the Home Department, The Times,* April 30, 1997; on the free movement of services *U v. W* [1997] 2 C.M.L.R. 431. *R. v. Human Fertilisation and Embryology Authority, ex p. Blood* [1997] 2 W.L.R. 806). A recent case of particular interest is *R. v. Chief Constable of Sussex, ex p. International Trader's Ferry Ltd* [1997] 3 W.L.R. 132. Owing to intense protests by animal rights groups in the first months of 1995, ITF was unable to export livestock to other Member States without the presence of a substantial police force at the port of export. In April 1995, the police informed ITF that in view of the costs involved and its responsibilities to keep the peace in other areas, it would restrict police services to two consecutive days per week. In those days when police cover was not provided, the movement of livestock was effectively prohibited as the police announced that it would turn back livestock vehicles if it anticipated a breach of the peace. The Divisonal Court rejected ITF's claim that the Chief Constable had exercised his discretion unreasonably within the meaning of the *Wednesbury* test. It held however that the Chief Constable's decision was a measure having equivalent effect to quantitative restrictions on exports contrary to Article 34 of the Treaty and that it was not saved by Article 36. Balcombe L.J. held that a public authority may not rely on the effect of civil disturbances as affording a defence on grounds of public policy under Article 36, provided that the resources are available to deal with such disturbances and the cost of doing so is not disproportionate. On the facts of the case, the Chief Constable had made no effort to increase the financial resources available to him and was therefore unable to prove that he had inadequate resources to police the port on a regular basis. The judgment of the Divisional Court was reversed by the Court of Appeal. Kennedy L.J. held that the need to ensure proper policing and to prevent crime where matters of public policy within the meaning of Article 36 and that, in view of the finite manpower and financial resources at the disposal of the Chief Constable, the restriction on exports resulting from his decision complied with the principle of proportionality. Given that the dispute gave rise to issues not covered by the case law of the Court of Justice, it is surprising that the Court of Appeal did not even consider the possibility of making a preliminary reference. Also, one may have sympathy with the decision of the Divisional Court that the Chief Constable should have at least asked the police authority to seek special financial assistance from the Home Office, even if it was apparent that such assistance would not be forthcoming. First, a public authority is under a duty to use its best endeavours to obtain the necessary finance to enforce Community law. Secondly, a formal request for financial assistance would satisfy the requirements of legal certainty in that it would enable the trader concerned to know precisely which authority has taken the decision affecting his rights and the reasons for it, and therefore seek redress against the proper defendant. The decision of the Court of Appeal leaves open the fundamental issue to what extent a national law enforcement authority may deny protection to Community rights on the ground that it would require excessive public expenditure. (Leave to appeal has been granted by the House of Lords: see [1997] 1 W.L.R. 1092).

21–204C   References for preliminary rulings were made in several cases involving diverse aspects of Community law. In *R. v. Secretary of State for Employment, ex p. Seymour-Smith and Another* [1997] 1 W.L.R. 473, the applicants challenged the requirement of the Unfair Dismissal (Variation of the Qualifying Period) Order 1985, which made claims for unfair dismissal subject to a qualifying period of two years' employment, on the ground that it infringed Community sex equality law. The House of Lords, reversing the decision of the Court of Appeal, held that it was *acte clair* that a directive may not produce horizontal direct effect, that an individual had no right to a mandamus against the State requiring that a directive be implemented, and that declaratory relief was not appropriate on the circumstances of the case as it would not change the legal position of the applicants. The House of Lords referred to the Court of Justice the question whether the right of compensation for unfair dismissal constitutes "pay" for the purposes of Article 119 of the Treaty. In *R. v. Ministry of Defence, ex p. Smith* [1996] Q.B. 517 the Court of Appeal held that discrimination on grounds of sexual orientation was not prohibited by the Sex Equality Directive and refused to make a reference to the Court of Justice on the interpretation of the directive. In *R. v. Ministry of Defence, ex p. Perkins* [1996] 1 All E.R. 257, however, on facts similar to those in *Smith*, Lightman J. decided to refer the question whether the Equal Treatment Directive prohibits discrimination on grounds of sexual orientation. In deciding to make a reference, Lightman J. took into account in particular the judgment of the Court of Justice in *P v. S* [1997] I.R.L.R. 297 and considered that, on the circumstances of the case, little importance should be attached to the fact that in *Smith* the House of Lords had refused leave to appeal. A similar issue has been referred to the Court of Justice in

Grant v. South West Trains Ltd (unreported). The issue in that case is whether the applicant, a female employee, is the victim of sex discrimination because she has been refused by her employer certain travel concessions, which were available to her predecessor for his common law wife, on the grounds that her partner is of the same sex. The difference between Grant and Perkins is that, in the first, the applicant is engaged in a lesbian relationship whereas, in the second, the only relevant factor is the existence of a state of mind, namely orientation, and not a manifestation of it. Following the judgment in P v. S, it was inevitable that issues such as those referred in Grant and Perkins would arise.

By contrast, no reference for preliminary ruling was made in R. v. Ministry of Agriculture Fisheries and Food, ex p. First City Trading Ltd [1997] 1 C.M.L.R. 250 or in R. v. Human Fertilisation and Embryology Authority, ex p. Blood 1997] 2 W.L.R. 806. In the latter case, on the basis of the case law of the Court of Justice on Article 59, Lord Woolf M.R. held that refusal of the Human Fertilisation and Embryology Authority to allow the export of the sperm of a deceased man to another Member State for the purposes of artifical insemination was a restriction on the freedom to provide services which would be compatible with Community law only if the Authority were able to justify it in the public interest.

PART VI

JUDICIAL REVIEW IN CONTEXT

CHAPTER 22

PLANNING

Introduction

[Note 2, delete and substitute "Now Secretary of State for the Environment, **22–002**
Transport and the Regions". Henceforth:]

"The Secretary of State".

[Note 3, delete "V. Moore, A Practical Approach to Planning Law (4th ed., 1994)"
and substitute:]

"V. Moore, *A Practical Approach to Planning Law* (6th ed., 1997).

The Development Plan

The content of development plans

[Note 11, delete: "A certificate of conformity is required under section 36(4) of the **22–010**
Act", and substitute:]

"s. 36(4); a certificate of conformity is required under s. 46(2) of the Act."

Public participation and inquiries into plans

[Note 25, insert after "Reg. 16 of the Development Plan Regulations.",:] **22–016**

See *Miller and Others v. Wycombe District Council* ([1997] J.P.L. 951) (part of
authority's local plan quashed where there had been a deficiency of reasons
given for the decision made to disagree with Inspector's findings).

Delete "Today it may be said that this procedure rarely effects rights, direct interests or **22–017**
legitimate expectations at this stage (they might be affected at the stage of development
control, which we shall consider below). In any event, appeal to common law
principles of fairness would be unlikely to succeed in view of the existence of an
extensive statutory code" and substitute:]

Although it may be said that this procedure does not generally affect rights, direct interests or legitimate expectations at this stage (they might be affected at the stage of development control, which we shall consider below), there is, nevertheless, an obligation on those who both propose and decide on the content of the plan to act fairly in considering objections to it. Appeals to the common law principles of fairness have been successful, notwithstanding the existence of an extensive statutory code. [Moore, pages 63–4)]

[Note 30: insert after "See Chap. 3 paras 3–013–3–018 above":]

"See, *e.g. Harlowby Estates Ltd and Another v. Harlow D.C.* [1997] J.P.L. 541 (provisions of local plan which included the applicant's land in green belt quashed following finding that inquiry failed to address objections raised by the applicant, or alternative proposals. The need to act fairly required that a further inquiry should have been held.)"

DEVELOPMENT CONTROL

22–018   *[Note 36: insert after "See, e.g. St Albans D.C. v. Secretary of State for the Environment [1993] J.P.L. 374":]*

"; *Loup (M.D.T.) v. Secretary of State for the Environment and Salisbury D.C.* [1996] J.P.L. 22 (where a development plan has been newly approved, the policies in it will have more weight in the scale than policies the relevance or force of which have been overtaken by events)." And see *City of Edinburgh Council v. Secretary of State for Scotland* [1997] 1 W.L.R. 1447 (H.L.)—the weight to be accorded respectively to the development plan and other material considerations could only be overridden by the Courts where the decision-maker had taken into account irrelevant considerations, had failed to take into account relevant considerations or had acted irrationally or perversely).

[Delete "However, it was always assumed that there was in general, and outside of specially protected areas, a presumption in favour of permitting development unless the development would 'cause demonstrable harm to interests of acknowledged importance.'" and substitute:]

It was presumed that there was in general, and outside of specially protected areas, a presumption in favour of permitting development unless the development would "cause demonstrable harm to interests of acknowledged importance". However, this formulation has been replaced with a weaker requirement that "Those deciding such planning applications or appeals should always take into account whether the proposed development would cause demonstrable harm to interests of acknowledged importance".

[Note 37: delete "See, e.g. P.P.G. 1 (1992), paras. 25–28" and substitute:]

Compare P.P.G. 1 (1992), paras. 25–28, and P.P.G. 1 (1997), para. 40.

Pre-application procedures

[Note 39: delete "Art. 8 of the General Development Order (Town and Country   **22–020**
Planning (General Permitted Development) Order 1995 (S.I. 1995 No. 418)" and
substitute:]

Art. 8 of the Town and Country Planning (General Development Procedure) Order 1995 (S.I. 1995 No. 419).

[Note 40: insert after ". . . E.C. Directive No. 85/337":]

, as amended by E.C. Directive No. 97/11'.

[Delete ". . . Department of the Environment. . ." and substitute:]   **22–023**

Department of the Environment, Transport and the Regions. . .

[Note 48: delete ". . . ECG Construction Ltd v. Secretary of State for the
Environment [1994] E.G.C.S. 143" and substitute:]

ECC Construction Ltd v. Secretary of State for the Environment [1994] J.P.L. 322.

[Add the following new paragraph after 22–023:]

A further example of the expansion of planning's concerns is environmental protection. Although the environmental effects of a development has always been a material consideration, the implementation of the E.C. Directive on Environmental Assessment has meant that certain projects must be subject to a more formalised environmental assessment procedure. (See Directive 85/337/EEC on the assessment of the effects of certain public and private projects in the environment [1985] O.J. L175, p.40.) Under the main set of implementing regulations, the Town and Country Planning (Assessment of Environmental Effects) Regulations 1988, (S.I. 1988 No. 1199, as amended), a local planning authority must not grant planning permission for any development of land to which the Regulations apply, unless they first take into account environmental information. The weight to be given to this environmental information and the power to control adverse environmental effects under pollution control legislation in determining applications for planning permission is a matter for the particular decision maker. (*Gateshead MBC v. Secretary of State for the*

Environment (1993) 67 P.&C.R. 179, (the environmental impact of emissions into the atmosphere was a material consideration in determining planning applications, but so too was the existence of pollution controls). Planning policy guidance has since confirmed that the planning and pollution control regimes are complementary, and that the dividing line between the two systems is not always clear, but that the planning system should not be operated so as to duplicate pollution controls. (See Planning Policy Guidance Note 23, *Planning and Pollution Control* (1994).

Conditions

22–027   *[Add to Note 53:]*

See Circular 11/95 as "The Use of Conditions in Planning Permission".

PLANNING BY AGREEMENT

22–036   *[Note 77: delete "This approach is similar to that set out in Circular 16/91 'Planning Obligations', which states (in para. B7) that 'Unacceptable development should never be permitted because of unrelated benefits offered by the applicant. . .', and applies (in para. B9) a test that when an obligation is acceptable, the extent of what is required should 'fairly and reasonably relate in scale and kind to the proposed development. Thus a developer may reasonably be expected to pay for or contribute to the cost of infrastructure which would not have been necessary but for his development, but his payments should be directly related in scale to the benefits which the proposed development will derive from the facilities to be provided. . ."' and substitute:]*

This approach is similar to that set out in Circular 1/97 "Planning Obligations", which states (in para. B2) that planning obligations "should only be sought where they are *necessary* to make a proposal acceptable in land-use planning terms", and applies (in para. B12) a test that when an obligations is acceptable, the extent of what is sought or offered should be "fairly and reasonably related in scale and kind to the proposed development . . . Developers may reasonably be expected to pay for or contribute to the cost of infrastructure which would not have been necessary but for the development. The effect of such infrastructure investment may be to confer some wider benefit but payments should be directly related in scale to the benefit which the proposed development will derive from the facilities to be provided. . .".

[Note 81:]

The *Tesco* case is now reported at [1995] 1 W.L.R. 759. Add at the end of the note: see the critical view of planning obligations contained in the third report of the Committee on Standards in Public Life, Cm. 3702–1 (July 1997), Vol. 1, Chap. 6 and Appendix 2.

[Note 85: insert after "s. 171C and 171D",:]   **22–038**

; *R. v. Teignbridge District Council ex p. Teignmouth Quay Co. Ltd* [1995] J.P.L. 828.

[Note 87: delete "Or that the steps required by the notice to be taken are exceeded what is necessary to remedy the breach. Ibid. s. 172(2)." and substitute:]

Or that the steps required by the notice to be taken exceed what is necessary to remedy the breach. *Ibid.* s. 174(2).

[Note 92: insert after ". . .Runneymede D.C. v. Harwood [1994] J.P.L. 724",:]   **22–039**

and where there are difficulties in ascertaining precisely who has the power to remedy the breach (*London Borough of Hillingdon v. Guinea Enterprises Ltd* [1997] J.P.L. B11.

APPEALS

[Note 97: delete "In 1993/94 14,113 appeals were decided in England. Report of   **22–041**
the Planning Inspectorate, 1993/4", and substitute:]

in 1995/6 12,236 appeals were decided in England. Report of the Planning Inspectorate, 1995/6.

[Note 99: delete "Town and Country Planning (Determination of Appeals by Appointed Persons) (Prescribed Classes) Regulations 1981 (S.I. No. 804)" and substitute:]

Town and Country Planning (Determination of Appeals by Appointed Persons) (Prescribed Classes) Regulations 1997 (S.I. 1997 No. 420).

CHAPTER 23

REVENUE

Appeals Tribunals

Note 19:]   23–006

ohn Dee Ltd v. Customs and Excise Commissioners was upheld by the Court of
\ppeal: see [1995] S.T.C. 941. The VAT Tribunal's jurisdiction in cases
·oncerned with appeals about the provision of security should be regarded
ıs appellate as opposed to supervisory. The Court preferred describing the
urisdiction as appellate in order to emphasise the fact that the Tribunal's
urisdiction is statutory and the grounds upon which the Tribunal can
ıllow an appeal are therefore dependent upon the correct construction of
he provisions conferring jurisdiction upon it. However, as counsel for the
Commissioners noted, in cases where the Tribunal cannot completely
·eassess the position in the light of all the evidence before them, the
grounds upon which the Tribunal can interfere with a decision are likely to
)e similar to, if not identical to, those upon which a Court acts in judicial
·eview proceedings.

Add to Note 21:]

;ee n. 19, above.

Add to Note 22 after Shepherd (Lon/93/1197) [1994] S.T.I. 543:]

This decision of the VAT Tribunal must now, however, be considered
vrongly decided in the light of the High Court decision in *Customs and
ixcise Commissioners v. Arnold* [1996] S.T.C. 1271.

Non-appellate Proceedings in the High Court

Original jurisdiction

Add new paragraphs:]   23–007

In *British Steel v. Customs and Excise Commissioners* [1996] 1 All E.R. 1022
British Steel claimed that it was entitled to a refund of duty that it had paid

on oil on the basis that it was "an approved person" using the oil for a qualifying purpose. It commenced proceedings for a refund on that basis. The Commissioners did not consider it was using the oil for a qualifying purpose and therefore had never approved British Steel as an "approved person". Laws J. stated that the proceedings were misconceived, British Steel had to be an "approved person" before it had a private law right to the money and the refusal of approval was a public law decision which had to be challenged in judicial review proceedings. The Court of Appeal allowed an appeal, on the basis that British Steel might be able to prove that it was an "approved person" and if it could it would have a restitutionary claim: see [1997] 2 All E.R. 366.

In *R. v. Customs and Excise Commissioners, ex p. Kay* [1996] S.T.C. 1500 Customs decided not to refund overpayments of VAT because of impending legislation that restricted claims to sums overpaid in the preceding three years. Declaratory relief was granted that the applicants were entitled to payment forthwith and that the Commissioners could not rely on the proposed legislation to delay making repayments.

[Note 25:]

R. v. Inland Revenue Commissioners, ex p. Barker is now reported at [1994 S.T.C. 731. (Taxpayer sought to argue that he was not, on the proper construction of Taxes Management Act 1970, s. 86 liable to pay interest on the sums assessed. Latham J. considered that the question of whether taxpayer was liable to pay the interest was a matter of private law. All the court was doing was calculating a debt).

Judicial review proceedings and the courts' supervisory jurisdiction

Jurisdiction

23–010   *[Add:]*

In *R. v. Inland Revenue Commissioners, ex. p. Calagar* [1995] S.T.C. 74 Popplewell J. considered that the High Court in judicial review proceedings had jurisdiction to consider a challenge to an assessment on the basis that the Inspector had made an error of law. However he considered that the availability of a satisfactory appeal procedure meant that the Court as a matter of discretion should refuse relief. The decisions of the Court of Appeal in *Inland Revenue Commissioners v. Atkin* [1990] 1 W.L.R. 1374 and *Inland Revenue Commissioners v. Napier* [1993] S.T.C. 815 were not cited to the Judge. Popplewell J. considered that he had jurisdiction because one of the grounds of review was error of law. However, if the error of law is jurisdictional it should be possible to raise it as a defence to enforcement proceedings. The decisions may possibly be reconcilable by reference to

ıe High Court's jurisdiction to review non-jurisdictional errors on the
ıce of the record.

)iscretion

4dd:]   **23–013**

ı *R. v. Inland Revenue Commissioners, ex. p. Calagar* [1995] S.T.C. 741
'opplewell J. did not consider that the fact that the decision raised difficult
oints of international law of political sensitivity which could go to the
Iouse of Lords was an "exceptional" reason justifying using the judicial
:view procedures in preference to appealing to the Commissioners.

Note 53:]   **23–014**

'he VAT Tribunal decision in *Shepperd* [1994] S.T.C. 543 must be
onsidered wrongly decided in the light of the High Court decision in
:ustoms and Excise Commissioners v. Arnold [1996] S.T.C. 1271.

GROUNDS OF REVIEW

:onfidentiality

4dd:]   **23–021**

ı *R. v. Inland Revenue Commissioners, ex p. Continental Shipping* [1996]
.T.C. 813 the applicants sought to challenge a notice issued under Taxes
Aanagement Act 1970, s. 20 requiring their bank to furnish the Revenue
/ith copies of their bank statements on the basis that the Revenue had
ıiled to notify the taxpayers, whose affairs were being investigated, of the
:ason for seeking the notice. Tucker J. questioned the applicants' standing,
ince the notice was to be sent to the taxpayers as opposed to the
pplicants, so it was difficult to see what wrong they had suffered.
.lthough he accepted there had been a technical breach of the statutory
:quirements, since requirements of confidentiality meant that the notice
ould not have provided any useful information, he refused to grant any
:lief as a matter of discretion.

"he need for flexibility and fairness in the administration of taxes

Note 77:]   **23–023**

'he decision in *R. v. Inland Revenue Commissioners, ex p. Unilever* was upheld
y the Court of Appeal: [1996] S.T.C. 681.

23–024   *[Note 78:]*

One factor relied upon in *R. v. Inland Revenue Commissioners, ex p. Allen* [1997] S.T.C. 1141 for refusing relief was that the Enquiry Branch Manual had not been published.

[Add new paragraphs:]

In *R. v. Customs and Excise Commissioners, ex p. Kay* [1996] S.T.C. 1500 Keene J. held that the Commissioners' duties of care and management did not authorise them to deliberately delay making repayments which were due because legislation was envisaged which would restrict claims to overpayments made in the preceding three years and would therefore result in the Commissioners ceasing to be liable to pay the sums in question. In the case of opticians, the Commissioners were also held to be acting unfairly in seeking to restrict claims, given the fact that they had publicly stated that they would allow claims up until March 2001. The Judge noted that the position might be different after legislation had been enacted limiting claims to three years, although unfairness might even then arise if the Commissioners had a discretion not to apply the three year limit.

In *R. v. Customs and Excise Commissioners, ex p. Littlewoods* [1997] S.T.C. 317 the applicants challenged proposed changes to VAT retail schemes which would preclude them from using Scheme B from March 1, 1997. It was argued that by failing to include any transitional provisions exempting outstanding balances from VAT, the changes were *ultra vires* since they would result in double taxation and were inconsistent with assurances given by Customs that they would not seek to impose VAT on outstanding balances if a trader ceased to use scheme B. Tucker J. rejected these submissions. He considered that

> "where there has been a change in the law, or where there has been new judicial interpretation of the law. . . then the commissioner should not be bound by assurances given in different circumstances based on a different view of the law which has been held to be mistaken. This is especially so when. . . the public interests require that there should be a change in policy."

He went on to note that the applicant had not suffered any detriment as result of the assurance. It is considered that the fact that there has been new judicial interpretation of the law should not automatically make it fair for the Commissioners to depart from previous assurances. Indeed in relation to past transactions it would invariably be unfair for the Commissioners to seek to alter the basis upon which they are taxed. These remarks were not commented upon in the Applicants successful appeal.

CHAPTER 24

PRISON DISCIPLINE

The Legal Framework of Prison Administration

Circular Instructions issued after 1994 were renamed Advice and Instruc-   **24–001**
tions to Governors; those issued since January 1997 are called Prison
Service Instructions.

The Prison Disciplinary System

[Add to Note 12:]   **24–003**

The fullest account of the work of the Prisons Ombudsman is to be found
in: Prisons Ombudsman, *Annual Report 1995* (laid before Parliament on
October 23, 1996). This reports that during the first 12 months, the
Ombudsman received 2,050 complaints, in respect of which 424 full
investigations were completed and 44 per cent of these were upheld. The
Ombudsman's recommendations were wholly or partially accepted by the
prison authorities in 90 per cent of cases. See also, Prisons Ombudsman,
Annual Reports 1996.

Conclusions

[Add:]   **24–016**

Applications for judicial review have been extended into other areas of
prison management, including the following:

> Categorisation: see R. v. Secretary of State for the Home Department, ex p.
> Duggan [1994] 3 All E.R. 277 (since the maintenance of category A
> status directly affected a prisoner's liberty, fairness required that,
> subject to public interest immunity, the gist of the reports should be
> revealed to enable the prisoner to comment, and reasons should
> subsequently be provided); R. v. Governor of Maidstone Prison, ex p.
> Peries, [1998] C.O.D. 150 (procedural fairness did not require that all
> the safeguards of Duggan be applicable to all categories of prisoners as
> there was a distinction between category A and other prisoners; the
> applicant was entitled to reasons after the decision affecting his

classification, but there was no entitlement to prior notification o relevant material); *R. v. Secretary of State for the Home Department, ex p Hepworth* [1996] C.O.D. 330; *R. v. Secretary of State for the Hom Department, ex p. Murphy* [1997] 8 C.L. 438; *R. v. Secretary of State for th Home Department, ex p. Sullivan, The Independent,* July 21, 1997; *R. v Secretary of State for the Home Department, ex p. Hepworth* [1998] C.O.D 146; *R. v. Secretary of State for the Home Department, ex p. McAvoy* [1998 C.O.D. 148.

Closed visits (*i.e.* where there is a glass screen between the visitor and the prisoner): see *R. v. Secretary of State for the Home Department, ex p O'Dhuibhir* [1997] C.O.D. 315 (Court of Appeal holds closed visits to be lawful as they did not impede the flow of information between solicitor and his client. The decision of Latham J. in *R. v. Secretary of State for the Home Department, ex p. Simms and O'Brien* [1997] C.O.D 217 was doubted).

Home leave: see *R. v. Secretary of State for the Home Department, ex p Hargreaves* [1997] 1 W.L.R. 906 (a challenge to Home Secretary* policy to tighten arrangements for home leave on ground that i frustrated prisoners' legitimate expectations was rejected; the most prisoner could legitimately expect was that their case would b examined individually in the light of whatever policy the Hom Secretary saw fit lawfully to adopt).

Random sampling: see *R. v. Secretary of State for the Home Department, e p. Temayne* [1996] 9 C.L. 491 (Home Secretary's decision to introduc random urine sampling of prisoners was not irrational since it acted a a deterrent).

Restrictions on access to the media: *R. v. Secretary of State for the Hom Department, ex p. Maber* [1996] 6 C.L. 300 (leave to challenge Standing Order 5G, r.2B, which prohibits prisoners contacting the media b telephone, was refused); *R. v. Secretary of State for the Home Departmen ex p. Simms and O'Brien, The Times,* December 9, 1997 (C.A. overruling [1997] C.O.D. 217) (blanket prohibition on use by journalist of material gathered on visit to a prisoner did not unlawfull interfere) with the prisoner's right to free speech). The approach o Latham J. in [1997] C.O.D. 217 has also been doubted by the Cour of Appeal in *R. v. Secretary of State for the Home Department, ex p O'Dhuibhir* [1997] C.O.D. 315). And note *R. v. Secretary of State for th Home Department, ex p. Leech (No.2)* [1994] Q.B. 198.

Searching: see *R. v. Secretary of State for the Home Department, ex p Zulfikar,* November 23, 1995 (unreported, C.A.) (leave to challeng governor's policy of strip-searching prisoners after every visit refused even having regard to the applicant's religious beliefs, the rigi application of the policy was not considered to be *Wednesbury* unrea sonable); *R. v. Governor of H.M. Prison Whitemore, ex p. Main* [1997 C.O.D. 400 (instruction to search cell and legal correspondence i absence of prisoner was not unlawful).

Scheme of privileges: see *R. v. Secretary of State for the Home Department,
ex p. Hepworth* [1998] C.O.D. 146 (Laws J. accepts that court has
jurisdiction to review a withdrawal or refusal of "enhanced status"
within a prison's scheme of privileges, but warns that there "are plain
dangers and disadvantages in the court's maintaining an intrusive
supervision over the internal administrative arrangements by which
prisons are run". Something akin to bad faith or crude irrationality
would have to be shown).

Add:]   **24–017**

Traditionally, neither the material before the Parole Board nor the reasons
for their decisions were disclosed. Consequently, there were few applications for judicial review of their decisions. Since the policy changed as a
consequence of the provisions of the Criminal Justice Act 1991, however,
applications have greatly increased. See, *e.g. R. v. Secretary of State for the
Home Department, ex p. Zulfikar*, July 21, 1995 (unreported) (decision of
Parole Board to refuse parole on ground that the prisoner had not
addressed his offending behaviour was struck down on the basis that the
reasoning was irrational); *R. v. Parole Board, ex p. Watson* [1996] 1 W.L.R.
906 (public safety test was applicable to the decision to recall prisoner on
revocation of a licence); *R. v. Secretary of State for the Home Department, ex p.
Lillycrop, The Times*, December 13, 1996 (fairness dictated that the Parole
Board should summarise reasons why parole was not recommended); *R. v.
Secretary of State for the Home Department, ex p. Hepworth* [1998] C.O.D. 146
relevance of prisoner's continued denial of guilt to Parole Board's
decisions to recommend release).

Add to Note 63:]

S. Creighton and V. King, *Prisoners and the Law* (1996).

CHAPTER 25

IMMIGRATION

[Add to Note 1:]

In 1995 over a third (1,220 out of 3,604) of all applications for leave to apply for judicial review received by the Crown Office concerned immigration matters: see Lord Chancellor's Department, *Judicial Statistics of England and Wales 1995* (Cm. 3290, 1996).

TYPES OF DECISION

[Add:]

25–002

A quite separate regime applies to nationals of the Member States of the European Economic Area. Their rights of entry and residence are governed by European law. For many years the courts and Immigration Appeal Tribunal strained to relate these rights to the categories and structure of the Immigration Act 1971. Special provision is now made in domestic law by the Immigration (European Economic Area) Order 1994 (S.I. 1994 No. 1895) although neither this nor the Immigration Rules deal comprehensively with those who are nationals of states with association (or similar) agreements with the European Union and have some rights of entry as a result.

ADMINISTRATIVE APPEALS

[Add:]

25–007

Asylum appeals are heard by a sub-group of adjudicators known as "special adjudicators": Asylum and Immigration Appeals Act 1993, s. 8.

An adjudicator must also allow an appeal if the decision was not "in accordance with the law": Immigration Act 1971, s. 19(1)(a). This gives the appellate authorities at least some scope to consider whether the immigration authorities acted in accordance with established principles of administrative or common law: *Secretary of State for the Home Department v. Dhubi Saleban Abdi* [1996] Imm. A.R. 148. Special adjudicators probably do not have this power since their task is confined to examining whether the

215

impugned decision would be contrary to the United Kingdom's obligation under the Refugee Convention: Asylum and Immigration Appeals Ac 1993, s. 8.

25–008   *[Add:]*

The "destination appeal" referred to in the text will only be available to an illegal entrant who has entered the United Kingdom in breach of : deportation order: Immigration Act 1971, s.17(1)(c). In certain circum stances those refused leave to enter or threatened with deportation may also appeal on "destination" grounds: *ibid.*

25–009   *[Add:]*

An asylum applicant whose claim is refused because he can be sent to Member State of the European Union or another state designated by th Secretary of State as safe (colloquially known as a "white list" country), can likewise only contest the safety of that country on appeal after he has lef the United Kingdom: Asylum and Immigration Act 1996, s. 3(2).

25–010   *[Note 14 should read:]*

See ss. 12 and 13 of the 1993 Act and the attenuated rights of appeal fo asylum seekers in s. 8 of and Sched. 2 to the Act. The rights of appeal fo asylum seekers have been further restricted by Asylum and Immigration Act 1996, ss. 1–3.

25–011   *[Add:]*

The date of decision is *not* the relevant time in asylum appeals. Th appellate authorities must take account of any change in circumstances in the country in question since the Secretary of State's decision or, in th case of the Tribunal, since the Special Adjudicator's determination: *Sand ralingham and Ravichandran v. Secretary of State for the Home Department* [1996 Imm. A.R. 97.

Even after the appeals process has been exhausted, there may be change of circumstance or new evidence may become available. Th immigration authorities will consider further representations, but if thes are also unsuccessful, does the asylum-seeker have a further right o appeal? The Court of Appeal has held that the question in the first place i for the Secretary of State to decide. The acid test is whether, comparing th new claim with that which had been earlier rejected and excluding materi: which the claimant could reasonably have been expected to rely on in th earlier claim, the new claim was sufficiently different from the earlier on to admit a realistic prospect that a favourable view would be taken of th new claim despite the unfavourable conclusion reached on the earlie

laim: *Onibiyo v. Secretary of State for the Home Department* [1996] Imm. A.R.
70. If the Secretary of State again rejects the application for asylum and
oes not accept that it constitutes a "new claim" with a further right of
ppeal, his decision may be challenged on judicial review. However, the
ourt will not decide for itself whether the claim is "new" but subject the
ecretary of State's decision to *Wednesbury* scrutiny (or examine whether
or any other reason it is unlawful): *R. v. Secretary of State for the Home
Department, ex p. Ravichandran (No. 2)* [1996] Imm. A.R. 418.

Add:]   25–012

lthough Home Office Presenting Officers represent immigration author-
ies in the great majority of appeals, in cases of particular importance, the
Iome Office has begun to instruct counsel. On the appeal of Dr
l'Massari, two counsel appeared on either side before Judge Pearl, the
Chief Adjudicator (March 5, 1996, *Butterworths Immigration Law Service*
(431)).
   The Refugee Legal Service, as well as the Immigration Advisory Service,
epresent claimants on asylum appeals.

Add:]   25–013

he Court of Appeal has confirmed that the Immigration Appeal Tri-
unal's jurisdiction is not confined to errors of law and that it may review
n adjudicator or special adjudicator's findings of fact. Of course, as with
ny other appellate body, the Tribunal must generally respect findings
vhich rely on an assessment of witnesses who gave oral evidence at first
nstance: *Borissov v. Secretary of State for the Home Department* [1996] Imm.
\.R. 524.

ACCESS TO JUDICIAL REVIEW

Note 19:]   25–014

he right of appeal to the Court of Appeal is under Immigration Act 1993,
. 9 (not s. 11).

Add:]

\ppeal lies against a "final determination" of the Immigration Appeal
Tribunal. This phrase does not include a determination refusing leave to
ppeal *to* the Tribunal: see *El Assall v. Secretary of State for the Home
Department, The Times,* March 1, 1995 following *Bland v. Chief Supplementary
3enefit Officer* [1983] 1 W.L.R. 262. There is no "final determination" either
vhere the Tribunal grants leave but remits the matter to be heard *de novo*

by an adjudicator or special adjudicator: *R. v. Immigration Appeal Tribuna* *ex p. Jebunisha Patel* [1996] Imm. A.R. 161. Nor is the Tribunal' determination of an appeal on a preliminary issue a final determination c the appeal (at least where it decides that the appellate authorities hav jurisdiction to hear the appeal): *Secretary of State for the Home Department* **i** *Dahir and Abdi* [1995] Imm. A.R. 570. In these cases, the proper route t challenge the Tribunal's decision for error of law is still an application fc judicial review. In *Dahir and Abdi* with the consent of the parties, the Cou of Appeal went on to consider the substantive point of law as though th Secretary of State had applied for judicial review. It sat for both purposes a a Court of Appeal, deciding that it was superfluous and unnecessary for th application for leave to apply for judicial review to be formally dismissed b one member of the court (in his capacity as a judge of the High Court) an then renewed before the other two (see Sir Ralph Gibson at p. 576).

25–015   *[Add:]*

Naturalisation and other decisions involving the exercise of a discretion b the Secretary of State under the British Nationality Act 1981 are nc subject to appeal to, or review in, any court: British Nationality Act 198 s. 44(2). However such is the influence of *Anisminic* that the Secretary c State did not even seek to argue that this provision ousted the power of th court to consider whether the Secretary of State had acted within hi jurisdiction in refusing to issue a naturalisation certificate: *R. v. Secretary* **i** *State for the Home Department, ex p. Fayed* [1997] 1 All E.R. 228 and see par 25–021 below.

GROUNDS FOR JUDICIAL REVIEW

Illegality

25–018   *[Add:]*

In February 1996 the Secretary of State for Social Security amended th Income Support (General) Regulations 1987 so as to exclude from benef asylum seekers who did not make their applications for asylum immedi ately on arrival or whose claims for asylum were rejected by the Hom Office and who were awaiting the determination of their appeals: see Soci Security (Persons From Abroad) Regulations 1996, reg. 8. In *R. v. Secretar of State for Social Security ex p. Joint Council for the Welfare of Immigrants* [199 1 W.L.R. 275, the Court of Appeal held that the amendments were *ult vires*. It was permissible for the Secretary of State to seek to discourag asylum-seekers, but the effect of the amendment was to render their righ under other legislation nugatory. The Asylum and Immigration Appea Act 1993 gave them a right to seek asylum and to pursue appeals again

refusal by the immigration authorities. The effect of the amendments was
that they would be forced to live in penury if they were to exercise these
rights. Simon Brown L.J. said:

> "Parliament cannot have intended a significant number of genuine
> asylum-seekers to be impaled on the horns of so intolerable a
> dilemma: the need either to abandon their claims to refugee status or
> alternatively to maintain them as best they can but in a state of utter
> destitution. Primary legislation alone could in my judgment achieve
> that sorry state of affairs."

However, within months Parliament saw fit to do just that and in the
Asylum and Immigration Act 1996, s. 11 and Sched. 1 it authorised (with
minor changes) the Regulations which had previously been struck down.
As very much a last resort asylum-seekers in such a position may be
eligible to "care and assistance" from local authorities under the National
Assistance Act 1948 see *R. v. Hammersmith and Fulham L.B.C., ex p. M, The
Times*, February 19, 1997.

The Home Secretary's policy of regularly refusing asylum seekers
permission to work while waiting for their appeals to be heard was declared
unlawful and had to be reconsidered: *R. v. Secretary of State for the Home
Department, ex p. Jammeh, The Times*, September 11, 1997.

Procedural propriety

[Add:]   25–021

The introduction of a wider right of appeal for asylum-seekers in the
Asylum and Immigration Appeals Act 1993 has led the courts to take a
narrower view of implied procedural obligations. Thus it is not incumbent
on a special adjudicator to draw the appellant's attention to inconsistencies
between statements made in interview to the Home Office or on the
original asylum application and evidence at the hearing of the appeal: *R. v.
Immigration Appeal Tribunal, ex p. Williams (Joseph)* [1995] Imm. A.R. 518.
Similarly, it is for the appellant to decide how to present his evidence and a
special adjudicator is not required before making his own assessment of an
expert's written report to warn the appellant and give him an opportunity
to call the maker: *R. v. Secretary of State for the Home Department, ex p.
Khanafer* [1996] Imm. A.R. 212. Where the asylum-applicant has a full right
of appeal before a special adjudicator the court will not ordinarily
investigate allegations that unfairness in the initial interviewing process led
to the applicant being deprived of a proper opportunity to put his case at
that stage. A *de novo* hearing before an adjudicator will overshadow the
earlier complaint (even if justified): *R. v. Secretary of State for the Home
Department, ex p. Sesay* [1995] Imm. A.R. 521.

The Asylum Appeals Procedure Rules require the Secretary of State to
produce the original or copies of any notes of interview with the appellant

and of any other documents referred to in the decision being appealed: r. 5(8). Adjudicators and special adjudicators can require either party to provide particulars of its case. However, a majority decision of the House of Lords has held that there is no further power to require the immigration authorities to give discovery of relevant documents: *Abdi and Gawe v Secretary of State for the Home Department* [1996] 1 W.L.R. 298. Moreover, the bald statement of the Secretary of State that he has knowledge of a particular country's immigration policies and practices and has experience of returning passengers to that country and has no reason to believe that the authorities of that country would not comply with their obligations under the Refugee Convention was some evidence in support of his certificate that an asylum applicant could be safely returned to that country (*ibid.*).

It is elementary that a judge ought only to consider material of which both parties are aware and in respect of which they have had an opportunity to make representations. In asylum appeals, special adjudicators usually have available one or more reports about the country in question and sometimes other material as well. This is especially common in "safe third country" cases. Special Adjudicators need to be vigilant to ensure that applicants' representatives have access to such bundles. They should draw attention to reports or documents which they regard as particularly relevant and refer to any document, determination or decision on which they are minded to rely. Failure to do this will not necessarily lead to the determination being quashed (if the court is persuaded that the applicant was not prejudiced by the omission): *Imre Fulop v. Secretary of State for the Home Department* [1995] Imm. A.R. 323. There is an exceptional statutory derogation from the principle of disclosure for evidence concerning forged documents which it would not be in the public interest to disclose to appellants: Immigration Act 1971, s. 22(4) and see *R. v. Secretary of State for the Home Department, ex p. Begum (Saira)* [1995] Imm. A.R. 407.

In the context of naturalisation the Court of Appeal has held that the Home Secretary had a duty to act fairly which the court could police notwithstanding an ouster clause in the British Nationality Act (see paragraph 25–015 above). The statute also provides expressly that the Home Secretary is not obliged to give reasons for such decisions. However, the Court of Appeal also held that the common law duty to act fairly might nonetheless require him to alert the applicant to matters of concern so as to enable effective representations to be made: *R. v. Secretary of State for the Home Department, ex p. Fayed* [1997] 1 All E.R. 228; see also a like duty where the Secretary of State is minded to refuse entry to a person because his exclusion would be contrary to the public good: *R. v. Secretary of State for the Home Department, ex p. Moon* (1996) 8 Admin. L.R. 477.

25–022   *[Add:]*

The Asylum Appeal (Procedure) Rules 1993, r. 32 deem any notice sent by post to have been received on the second day after it was sent. The

Divisional Court has held that this precludes any evidence that the notice was in fact received at some other time or not at all: *R. v. Secretary of State for the Home Department, ex p. Sasikath* [1997] Imm. A.R. 83. The same case confirmed an earlier decision (*R. v. Secretary of State for the Home Department, ex p. Sivanatharaja* [1995] Imm. A.R. 52) that such service on the appellant himself alone would be effective even though it was known that the appellant was represented. This can have the harsh consequence that an appeal may be dismissed in the absence of the appellant (see Regulation 25 of the 1993 Rules) at a hearing of which he himself has had only a fictional notice and of which his representative has not even had that.

Unreasonableness

[Add:]   **25–024**

In *Raghbir Singh v. Secretary of State for the Home Department* [1996] Imm. A.R. 507 the Court of Appeal applied a similarly deferential attitude to deportation decisions taken on "other reasons of a political nature" which also preclude an appeal: Immigration Act 1971, s.15(3). *R. v. Secretary of State for the Home Department, ex p. Chahal* [1995] 1 W.L.R. 526 was a further case in which the Court of Appeal entertained only limited argument as to the Secretary of State's conclusion that the appellant's deportation would be conducive to the public good on grounds of national security. Chahal, a Sikh activist claimed that he would be tortured if he was returned to India (as he had been in the past). The English courts upheld the Home Secretary's claim that, whatever the merit of his fear of persecution, Articles 22(2) and 32(2) of the Refugee Convention permitted his deportation because there were reasonable grounds for regarding him as a danger to the security of the United Kingdom. However, the European Court of Human Rights subsequently found that his removal to India would be a violation of his right under Article 3 of the European Human Rights Convention since there was convincing evidence that this would lead to him being tortured or suffering inhuman or degrading treatment or punishment. The prohibition on such treatment was absolute whether the respondent state was directly responsible for it or indirectly responsible by sending the applicant to another territory where there was good reason to believe that he would be exposed to it: *Chahal v. United Kingdom* (1997) 23 E.H.H.R. 413. The United Kingdom government accepted the decision and released Chahal.

[Add:]   **25–026**

It is not necessarily fatal to an application for judicial review that the error of law was not taken by the applicant before the authority whose decision is under review. However, in order to be granted leave to apply for judicial review, the applicant must show more than that the point was "arguable". If a Special Adjudicator's decision is being impugned, the point must have been an obvious one of Convention law which was readily discernable and which favoured the applicant. If the applicant seeks to challenge a refusal of leave to appeal by the Tribunal, it must be properly arguable that the point not raised in the grounds of appeal to the Tribunal had a strong prospect of success if leave to appeal had been granted: see *R. v. Secretary of State for the Home Department, ex p. Robinson* [1997] 1 W.L.R. 182 (C.A.) and *R. v. Special Adjudicator, ex p. Kerrouche* [1998] I.N.L.R. 88 (C.A.).

Differences of procedure in considering asylum applications amongst the very large numbers of parties to the Refugee Convention are inevitable. In addition, since there is no multinational court with the power to give definitive interpretations of the Convention's meaning, it is not surprising that in some respects constructions of the Convention have diverged. However, the courts have held that a different procedure (which led a third country to refuse asylum) would only be relevant if it was contrary to the English court's view of substantive justice. A different interpretation of the Convention would only matter if the third country's interpretation was sufficiently different from that in English law to be outside the range of possible interpretations: *R. v. Secretary of State for the Home Department, ex p. Chiper* [1995] Imm. A.R. 410 and *R. v. Special Adjudicator, ex p. Kerrouche,* July 31, 1997 (unreported, C.A.).

25–027   *[Add:]*

The 1993 Act gave a "fast track" right of appeal against the Secretary of State's certificate that an asylum-applicant could be removed to a safe third country. Very short time limits are set for each stage of the appeal process (see now asylum Appeals (Procedure) Rules 1996, Regulations 5, 6, 9 and 11) and there is no appeal to the Immigration Appeal Tribunal if the Special Adjudicator upholds the certificate: 1993 Act, Schedule 2, paragraph 5(7) as substituted by Asylum and Immigration Appeals Act 1996, s.1.

The absence of an appellate route causes difficulties where the determinations of special adjudicators as to the safety of particular countries differ. This may be due to different evidence, but inconsistencies are unsatisfactory where the material is essentially the same. Judicial review is the only judicial mechanism for resolving the problem and it has yet to find a clear way of doing so. The principle that a special adjudicator should give reasons for failing to follow an earlier determination of another special adjudicator on the same question (*Gnanavaratharan v. Special Adjudicator* [1995] Imm. A.R. 64) has not been followed by the Court of Appeal in *Sinathamby Kumar v. Secretary of State for the Home Department* [1996] Imm. A.R. 548. The later case was decided a week after the Divisional Court had relied on *Gnanavaratharan* to resolve sharply differing views amongst special adjudicators as to whether Belgium was a safe third country. It held that Belgium was not safe: *R. v. Special Adjudicator, ex p. Turus, Bostem and others* [1996] Imm. A.R. 388.

Add:]   **25–029**

The Immigration Rules were intended to be a statement of the practice to
be followed in the administration of the Immigration Act: Immigration Act
1971, s. 3(1). However, policies and practices outside the Rules have
proliferated. Their status is often ambiguous. Thus in *Secretary of State for the
Home Department v. Hastrup* [1996] Imm. A.R. 616 the Court of Appeal
categorised a document which set out the Department's policy on spouses
and children and which was intended to reflect the United Kingdom's
obligations under Article 8 of the European Convention on Human Rights
as no more than an internal document and which could therefore not give
rise to a legitimate expectation that its terms would be applied (this was
conceded by the applicant). Yet this "internal document" was widely
known and had been referred to and relied upon in numerous judicial
review applications in the past (some of which had been successful, *e.g.*
R. v. Secretary of State for the Home Department, ex p. Urmaza [1996] C.O.D.
479; *R. v. Secretary of State for the Home Department, ex p. Amankwah* [1994]
Imm. A.R. 240, and some of which had set out extensive extracts from the
document). In *Hastrup* the Court of Appeal noted that the policy document
did not purport to set out universal or inflexible practices and the court
thought that whether the Home Secretary intended to use the leeway
which the document catered for, or whether he intended to depart from it,
he was free to do so on condition (a) that he had regard to his generally
stated policy and (b) that he gave reasons for either departing from them or
exercising an unusual course within them.

CHAPTER 26

PUBLIC SECTOR HOUSING

The Local Housing Authority and its Powers

[Add:]   26–002

The Housing Act 1996, discussed below, makes significant changes to the powers and duties of local housing authorities.

[Add:]   26–003

Part I of the Housing Act 1996 now provides for a register of regulated "social landlords" (housing associations and newer types of social landlords) supervised by "the Corporation" (formerly the Housing Corporation). The 1996 Act establishes a right of appeal to the High Court from some of the decisions of the Corporation; in other situations an application for judicial review will be the appropriate method to challenge the legality of its decisions. It is possible that, in some circumstances, public functions carried out by the social landlords themselves may be subject to judicial review: on amenability to judicial review generally, see above paragraph 3–023 *et seq.*

Homelessness

[Add:]   26–006

The provision in the Housing Act 1996 of a new statutory right to an internal review of homelessness decisions, together with a right of appeal on point of law to the county court, will significantly reduce the number of applications for judicial review: see below, paragraph 20–014A.

Substantive law

[Delete and substitute:]   26–007

Responsibilities towards the homeless are now imposed upon local housing authorities by Part VII of the Housing Act 1996. Part III of Housing Act

1985 is repealed. The 1996 Act applies to applications for assistance made on or after January 20, 1997 while the Housing Act 1985 continues to apply to those whose application were made before that day. The main concepts of homelessness (section 175), priority need (section 189) and intentional homelessness (section 191) remain broadly, though not exactly, as under Part III of the 1985 Act.

Section 185 of the 1996 Act provides that "persons from abroad" (people subject to immigration control) are not eligible for assistance unless they fall within a class prescribed by regulations: see Homelessness Regulations 1996 (S.I. 1996 No. 2754). Further, such persons are to be disregarded in determining whether eligible persons are homeless or in priority need: section 185(4). Exclusion of in-country asylum seekers from access to any part of the system of public housing (and from eligibility for state benefits) led the Court of Appeal to conclude that they could reach such a condition of destitution as to qualify for "residential accommodation" under section 21 of the National Assistance Act 1948: see *R. v. Hammersmith and Fulham L.B.C. and others, ex p. M and others* (1997) 9 Admin. L.R. 504.

[Note 14:]

See now Housing Act 1996, Part VII.

26–008 *[Note 15:]*

See now Housing Act 1996, s. 184.

[Note 16:]

See now Housing Act 1996, s. 188 (interim duty to accommodate in case of priority need). *R. v. Brent L.B.C., ex p. Awua* is now reported at [1996] 1 A.C. 55. The *ejusdem generis* rule has no application for the purpose of construing "other special reason" which is a free-standing category. Accordingly destitute asylum seekers are capable of being "vulnerable" for the purposes of the Act: *R. v. Kensington and Chelsea R.L.B.C., ex p. Kihara* (1997) 9 Admin. L.R. 25.

20–009 *[Note 17:]*

Homelessness is now defined by Housing Act 1996, s. 175.

[Note 18:]

On priority need, see now Housing Act 1996, s. 185(4)(b).

[Note 19:]

On intentional homelessness, see now Housing Act 1996, ss. 190–191.

Delete and substitute:]

If the authority decides (i) it is "satisfied" that the applicant is homeless
and in priority need, (ii) that it is "not satisfied" that the applicant became
homeless intentionally, and (iii) it is satisfied "that other suitable accommodation is available" for the occupation of the applicant in the district, the
"full housing duty" is now "to provide the applicant with such advice and
assistance as the authority consider is reasonably required to enable him to
secure such accommodation": Housing Act 1996, s. 197. This is in addition
to the new and more general duty in section 179 to "secure that advice and
information about homelessness, and the prevention of homelessness, is
available free of charge to any person in their district".

Where other suitable accommodation is *not* available, the duty upon the
authority is to secure that accommodation is made available to fully
qualifying applicants for a minimum period of two years: section 193. The
duty terminates if: the applicant refuses any offer of suitable accommodation under Parts VI or VII after having been informed of the consequences; he ceases to be "eligible"; he becomes intentionally homeless
from the accommodation provided; he accepts an offer of accommodation
under Part VI; or he otherwise voluntarily leaves: s. 193. After this two year
period the authority has a discretion to continue to house the applicant, but
must not do so unless he continues to have a priority need and there is no
other suitable accommodation available in the district: s. 194. No authority
may provide accommodation for more than two years out of any three
under Part VII of the 1996 Act unless it is in a hostel or is a private sector
leasing arrangement: s. 207. The effect is likely to be that homeless families
live in short term and/or relatively poor accommodation while their
applications to be allocated secure housing accommodation under Part VI
are processed. There is no general legal requirement that accommodation
made available to an applicant in discharge of its duty under the Act need
by settled or permanent although it must not expose the applicant to the
threat of further homelessness within 28 days without alternative accommodation being available. There is accordingly nothing inherently unlawful
in the offer of assured shorthold accommodation: *R. v. Wandsworth L.B.C.,
ex p. Mansoor and Wingrove* [1997] Q.B. 953.

Note 21:]

See now Housing Act 1996, s. 184(3).

The Code

Note 24:]

See now Housing Act 1996, s. 182.

[Note 25:]

R. v. Brent L.B.C., ex p. Awua is now reported at [1996] 1 A.C. 55.

26–013– *[Delete these paragraphs:]*
26–014

JUDICIAL REVIEW

[Add new paragraph 26–014A:]

Introduction

26–014A Following recommendations by the Law Commission and by Lord Woolf
in *Access to Justice*, the Housing Act 1996 now provides two forms of redress
for people claiming to be eligible for assistance: first, there is a right to
request an internal review by the local housing authority of decisions taken
in carrying out its housing duties towards the homeless (s. 202); and,
secondly, a right of appeal on a point of law to the county court (s. 204).
These new provisions will heavily circumscribe the need for applicants to
apply for judicial review: see paragraph 20–019 above on the general
significance of alternative remedies. The local authority has a discretion,
not a duty, to provide accommodation pending an internal review or
appeal: s. 199.

Illegality and irrationality

26–019 *[Note 44:]*

The Court of Appeal decision in *R. v. Kensington and Chelsea R.L.B.C., ex p.
Ben-el-Mabrouk* is now reported at (1995) 27 H.L.R. 564.

Procedural impropriety

26–024 *[Add to Note 52:]*

See also *R. v. Barnet L.B.C., ex p. Babalola* (1995) 28 H.L.R. 196.

Reasoned decisions

26–027 *[Replace "section 64" with:]*

section 184 of the Housing Act 1996.

Add:]

There is no express requirement to give reasons why accommodation offered to an applicant in discharge of the authority's obligations is 'suitable" for the applicant for the purposes of section 69 of the Housing Act 1985 (see now sections 193 and 197 of the Housing Act 1996). Having regard to the difficulties inherent in allocating scarce resources, the courts will not normally impose a duty on an authority to give reasons unless, perhaps, the decision is "demonstrably out of line with the housing policy of the relevant council": *R. v. Kensington and Chelsea R.L.B.C., ex p. Grillo* (1996) 8 Admin. L.R. 165.

Note 63:] **26–030**

R. v. Islington L.B.C., ex p. Hinds (1994) 27 H.L.R. 65 was reversed by the Court of Appeal: see now (1995) 28 H.L.R. 302. In *R. v. Westminster C.C., ex p. Ermakov* [1996] 2 All E.R. 302, after a careful review of the authorities, the Court of Appeal held that although the court would admit evidence to elucidate or, exceptionally, correct or add to reasons given by an authority it would be very cautious about doing so. It would generally admit evidence to elucidate reasons where there had been an error in transcription or expression, where words had been inadvertently omitted, or where the language used lacked clarity—but not evidence tending to show that the real reasons for the decision were different from the reasons sent to the applicant. Where the reasons set out in the decision letter were manifestly flawed the decision letter would be quashed and the court would not refuse relief on the strength of reasons adduced in evidence after the commencement of proceedings.

HOUSING ALLOCATION

Note 69:] **26–033**

A "reasonable preference" may mean no preference at all. The authority may exclude members of the statutorily preferred groups from its housing waiting list on proper grounds such as rent arrears: *R. v. Wolverhampton L.B.C., ex p. Watters* (1997) 29 H.L.R. 931.

Remedies

Add to Note 77:] **26–037**

See also *R. v. Newham L.B.C., ex p. Ajayi* (1994) 28 H.L.R. 25.

Add:] **26–038**

In *O'Rourke v. Camden L.B.C.* [1997] 3 W.L.R. 86 the House of Lords overruled *Thornton v. Kirklees M.B.C.* [1979] Q.B. 626 and held that a local housing authority which had reason to believe an applicant might be homeless and in priority need but which failed in its statutory duty to provide the applicant with interim accommodation pending inquiries did not commit the tort of breach of statutory duty; the applicant had no action for damages in such circumstances.

CHAPTER 27

SOCIAL SECURITY

THE STRUCTURE OF DECISION-MAKING

Insert new paragraph after 27–003:]

27–003

In *R. v. Oxford Social Security Appeal Tribunal, ex p. Wolke* [1996] C.O.D. 418 a refusal of income support was challenged by an application for judicial review rather than by following the normal appeal route. Popplewell J. was prepared to hear the case notwithstanding the failure to use an alternative statutory remedy. Both parties agreed to this course because the issue was one of simple statutory construction. But this is often the case in social security. Moreover, it had not previously been thought that an exception existed to the alternative remedy bar to an application for judicial review merely because both parties agreed that the latter was the more appropriate procedure. However, as this question is one of discretion rather than of jurisdiction, the consent of the parties must be a relevant factor. It cannot (or should not) be conclusive especially when the resources of the Crown Office are very stretched and a specialist appellate mechanism exists to resolve all issues of fact and law with an ultimate appeal to the Court of Appeal.

27–006

Insert new paragraph after 27–006:]

In *R. v. Secretary of State for Social Security, ex p. Sherwin* (1996) 32 B.M.L.R. 1 an attack was mounted on a decision of an employee of the Department of Social Security (working within the Benefits Agency but acting on behalf of the Secretary of State) to suspend benefit pending an appeal. The argument was that the rule against delegation and the application of the *Carltona* principle (on which, see paragraph 6–113 above) made the action of the individual decision-maker unlawful. Such person was acting in the name of the Secretary of State as permitted by *Carltona* but the Agency was largely autonomous and the Secretary of State no longer answered questions in Parliament about its day to day activities. The Divisional Court held that the employee remained a civil servant, was aware that he was acting for the Secretary of State and that his act was not outside the *Carltona* principle. The Court of Appeal later refused leave to appeal. Given the constitutional importance of this case the judgments of the Divisional Court dealt very tersely with the analysis of *Carltona* presented by the applicant. See further Mark Freedland, "The Rule against Delegation and the *Carltona* Doctrine in an Agency Context" [1996] P.L. 19.

RESOURCE ALLOCATION IN SOCIAL SECURITY

27–020   *[Insert new paragraph after 27–020:]*

Resources and public law duties

In *R. v. Gloucestershire C.C., ex p. Barry* [1997] A.C. 584 the House of Lords held by a bare majority that a duty to assess and then meet the needs of an elderly and disabled individual for personal social services was conditioned by the resources available to the authority in question. Section 2(1) of the Chronically Sick and Disabled Persons Act 1970 imposes a duty on an authority if satisfied that it was necessary to make arrangements to meet an individual's needs, to make those arrangements. The applicant had been assessed as needing certain services but was later told that resource limitations prevented them from continuing to meet them in full. The Court of Appeal had held that the authority was not entitled to take account of its resources when assessing or reassessing whether it was necessary to make arrangements in order to meet the needs of an individual (see [1996] 4 All E.R. 421). The House of Lords, in reversing this decision, held that needs were to be assessed in the context of many relevant factors including acceptable standards of living, the nature and extent of the disability and the relative cost balanced against the relative benefit and the need for it. In making its assessment the authority had to consider what the impact would be upon its resources. This, in turn, would depend upon its financial position. In brief, what appeared to be an absolute duty had to be read in the context of the cost of that meeting that need. For the minority this was an impermissible reading of the statute that would, in effect, reduce a clear duty to a mere power. The decision was clearly taken on policy grounds the majority believing that it would be unrealistic to impose a duty that an authority did not have the resources to meet. This raises very difficult questions about the use of mandatory language in statutes, the proper approach to the interpretation of social legislation and the dilemma created for the implementation of social policy at a time when resources are limited.

Jowitt J. followed the above general approach to the interpretation of social legislation in *R. v. Sefton M.B.C., ex p. Help the Aged Ltd and others* [1997] C.O.D. 387. Here the duty was to provide accommodation under Part III of the National Assistance Act 1948. An authority with limited resources effectively rationed entry into such accommodation by reference to harsher financial criteria than would apply in the assessment of means and of the payment to be made (under regulations) for such accommodation if it were provided. This was held to be a lawful approach. It appears that the House of Lords was laying down a general rule for the interpretation of social legislation imposing apparent duties and the case may be followed in relation to other statutory duties. But, ultimately, the construction of each statute is a question arising upon that statute alone and generalisations can be dangerous. It is also a fact that Parliament frequently does not make clear its intentions with regard to the relationship between duties and available resources because that would raise acutely difficult political issues that are more conveniently left for the future and the courts. On appeal, the Court of Appeal reversed the decision of Jowitt J.: see [1997] 3 W.L.R. 884. Applying *Barry*, the court held that there was indeed a limited subjective element in making the assessment whether the ailments of the person concerned did or did not establish a "need for care and attention". In the present case, however, it was clear that the local authority accepted that the individual applicant met their own threshold as a person in need of care and attention. It was therefore unlawful for a local authority to decide, notwithstanding this, that they were not prepared to meet that need.

Resource allocation in health care

Two recent cases in which the Divisional Court have considered whether the policy adopted by health authorities and individual hospitals in relation to types of treatment offered has been lawful. In *R. v. East Lancashire Health Authority and others, ex p. B* [1997] C.O.D. 267 Jowitt J. held that a decision not to fund certain treatment for children was not reached in breach of a legitimate expectation that it would be adopted. Further, that there had been no fettering of discretion where the individual applicants had not asked to be exempted from the general policy not to fund the particular treatment and that, even if this could be shown in the future, the prospect of demonstrating *Wednesbury* unreasonableness was meagre. In *R. v. North Derbyshire Health Authority, ex p. Fisher* (1998) 10 Admin. L.R. 27 an authority had disregarded, on financial grounds, a circular from the Secretary of Sate about making certain treatment available. Dyson J. held that this was unlawful and went on to order the authority to formulate a policy taking account of the circular within a short period of time. This came very close to ordering the authority to provide the treatment previously denied as the facts showed that the only reasonable course would have been to implement the circular and the reasons given for not doing so were regarded as disingenuous by the judge. Both of these cases should be seen as primarily decided on their facts but they do show both the limits of, and the occasion for, judicial intervention in day to day health care decisions.

PROBLEMS OF DELEGATED LEGISLATION AND OF VIRES

27-024 *[Insert new paragraphs after 27-024:]*

In *R. v. Secretary of State for Social Security, ex p. Joint Council for the Welfare of Immigrants* [1997] 1 W.L.R. 275 the Court of Appeal held unlawful amendments to social security regulations which would have denied benefit to asylum seekers who were refused leave to enter or remain as a refugee pending an appeal. The court characterised the effect of the law as a grave interference with both statutory and basic human rights to a subsistence income. Only primary legislation could achieve such an objective. The decision was promptly reversed by section 9 of the Asylum and Immigration Act 1996. However, in *R. v. Westminster C.C., ex p. A and others, The Times,* February 19, 1997 it was held that an authority might often have a duty under National Assistance legislation to provide basic housing to such persons pending the hearing of their appeals. These cases show the complex interaction between long standing social legislation and more immediate political objectives of limiting the rights of certain individuals or groups of access to welfare benefits.

In *R. v. Secretary of State for Social Security, ex p. Sutherland* [1997] C.O.D. 222 Laws J. held *ultra vires* a provision in regulations permitting suspension of benefits in one case where a general question about entitlement to that benefit was being tested within the social security appeal process. An apparently wide enabling power to make regulations about suspension of benefit in cases where a question arises as to entitlement was construed as extending only to an existing case and not to one that might be affected by a decision of a Social Security Commissioner in another, test, case. Laws J. conceded that the construction for which the respondent argued would be convenient and would avoid the respondent having to appeal every case in which the test case propositions might arise from a tribunal to a Commissioner. But legality was most important and a Minister had to adhere strictly to the powers given to him by Parliament.

CHAPTER 28

TREATIES AND FOREIGN AFFAIRS

Treaties and legislation

[Add to Note 32:]   **28–023**

Nevertheless, the High Court of Australia in *Minister for Immigration and Ethnic Affairs v. Teoh* (1995) 128 A.L.R. 353 found a treaty which had not been the subject of legislation to be within the purview of the court, holding that ratification by Australia created a legitimate expectation that administrative decision-makers would act in conformity with the requirements of the treaty in the absence of any statutory or executive indication to the contrary. Such legitimate expectation did not, however, compel action consistent with the treaty's provisions; but procedural fairness would require notice and an opportunity to make representations if a course of action inconsistent with those provisions were proposed. See also: R. Piotrowicz, "Unincorporated treaties in Australian Law" [1996] P.L. 190 at 194 quoting a statement made on behalf of the Australian Government expressing its general rebuttal of any such expectation for existing and future treaties; A. Lester, "Government compliance with international human rights law: a new year's legitimate expectation" [1996] P.L. 187, who considers it uncertain whether English courts would follow *Teoh*; and Murray Hunt, *Using Human Rights in English Courts* (1997), pages 242–261.

[Add to Note 34:]

See also *R. v. Secretary of State for Social Security, ex p. Joint Council for the Welfare of Immigrants* [1997] 1 W.L.R. 275.